NOVELL'S GUIDE

TO NETWARE®
LAN Analysis

LAURA CHAPPELL

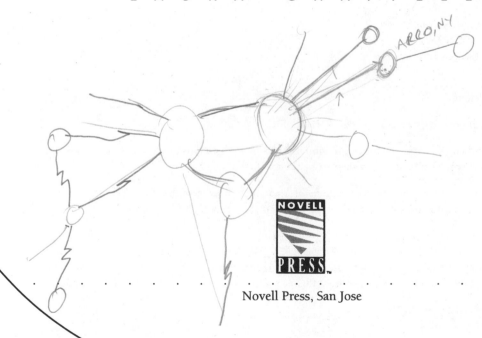

NOVELL
PRESS™

Novell Press, San Jose

PUBLISHER: *Peter Jerram*
EDITOR-IN-CHIEF: *Dr. R.S. Langer*
SERIES EDITOR: *David Kolodney*
ACQUISITIONS EDITOR: *Dianne King*
PROGRAM MANAGER: *Rosalie Kearsley*
DEVELOPMENTAL EDITOR: *David Kolodney*
EDITOR: *Dusty Bernard*
PROJECT EDITOR: *Michelle Nance*
TECHNICAL EDITORS: *Roger Spicer, Greg Mayfield, Dzung Nguyen, Josine Pentin*
NOVELL EDITORIAL ADVISORS: *Kelley Lindberg and Scott Lowe*
BOOK DESIGNER: *Helen Bruno*
PRODUCTION ARTIST: *Alissa Feinberg*
SCREEN GRAPHICS: *John Corrigan*
TYPESETTER: *Dina F Quan*
PROOFREADER/PRODUCTION ASSISTANT: *David Silva*
INDEXER: *Nancy Guenther*
COVER DESIGNER: *Archer Design*
NOVELL PRESS LOGO DESIGN: *Jennifer Gill*
COVER PHOTOGRAPHER: *Eric Harger*
Screen reproductions produced with SnapPRO!™
SnapPRO!™ is a trademark of Window Painters Ltd.

Library of Congress Card Number: 92-62329
ISBN: 0-7821-1143-2

Manufactured in the United States of America
10 9 8 7 6 5

Acknowledgments

Very special thanks to Roger Spicer for his unrelenting technical reviews and expertise as an editor on this project. With sincere gratitude, I wish also to thank Dan Hakes and Josine Pentin. Your enthusiasm for the technology is quite contagious!

My thanks also go to Rose Kearsley at Novell Press for her assistance in getting this project started and providing moral support during its creation. My appreciation to Dusty Bernard for her tireless reviews and helpful comments during the long days and many weekends required to complete this book. Also, thanks to the many at Sybex who initiated and supported this project persistently over the months—Michelle Nance, John Corrigan, David Kolodney, Dianne King, and Barbara Gordon.

Thanks also to Rick Romine at Novell for not kicking me out of my first encounter with the LANalyzer instructors and giving me a home run in baseball for my "Ethernet Frame" drawing. For their technical advice, assistance, and great senses of humor, thanks to Charlie Justus, Javier Martell, Bob Pratt, Greg Mayfield, Dzung Nguyen, Bob Ross, Wendy McCaw, John Rosdahl, Bill Gillman, Delyle Johnson, Dan Marshall, J.D. Marymee, Janice Perkins, and, of course, the infamous Christie Zervos.

Very special thanks to Steve Dauber and Steve Genova for helping this project get rolling and for revising my chapters...and revising...and revising....

For their continuous support and understanding of my work habits, I wish to express my gratitude to my friends and family, who have not forgotten me (even when I don't return their calls for weeks on end). You know who you are, I'm sure; I probably still owe you a call or two.

This book is dedicated to Jill, Tom, and Lindsey Faye Poulsen.

CONTENTS AT A *Glance*

TABLE OF *Contents*

*I*ntroduction

Working in a LAN environment is fundamentally different from working in a stand-alone environment. Cabling becomes the blood-stream of the network, and communications protocols are used to transfer data and resource management information from one system to another. As NetWare LANs increase in popularity, so does the need for more detailed information regarding protocol performance, troubleshooting, testing, and optimization.

Currently, there are no comprehensive books or classes that address the NetWare protocols as they are used on an Ethernet LAN. Since Ethernet is the most common implementation of NetWare networks, it seems logical to detail not only how NetWare communicates, but also how the Ethernet access method and cabling systems perform.

Who Should Read This Book

This book is designed for all current and new NetWare users who are interested in learning the basic through advanced steps of protocol analysis in order to troubleshoot, test, and optimize their NetWare Ethernet LANs. Whether you have years of NetWare experience or are still mastering console utilities, this book will help you learn and troubleshoot the communications that are occurring "behind the scenes" in NetWare.

If you are a network administrator, this book will guide you through the techniques to fully document your network performance and identify growth trends, cabling and server overload, and potential Ethernet and Net-Ware errors.

If you are a network technician, this book will provide you with an insight into Ethernet frame structures and cabling systems. You will become familiar with frame errors that indicate an overloaded network segment, a cabling problem, a faulty LAN driver, and a faulty transceiver. By examining the NetWare communications protocols, you will gain a thorough understanding of how the NetWare client/server communications system works, as well as how to optimize it.

For the instructor who presents technical lectures on the NetWare operating system and support, this book will address many of the common questions asked in class. Used as supplemental instructional material, this book will provide greater insight into the Ethernet media access method and NetWare communications for beginning through advanced students.

What You'll Learn

In this book, you will learn the basics of Ethernet cabling and frame structures. You will gain a thorough understanding of errors that occur on Ethernet LANs and their effect on performance.

You will also learn about NetWare communications that provide services such as routing and server information, file and printer access, bindery access, connection-oriented and connectionless communications, large file transfer, diagnostics and configuration information, connection validation, serialization information, and network messaging.

This book also provides you with a comprehensive list of protocol analysis features and tools that are used to document network health and performance, test network cabling and server capabilities, optimize network performance, and troubleshoot Ethernet and NetWare communications.

The Tools Presented in This Book

This book will introduce you to two protocol analyzers: the LANalyzer for NetWare and the LANalyzer. Each analyzer offers a range of capabilities for examining networking protocols.

The LANalyzer for NetWare is a Windows-based product and uses a GUI (Graphical User Interface). Whenever a screen shot has characteristics of this interface, you are looking at a demonstration of the LANalyzer for NetWare, as in Figure I.1.

FIGURE I.I

The LANalyzer for NetWare uses the Windows graphical user interface.

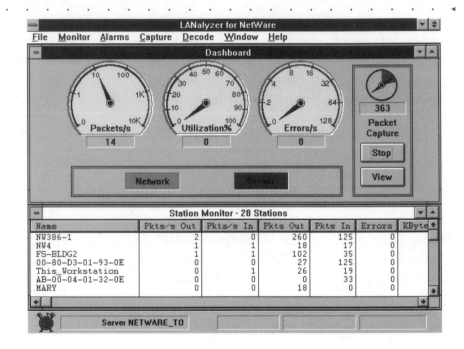

The LANalyzer, on the other hand, uses the traditional NetWare interface and presents a text-based screen. Whenever a screen shot depicts a text-based screen, you are looking at the LANalyzer product, as shown in Figure I.2.

For more information on the LANalyzer for NetWare and the LANalyzer, refer to Appendix C.

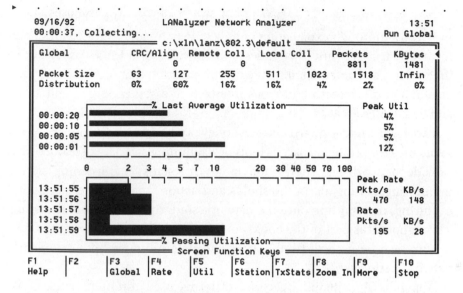

FIGURE 1.2

The LANalyzer uses the traditional NetWare interface.

How This Book Is Organized

This book is separated into four parts, covering the media access method; NetWare protocols; performance benchmarking, testing, and optimization; and, finally, protocol analyzer features.

Part I, "Ethernet/802.3 LANs," details the Ethernet frame structures used in the NetWare environment, including Ethernet_802.3 (Ethernet "raw"), Ethernet_802.2, Ethernet_SNAP, and Ethernet_II. Part I also details cabling system configuration requirements and limitations, as well as cable testing. Finally, Part I presents a complete listing of frame errors seen on NetWare LANs, along with their potential causes and possible solutions.

Part II, "NetWare Protocols," examines the NetWare protocols, such as Routing Information Protocol (RIP), Service Advertising Protocol (SAP), Internetwork Packet Exchange (IPX), Sequenced Packet Exchange (SPX), and NetWare Core Protocol (NCP). Also included in Part II is an analysis of the Burst Mode, Watchdog, and serialization protocols. Finally, the Diagnostic Responder Configuration Request and Response formats are defined and used for troubleshooting a NetWare LAN.

NOTE
Throughout this book, many hexadecimal values are represented with a preceding "0x." Hardware and software addresses in the NetWare environment are shown in their hexadecimal format throughout this book, even if they do not contain the preceding "0x" indicator.

Part III, "Performance Benchmarking, Testing, and Optimization," provides a thorough explanation of how to benchmark your network's performance, test network capabilities, and optimize your LAN. Also included in Part III is a chapter detailing the communication that occurs during successful and unsuccessful attempts to attach to a server, log in, and create and delete files.

Part IV, "Protocol Analyzers—Overview and Features," summarizes the many uses for protocol analysis tools by examining a variety of features that provide network short-term and long-term statistics gathering, station monitoring, setting alarm thresholds and actions, packet filtering, packet capturing, transmitting onto the network, and, finally, protocol decoding. Throughout this part of the book, you are provided with examples of how features can be used to troubleshoot and determine methods to enhance network performance.

Appendix A contains a glossary of terms used throughout the book. Terms defined in the glossary appear in italics within the text. Appendix B lists books and articles used in the research of this book and recommended for further study. Appendix C provides information on Novell's LANalyzer for NetWare and LANalyzer products. Appendix D contains a hexadecimal-decimal-binary conversion chart.

With this book at hand, most NetWare communications and Ethernet performance issues can be easily solved. Using this book in conjunction with a protocol analyzer attached to your own network, you will be capable of tracking network trends, configurations, and performance characteristics. Upon completion of this book and the many analysis techniques presented here, you will have acquired a thorough understanding of the NetWare communication system on an Ethernet LAN.

Ethernet/ 802.3 LANS

Part I addresses physical configurations and specifications of Ethernet LANs.

Chapter 1 provides a brief history of Ethernet and 802.3 standards, an explanation of how stations transmit and receive packets on an Ethernet network, and an outline of steps to test a station's ability to transmit and receive packets on a segment.

Chapter 2 looks at performance considerations for networks using carrier sense multiple access/collision detection (CSMA/CD) as the media access method; how to characterize bandwidth utilization, monitor usage of the cabling system, stress-test network segments, and solve performance problems resulting from overloaded cabling segments.

Chapter 3 examines the cabling specifications for 10Base5 (thick-net), 10Base2 (thinnet), and 10BaseT (twisted-pair) networks and defines such common cabling problems such as opens, shorts, and excessively long segments.

Chapter 4 discusses the four Ethernet frame types used in the Net-Ware environment: Ethernet_802.3, Ethernet_802.2, Ethernet_SNAP, and Ethernet_II. You learn to capture server and workstation packets that indicate what frame type has been loaded.

Chapter 5 explains errors caused by hardware and software problems, such as poorly written drivers, malfunctioning network interface cards, and faulty transceivers.

CHAPTER 1

Overview of
Ethernet LANS

When installing a NetWare LAN, users must select a network access method that fits their specific needs. This network access method determines the type of network interface cards that are placed in the workstations (Ethernet, Token Ring, ARCnet, and so on), how workstations access the cabling system, and how data is prepared and sent across the network.

There are three common access methods seen on today's NetWare LANs:

- ▸ Carrier sense multiple access with collision detection (CSMA/CD)

- ▸ Token-passing ring

- ▸ Token-passing bus

Ethernet LANs use the CSMA/CD method, while Token Ring and ARCnet use token-passing ring and token-passing bus, respectively.

Currently, most NetWare LANs are Ethernet (CSMA/CD) systems; however, Token Ring networks have been steadily rising in popularity over the past year. ARCnet LANs are still holding third place in this "war" between the network access options.

These three access methods have unique ways of communicating over the network. On a CSMA/CD network, all workstations share a common cabling system, as shown in Figure 1.1. Because of this, they can (and sometimes do) send data at the same time on the cable. This causes data signals to collide on the network. Some steps must be taken to avoid sending at the

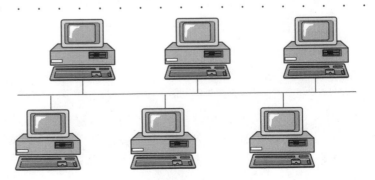

FIGURE 1.1

Ethernet network segment

same time as another workstation and to retransmit if the last message was involved in a collision. These steps are defined by the Institute of Electrical and Electronic Engineers (IEEE). The IEEE 802.3 CSMA/CD specifications are covered in this chapter.

Token Ring and ARCnet LANs do not allow workstations to transmit at the same time. To ensure this, a station must wait for permission to transmit data on the cabling system. Stations wait for a token before they can transmit. A *token* gives the station permission to transmit. Each workstation is given an equal chance to transmit on the cabling system since the token rotates around the network from station to station, based on the station node address (ARCnet) or physical wiring (Token Ring). This type of access method is called *deterministic* since the token is passed in a well-defined process that guarantees access to the network.

This chapter explains how workstations use the CSMA/CD access method to send messages on the network.

NOTE
The term "Ethernet" is used in this book to describe Ethernet II and 802.3 network specifications and functions, collectively.

Advantages and Disadvantages of Ethernet

The primary advantages of Ethernet include

- **Ease of installation:** All workstations can be connected to a segment using a simple T-connector or transceiver. Ethernet LANs do not require a hub to connect systems.

- **Well-known technology:** Ethernet networks have been prevalent in the industry for many years and are quite common.

- **Availability of inexpensive cards:** The price of Ethernet cards has dropped significantly over the past two years.

- **Various wiring configurations:** As shown in Chapter 3, Ethernet LANs can be configured using different cable types and cable layouts.

NOTE
Chapter 3 discusses how hub systems and RJ45 (telephone-type) connectors can be used, if desired.

The main disadvantages of Ethernet include

▶ **Decreasing throughput on heavily loaded LANs:** On CSMA/CD LANs, as the load on the network increases, performance decreases. Although many feel CSMA/CD is Ethernet's greatest feature, others believe it is Ethernet's primary weakness because a higher network load severely degrades performance.

▶ **Difficulty in troubleshooting:** Ethernet networks can be difficult to troubleshoot because of the common cabling system used. If there is a break in the cable, the entire LAN segment is down. It can be very difficult to isolate a single node that is responsible for generating errors and causing problems on the network.

Before you begin working on an Ethernet LAN, it's important to understand how the access protocol, CSMA/CD, works. This helps you interpret the statistics, errors, and utilization information that are presented by an analyzer and throughout this book.

How CSMA/CD Works: Transmitting

NOTE
For further details on the CSMA/CD protocol, refer to the IEEE 802.3 specifications.

Because of the common cabling system that CSMA/CD networks use, some rules must be set to avoid the situation of workstations transmitting at the same time. If multiple stations transmit simultaneously, however, there must also be some way for them to find out if their packet has been involved in a collision and when to retransmit. (The CSMA/CD protocol is similar to a party-line phone, where many people can be on the line, talking at the same time. If everyone talks at once, you hear garbled chatter. If everyone waits his or her turn, however, you can understand each speaker, one at a time.)

Stations follow five steps when transmitting on the CSMA/CD network. Each station must

I · Listen before transmitting

2 · Defer (wait) if the cable is busy

3 · Transmit and listen for collisions

4 · If a collision did occur, wait before retransmitting

5 · Retransmit or abort

STEP 1: LISTEN BEFORE TRANSMITTING

Stations continually monitor the cable segment for a "carrier on" signal, as shown in Figure 1.2. "Carrier on" is a signal on the cable, commonly recognized by a voltage indicating that the cable is in use. If a station does not notice "carrier on," it assumes the cable is free and begins transmission. (In terms of the party-line analogy mentioned earlier, this function is similar to listening on the phone line before speaking.) If the wire is busy ("carrier on") when a station transmits, the station's packet will collide with the existing signal on the wire.

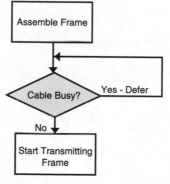

STEP 2: DEFER (WAIT) IF THE CABLE IS BUSY

In order to avoid collisions, stations must defer (wait) if they notice the cable is in use, as shown in Figure 1.3. A properly performing interface card will not intentionally transmit if it knows the cable is busy. (On a party line, if you hear someone talking, you wait until that person is finished before

FIGURE 1.3

*Stations defer if the wire
is busy.*

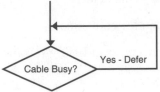

beginning to speak.) *Deferral time* is a set amount of time that a station must wait once the line becomes idle before attempting to retransmit.

STEP 3: TRANSMIT AND LISTEN FOR COLLISIONS

When the medium is clear ("carrier off") for at least 9.6 microseconds, a station may transmit, as you can see in Figure 1.4. Frames are transmitted in both directions down the cabling system.

FIGURE 1.4

*If the cable is free, the station
may begin transmission.*

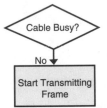

If another station on the segment has transmitted a packet at the same time, the packets collide on the wire, as shown in Figure 1.5. The packets involved in the collision are now only packet fragments on the cable. (If you began speaking at the same time as others on the party line, your conversations would collide, and the result would be a garbled message.) During transmission, therefore, the station listens for a collision on the segment. Collisions are recognized as a signal on the cable that is equal to or exceeds the signal produced by two or more transceivers simultaneously transmitting.

If a collision occurs but other stations haven't yet seen the collision signal, they may attempt to transmit. These stations would then be involved in yet another collision. To avoid this situation, stations involved in a collision ensure that all stations on the segment are aware that the cable is still busy by transmitting "jam," as illustrated in Figure 1.6. (*Jam* is specified as a minimum 32-bit transmission that cannot be equal to the CRC value of the prior transmission.) Stations involved in a collision increment their transmit attempt counter by one.

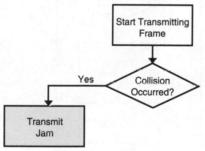

FIGURE 1.6
If a collision occurs, the stations involved transmit "jam."

STEP 4: WAIT BEFORE RETRANSMITTING

If stations retransmitted immediately after a collision, their second transmissions would also collide. It is necessary, therefore, to randomize the amount of time that stations must wait before attempting to retransmit.

In order to select when to retransmit, stations perform an algorithm that provides several available times when the station can attempt retransmission. This is called the *backoff algorithm*. Stations randomly select which time they will use, as shown in Figure 1.7. This reduces the chance of two or more stations retransmitting at the same time. (For example, on a party line, if two people begin talking at the same time, the messages are garbled. Both people will stop talking and then one will start up again as the other listens.)

Stations use the backoff algorithm to determine when they can attempt retransmission.

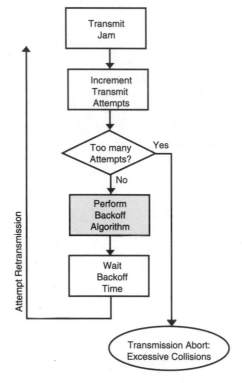

STEP 5: RETRANSMIT OR ABORT

If a station is on a busy segment, it may not be able to transmit without its packet colliding with another packet on the segment. A station may attempt to transmit up to 16 times before it must abort the attempt. Net-Ware v3.x servers display the number of aborted server transmissions in the MONITOR utility under LAN Driver Statistics as "ExcessCollisionsCount," as shown in Figure 1.8. If the station retransmits and there is no indication that the packet was again involved in a collision, the transmission is considered successful. (On a party line, if you spoke when the line was not busy, your voice would be heard clearly. If you attempted to get a message through but couldn't because the line was constantly in use, you might give up.)

After each successful transmission, a station can perform a test of its collision-detection function to ensure it is working correctly. This is called the *Signal Quality Error (SQE) test*. An SQE test is performed if the transceiver's SQE function is set to "on."

Understanding how stations access the medium helps determine whether the transmitting stations are accessing the medium efficiently and whether they are following all the rules of CSMA/CD. The flowchart shown in Figure 1.9 defines each of the steps that must be taken in order for a station to transmit on a CSMA/CD network. If a station does not follow

NOTE
All repeaters must have SQE disabled; enabled repeaters think collisions are occurring and "jam" the network.

NOTE
In Chapter 3, you will use the LANalyzer to identify stations violating the rules of CSMA/CD.

```
NetWare v3.11 (250 user) - 2/20/91          NetWare 386 Loadable Module

         ┌──────────────────────────────────────────────────────────┐
         │              Information For Server SALES1                 │
         ├──────────────────────────────────────────────────────────┤
         │ File Server Up Time:    0 Days  9 Hours 47 Minutes  6 Seconds │
         │ Utilization:             1     Packet Receive Buffers:   100 │
         │ Original Cache Buffers: 3,643   Directory Cache Buffers:  50 │
         │ Total Cache Buffers:    2,350   Service Processes:         2 │
         │ Dirty Cache Buffers:      0     Connections In Use:        2 │
         │ Current Disk Requests:    0     Open Files:               13 │
         └──────────────────────────────────────────────────────────┘

         ┌──────────────────────────────────────────────────────────┐
         │          NE2000 [port=320 int=2 frame=ETHERNET_802.3]      │
┌────┐   │ ▲  Hardware Receive Mismatch Count:              0         │
│NE20│   │                                                            │
│NE20│   │    Custom Statistics:                                      │
│    │   │      CarrierSenseLostCount                       0         │
│    │   │      UnderrunErrorCount                          0         │
│    │   │      ExcessCollisionsCount                       8         │
│    │   │      TransmitTimeoutCount                        0         │
│    │   │ ▼    TotalCollisionsCount                       197        │
└────┘   └──────────────────────────────────────────────────────────┘
```

FIGURE 1.8
The NetWare Monitor screen displays excessive collision counts.

FIGURE 1.9

Transmission flowchart

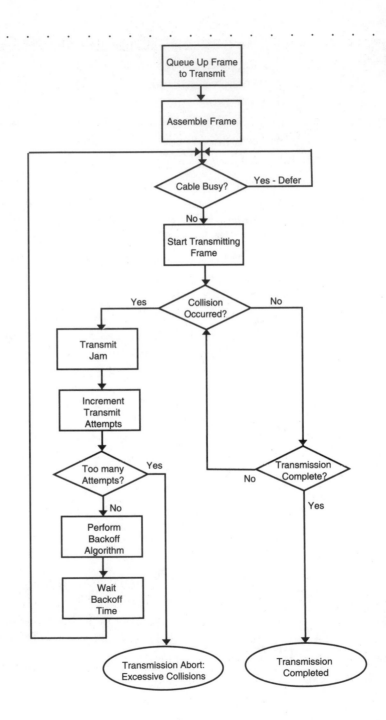

the steps outlined in the flowchart, it could cause the segment to become unusable.

How CSMA/CD Works: Receiving

Now that you have seen the process for transmitting on a segment, let's look at the receiving end. As discussed earlier in this chapter, when a station transmits a packet it is sent in both directions on the cabling system. An active station on a segment must perform these four steps:

1 · View incoming packets and check for fragments

2 · Check the destination address

3 · If destined for the local station, check the integrity of the packet

4 · Process the packet

STEP 1: VIEW INCOMING PACKETS AND CHECK FOR FRAGMENTS

On Ethernet LANs, all stations on the segment view each packet as it passes on the wire, regardless of whether the packet is addressed to that station. (This is similar to the party-line phone system. Even though conversations are not intended for you, you can hear them.) As shown in Figure 1.10, the receiving station checks the packet to ensure that it is the appropriate length (minimum 64 bytes) and not a fragment caused by a collision.

STEP 2: CHECK THE DESTINATION ADDRESS

After verifying that the packet is not a fragment, the receiving station next checks the destination address of the packet to see if it should be processed, as shown in Figure 1.11. If the packet is addressed to the local station, is a "broadcast," or is to a recognized "multicast" address, the station checks the integrity of the packet.

NOTE
Broadcast addressing is covered in Chapter 4.

FIGURE 1.10

*When viewing packets,
stations look for fragments.*

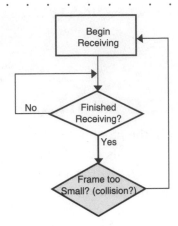

FIGURE 1.11

*Stations check the
destination address.*

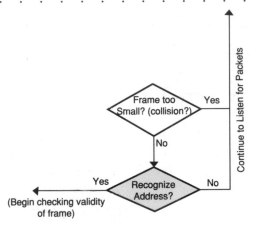

STEP 3: CHECK THE INTEGRITY OF THE PACKET

At this point, a receiving station knows the packet is not a fragment and is addressed to itself or to a recognized address. The station does not know, however, whether the packet is properly formed. Packets that have been corrupted on the cabling segment or were not properly formed by the transmitting station can still be read by receiving stations. To avoid processing these corrupt packets, the receiving station must check several of the packet's characteristics, as shown in Figure 1.12.

FIGURE 1.12
Packets are checked for integrity.

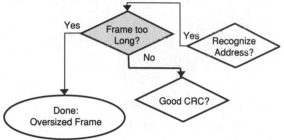

The first characteristic that must be checked is the length. If a frame is larger than 1518 bytes, it is considered an oversized frame. Oversized frames may be caused by a faulty LAN driver.

Packets may also be considered corrupt if one or more bits in the packet have been "swapped" from a 1 to a 0 or vice versa while traveling on the cabling system. If the packet is not oversized, the receiving station checks the packet to determine if the contents are the same upon receipt as they were at the time of transmission. This is called a *Cyclical Redundancy Check* (*CRC*). If the packet fails the CRC check, the receiver then verifies the alignment of the frame.

Misaligned packets do not end on an 8-bit boundary. All packets contain a set number of bytes (8 bits) and must end after a defined number of bytes. Packets that do not end on a byte boundary fail the alignment check. For example, a packet cannot be 72 bytes and 3 bits in length. It must be either 72 bytes or 73 bytes.

If the frame did not pass the CRC check but did end on an 8-bit boundary (proper alignment), it is considered a CRC error.

So far, you have checked the frame to see whether it is a fragment, whether it is too long, whether it contains a CRC error, and whether it is properly aligned. If the frame has successfully passed all these checkpoints, you must now perform the final length check.

The receiving station checks to see if the frame is too short. If the frame is less than 64 bytes but otherwise well formed, it is considered an undersized frame. Undersized frames may be caused by a corrupt LAN driver.

All these checkpoints ensure that packets are valid in length and content before being processed by the receiving station. If the frame fails to pass any of the above checkpoints, it will not be passed to a higher layer protocol for processing by the receiving station.

STEP 4: PROCESS THE PACKET

If the packet has made it successfully through all the checkpoints, as shown in Figure 1.13, it is considered a valid, well-formed, legal-sized frame. If a station is still experiencing communication problems, you must look further into the packet to find the problem. Perhaps a station is using the wrong frame type or has an error in the IPX/SPX header.

F I G U R E 1.13

Packets that have integrity will be processed.

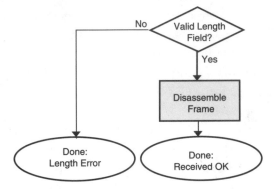

The flowchart shown in Figure 1.14 defines the steps that must be taken in order for a station to process a packet on a CSMA/CD network.

Testing a Station's Ability to Transmit and Receive

If stations have proper network connections, have no malfunctioning cards or transceivers, and follow the rules set forth by the CSMA/CD specifications, they should be able to transmit and receive properly formed frames.

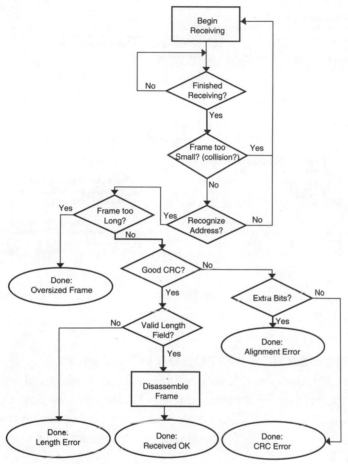

FIGURE I.14

Receipt flowchart

If a user is complaining that he or she cannot communicate on the network segment, a protocol analyzer can be used to test the station's ability to receive and transmit packets.

The LANalyzer's NODEVIEW application checks the connectivity of NetWare IPX client stations. (There is a separate application, SERVERVU, that tests the connectivity of NetWare file servers.)

The NODEVIEW application broadcasts a diagnostic packet, often referred to as a *ping* packet, as illustrated in Figure 1.15. Stations that have the Diagnostic Responder loaded must reply.

NOTE
The Diagnostic Responder is covered in detail in Chapter 11.

FIGURE 1.15

NODEVIEW broadcasts a

diagnostic packet on the

segment.

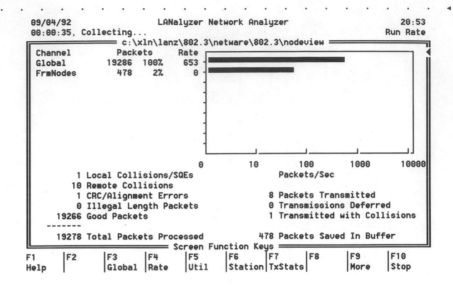

Responding stations are listed in the Station Monitor screen, as you can see in Figure 1.16.

STATIONS THAT RESPOND TO THE PING

If a station passes the IPX ping test but still has trouble communicating, perhaps the problem is an intermittent, or "flaky," connector. Check the connection. There might also be a problem with an upper-layer protocol such as IPX, SPX, or NCP. (These protocols are defined and tested in Part II of this book.)

STATIONS THAT DO NOT RESPOND TO THE TEST

If a station does not respond, it could indicate a problem with the station's configuration or its transmit or receive function.

Is IPX Loaded?

Before assuming the station has a bad card, transceiver, or connection, make certain that IPX is loaded. If IPX is not loaded, the client cannot

```
09/04/92                  LANalyzer Network Analyzer                    20 53
00:00:08, Collecting...                                             Run Station
                  c:\xln\lanz\802.3\netware\802.3\nodeview
Stations seen: 51
                       Packet Rate    Total Packets    Avg. Size     Errors
No.  Station Address    Rcv   Xmt      Rcv     Xmt      Rcv   Xmt    Rcv   Xmt
1    exos651575          0     0        50       0       64    -
2    novel11EFD61        0     0         0       1        -    64
3    exosF8F4F8          0     0         0       1        -    64
4    novel11E70F0        0     0         0       1        -    64
5    exosC22558          0     0         0       1        -    64
6    novel102D64E        0     0         0       1        -    64
7    exos565529          0     0         0       1        -    64
8    exos564688          0     0         0       1        -    64
9    novel1321A6B        0     0         0       1        -    64
10   exosC30670          0     0         0       1        -    64
11   novel1332248B       0     0         0       1        -    64
12   novel11E1047        0     0         0       1        -    64
13   exos524220          0     0         0       1        -    64
14   novel1190ED5        0     0         0       1        -    64
15   exos551009          0     0         0       1        -    64
16   novel11E1AA5        0     0         0       1        -    64
                            Screen Function Keys
F1      F2      F3      F4      F5      F6      F7      F8      F9      F10
Help            Global  Rate    Util    Station TxStats         More    Stop
```

F I G U R E I.16

Station Monitor screen displays responding stations.

respond to the test. Make certain the client has loaded either IPX.COM or IPXODI.COM. Try loading IPX at the client. If IPX is already loaded, you will receive the message "IPX already loaded."

Is the Diagnostic Responder Loaded?

Make certain that the Diagnostic Responder is loaded on the station. NetWare's Diagnostic Responder replies to the IPX ping packet that is transmitted by the NODEVIEW application.

To be certain that the Responder is loaded, unload IPX and reload without using any parameters. When you load IPX.COM or IPXODI.COM, the Diagnostic Responder is automatically loaded unless otherwise specified using parameters. To view available IPX load parameters, type **IPX ?** at the workstation. These options include

NOTE
For further information on Novell's Diagnostic Responder, refer to Chapter II.

IPXODI	Installs IPX, SPX, and the Responder
IPXODI D	Installs IPX and SPX but not the Responder
IPXODI A	Installs IPX but not SPX or the Responder

If you have verified that IPX and the Diagnostic Responder are loaded, check the following:

▸ The transceiver's transmit/receive LEDs, if any

▸ The transceiver cable (if using an external transceiver)

▸ The connection to the cable (transceiver attachment point)

If the transceiver, transceiver cable, and connection seem to be secure and functioning properly, replace the network interface card and run NODEVIEW again.

If the station responds after the card is replaced, the original card was most likely at fault. Verify that the card settings match the configuration in the NET.CFG file. If the station still does not respond, alternately swap out the transceiver, transceiver cable, and transceiver attachment point.

This chapter introduced three access methods: CSMA/CD, token-passing ring and token-passing bus. By stepping through the procedures for transmitting and receiving data on a CSMA/CD network, you have examined the five steps for transmitting and the four steps for receiving packets on an Ethernet network.

You've tested a workstation's ability to transmit and receive packets on the Ethernet segment by using the LANalyzer NODEVIEW application and learned how to determine whether a station will respond to an IPX diagnostic ping.

Chapter 2 analyzes the traffic on an Ethernet cable segment.

Performance Considerations for CSMA/CD

Chapter 1 examined the rules of CSMA/CD. If stations follow these rules, they should be able to transmit and receive packets on the wire. Unfortunately, there are several other factors that can affect a workstation's ability to transmit and receive on Ethernet LANs: utilization of the cabling system, errors on the LAN, inefficient configuration, and so on. This chapter analyzes the utilization of the network cabling system and provides methods for optimizing the network.

Defining Bandwidth Utilization

Consider the Ethernet cable segment as a freeway, as shown in Figure 2.1. During rush hour, the commute is slow because of the traffic. There is generally a higher number of accidents, which may block the road. Also, many freeways now control access by installing timed lights at the entrance ramps. When the light turns green, a car may enter the freeway.

FIGURE 2.1

Ethernet freeway

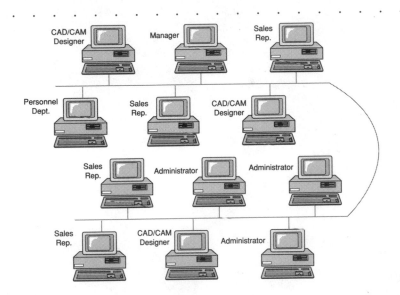

Rush hour on an Ethernet cable may occur at 8:00 A.M. and 5:00 P.M., when people are logging in or logging out. It may also occur when backup is performed across the network. During rush hour, you may find the network slower than normal. In an extreme case, you may not get access to the cable; it may always be busy.

If there is a lot of activity on the cable segment, you will experience collisions, as shown in Figure 2.2, as multiple stations attempt to transmit at the same time. Although collisions are considered normal for an Ethernet LAN, excessive collisions reduce the effectiveness of the network.

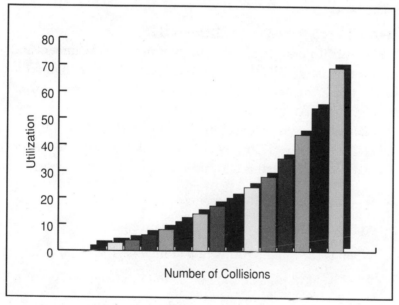

FIGURE 2.2

When utilization goes up, so do collisions

Generally, network personnel can tell when the network is extremely busy based on the response time observed at a workstation. However, this does not identify the cause of a sudden excessive network load. Protocol analyzers allow you to monitor your network usage; you can identify the times when the network is most active, determine typical network usage levels, and detect when the network is experiencing unusually high levels of traffic.

DETERMINING CURRENT BANDWIDTH UTILIZATION

On a freeway, the available bandwidth would be determined by the maximum number of vehicles that could use the freeway. The *current* bandwidth utilization is the amount of traffic the freeway is supporting at this time.

The maximum bandwidth available on an Ethernet LAN is 10 megabits per second. The bandwidth utilization is the amount of cable bandwidth currently in use. For example, a busy segment may be experiencing 60% utilization of the bandwidth, or 60% of 10Mb/s. To determine bandwidth utilization, analyzers look at the kilobytes per second in use as a percentage of the maximum possible. (One thousand kilobytes equal 1 megabyte.)

WHAT IS NORMAL UTILIZATION?

To determine if a condition is unusual, it is necessary to understand what "usual," or normal, is. All NetWare LANs have unique configurations and usage. "Normal" for one network may not be considered "normal" for another.

A *baseline* defines normal activity for a network. Baseline information that relates to the network bandwidth utilization should be documented and referred to often. With this information, you can answer these questions:

NOTE
Chapter 13 provides a comprehensive list of network characteristics that should be included in your baseline. This chapter looks specifically at the bandwidth utilization.

► Is your network load increasing?

► Are unusual peaks in utilization occurring?

► When is the cabling bandwidth at high peak and low peak?

► What types of protocols are using the bandwidth?

► Which users are taking up most of the bandwidth?

GATHERING AND INTERPRETING BASELINE INFORMATION

Running a protocol analyzer on the network segment for at least 24 hours creates a baseline against which you can compare future network activity.

In Figure 2.3, bandwidth information has been gathered for 24 hours using the LANalyzer for NetWare. You are viewing the time period beginning at 10:30 P.M. You can see that the peak utilization of the bandwidth occurs at 8:30 A.M.—a time when people are logging in to the network. This is typical of most LANs.

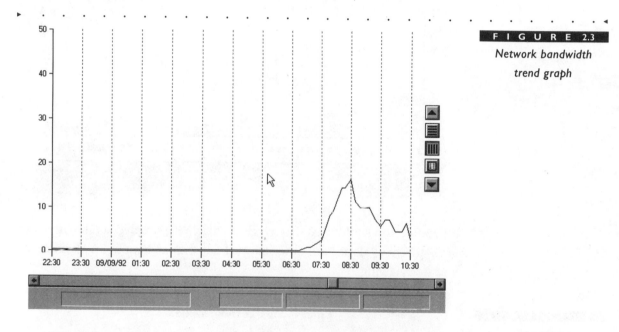

FIGURE 2.3

Network bandwidth
trend graph

In Figure 2.4, you are viewing the bandwidth utilization graph beginning at 11:30 A.M. There are two time periods that show increased network utilization, 5:00 P.M. and 9:00 P.M. The first peak occurs as users log out of the network. The second is during a network backup of all servers to a centralized location.

Monitoring network utilization throughout the day would be a tedious, time-consuming process unless you automated it. The LANalyzer and LANalyzer for NetWare allow unattended collection of network statistics that can be imported into common spreadsheets for later graphing and analysis. The LANalyzer and LANalyzer for NetWare also allow you to set

FIGURE 2.4

*Afternoon and evening
utilization trend*

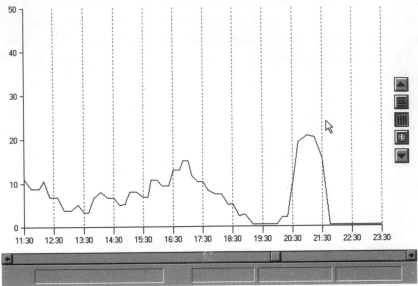

utilization thresholds that will trigger an alarm if exceeded, as shown in Figure 2.5. These alarms are time stamped and can be kept in an alarm report for later viewing.

FIGURE 2.5

*Setting the utilization
alarm threshold*

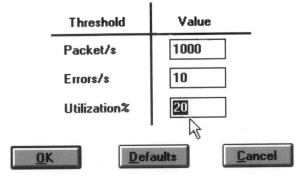

For example, the typical utilization of the network during the day ranges from 5% to 15%. During peak times, however, utilization can jump up to 18%. You can set an alarm at 20% utilization. When the 20% threshold is exceeded, the alarm is triggered.

Monitoring Changes in Bandwidth Utilization

If users begin to complain about performance, the baseline information you created will serve as a reference point for normal activity while you examine the current network performance.

In Figure 2.6, you can see that the network is experiencing some unusual activity. The utilization alarm has been triggered as well. If the utilization climbs high enough, users may begin to complain of network slowness. In Figure 2.7, the LANalyzer for NetWare was used to sort station activity by the number of kilobytes that have been transmitted to determine who is using most of the bandwidth.

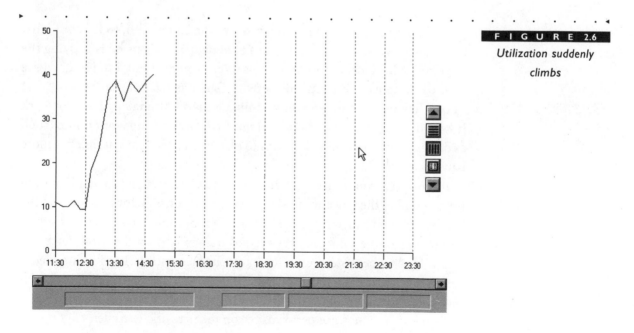

FIGURE 2.6

Utilization suddenly climbs

FIGURE 2.7

Sorting stations based on bandwidth utilization

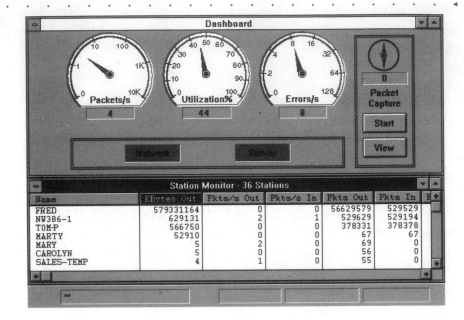

You can call Fred, who is using most of the bandwidth, to find out what type of activity he is performing on the network. Perhaps he is copying the contents of his local drive up to the server or performing intense database queries. If he can perform this activity (such as backing up local drives) during low-peak times, you may eliminate the additional load during work hours. If this is an activity that Fred must perform during work hours (such as database queries), you may need to place him on a segment that has more bandwidth available.

If, however, you notice the network bandwidth is higher overall for each time period of the day and no single user is responsible for overloading the bandwidth, you can assume the network has become busier as the result of an increase in the kilobytes per second transmitted on the cable segment. The cable has become the performance bottleneck. Perhaps you added a database server on the local segment that each user is accessing. This could cause additional traffic on the local segment.

If you wish to increase performance on the network, consider splitting the network into separate segments by using a bridge or router. By splitting the network cabling system into two separate segments, you are "load balancing" across two segments. Figure 2.8 illustrates utilization before splitting the segment, and Figure 2.9 illustrates utilization after splitting the segment. (Since a repeater transmits all traffic between segments, it would not relieve this type of situation.)

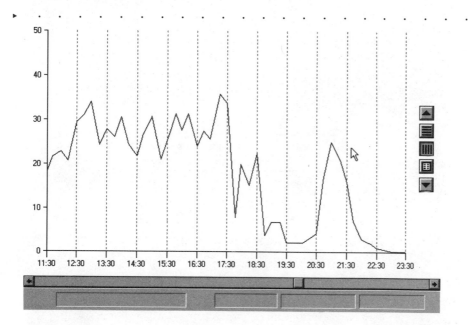

FIGURE 2.8

Utilization before

splitting the segment

After splitting the segment, you should monitor the utilization of each segment. If you have placed most of the power users on a single segment, performance may not be acceptable. You may wish to balance these users across two segments.

Using Bridges to Load Balance

Bridges connect network segments, as shown in Figure 2.10, and do not allow traffic across that is destined for a station on the local segment. A bridge maintains a list of hardware addresses for each of its network interfaces. The bridge creates this list by examining each packet's source address and adding the station to the appropriate interface table.

F I G U R E   2.9

Utilization on segments
after splitting the LAN

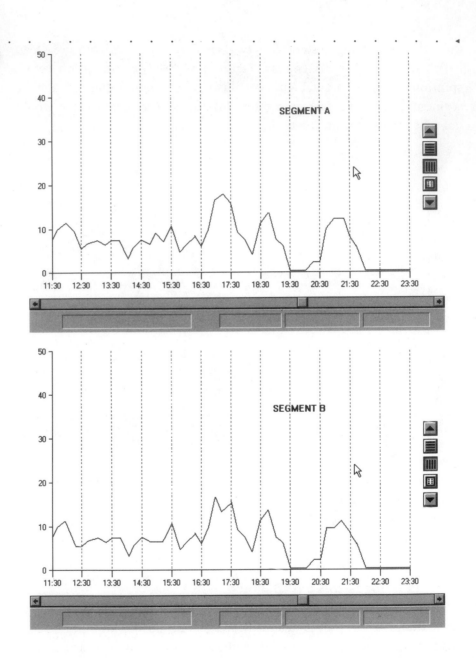

BRIDGE

Interface #1
Node Address List

ABC
DEF

Network
Address
C9-99-01-20

Interface #2
Node Address List

GHI
JKL

Network
Address
C9-99-01-20

Station
ABC

Station
DEF

Station
GHI

Station
JKL

Bridges maintain a list of stations on each segment.

For example, when station ABC transmits a packet, the bridge will see the packet on interface 1 and place station ABC in its table for interface 1. Station DEF transmits a packet, and its station address is placed in the bridge's interface 1 table as well. Stations GHI and JKL, however, will be added to the bridge's interface 2 table since their packets are received by interface 2.

The bridge will use this table to determine whether or not packets should be forwarded to another segment. If station ABC transmits a packet destined for station DEF, the bridge will look up the address in its tables. Since the destination station is located on the interface 1 side of the bridge, the packet will not be forwarded. If, however, station ABC transmits a packet to station GHI, the packet will be forwarded to the segment attached to interface 2.

Using Routers for Load Balancing

Routers separate network traffic based on a "software" address (network address). If you separate a large network into two distinct networks using a router, traffic is not passed onto another segment unless it is destined for a station on the other network.

Routers maintain information regarding the networks to which they are connected. For example, in Figure 2.11, the router is configured to connect two NetWare networks, AB-01-01-01 and CD-02-02-02. When a station on network AB-01-01-01 transmits a packet destined for a server on network CD-02-02-02, the router examines the destination network address contained

NOTE
Chapter 10 examines the routing information gathered from packets on the network.

FIGURE 2.11

*Routers forward packets
based on network
addresses.*

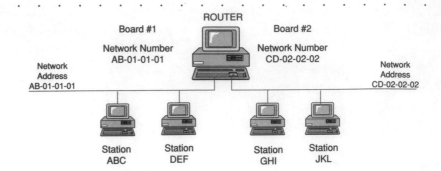

in the packet being transmitted and forwards the packet to the other network. If, however, the packet is destined for the local address network, it will not be forwarded.

The determination of whether to use a bridge or a router is based on several factors. Bridges are generally quicker than routers; however, not many bridge manufacturers can connect to two unlike networks (such as Ethernet and Token Ring). Routers, though generally slower, permit connectivity between unlike network types. Also, whereas bridges simply forward on packets not destined for the local segment, routers maintain tables of information about end-to-end connectivity, such as the next router to send a packet to for the shortest path.

Next you will look at individual bandwidth utilization and determine whether or not a network will support additional workstations on a single segment.

MONITORING INDIVIDUAL USE OF THE BANDWIDTH

To determine if a segment can support additional users, you must first determine how much bandwidth is being consumed by each user on the network. You can provide an approximate percentage of bandwidth in use by each station with a simple formula:

total bandwidth used÷number of nodes on segment

For example, if current overall bandwidth utilization is at 20% and you have 20 users, you can estimate that each user is using 1% of the bandwidth. Adding 20 more users at 1% each will increase overall bandwidth to 40%. This increase in utilization may create an unacceptable response time on the network because the cabling system is overloaded.

Although simple to perform, this formula is not very accurate. If you need to gather more exact statistics, you may wish to "filter" traffic from one or more users on the segment and average their utilization over time. For example, perhaps you currently have three graphics designers working on a segment, as shown in Figure 2.12. They are heavy bandwidth users because of the number of large graphics files they are transferring to and from the server. You need to know the average bandwidth each designer is using so you can estimate the effect of adding another graphics designer to the local segment.

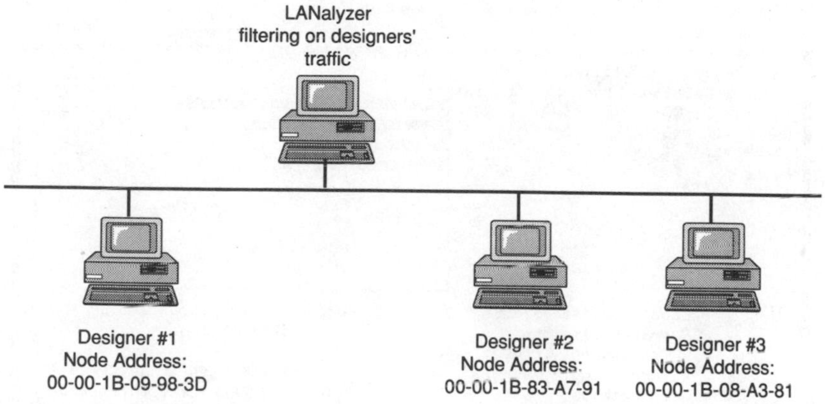

FIGURE 2.12

Graphics designers on segment

LANalyzer filtering on designers' traffic

Designer #1
Node Address:
00-00-1B-09-98-3D

Designer #2
Node Address:
00-00-1B-83-A7-91

Designer #3
Node Address:
00-00-1B-08-A3-81

To determine the approximate load that another designer will place on the network, you can first use the LANalyzer to determine how much of the bandwidth is in use by each of the existing designers.

By defining one receive channel for the traffic of each of the designers, you can determine the average bandwidth utilization for each designer.

As shown in Figure 2.13, tracking the designers over 24 hours will define the typical bandwidth utilization of each. Once this data has been gathered, it can be exported to a spreadsheet and plotted for comparative purposes.

From the information presented in Figure 2.14, you can see that each designer's average bandwidth during working hours (8:00 A.M. to 6:00 P.M.) is 9%.

Now that you know the approximate load per designer, you can use this information to simulate a 9% load on the network and record how often the new designer will have access to the medium on the first attempt to transmit. This is called a *load test*. Because you will not be transmitting the load to a specific device on the network, it is considered a *dumb load test*.

Note
In Chapter 13, you will see how to transmit an intelligent load to test a particular device on the network.

F I G U R E 2.13

Designers use an average of 9% bandwidth each.

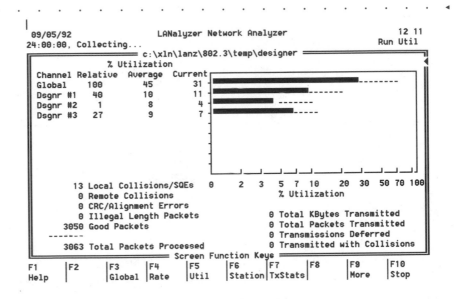

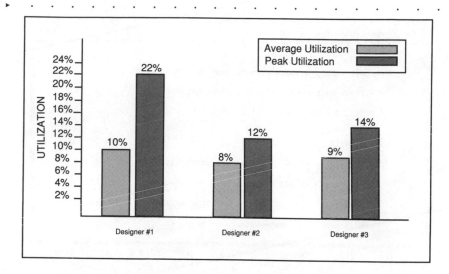

FIGURE 2.14

Spreadsheet comparison
of designers' use

Testing Access to the Medium
(Load Test)

You have now determined that the designers use an average of 9% of the bandwidth. Using the LANalyzer, you can transmit the same load and monitor network performance.

The LANalyzer's GENLOAD application permits you to generate a dumb load on the segment. In Figure 2.15, it is specified that a 9% load of NetWare IPX packets is to be sent to node address 00-00-00-00-00-00.

After starting the application, you can view the TxStats statistics, shown in Figure 2.16, to see that 74% of the time packets are transmitted successfully on the first attempt. This seems reasonable.

Now let's perform the same test generating a 27% load on the segment to simulate the addition of three designers. The TxStats statistics show that the number of successful first attempts to transmit has decreased to 62% (Figure 2.16, Screen 2). As utilization has increased, so has the number of collisions on the local segment. This additional load may not be acceptable for the network. Users will notice slowness when accessing servers or routers on the segment. (From our earlier analogy, this is like driving in rush-hour traffic.)

FIGURE 2.15

Setting up GENLOAD to transmit a 9% load

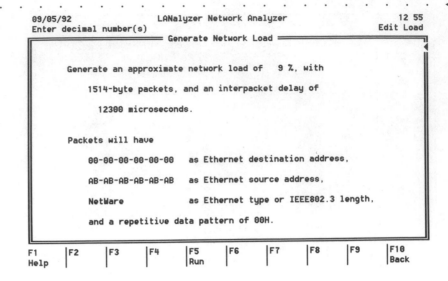

```
09/05/92                    LANalyzer Network Analyzer                12 55
Enter decimal number(s)                                             Edit Load
                         ═══ Generate Network Load ═══

     Generate an approximate network load of   9 %, with

        1514-byte packets, and an interpacket delay of

           12300 microseconds.


     Packets will have

        00-00-00-00-00-00    as Ethernet destination address,

        AB-AB-AB-AB-AB-AB    as Ethernet source address,

        NetWare              as Ethernet type or IEEE802.3 length,

        and a repetitive data pattern of 00H.



F1      |F2    |F3    |F4    |F5    |F6    |F7    |F8    |F9    |F10
Help    |      |      |      |Run   |      |      |      |      |Back
```

Stress-Testing the Network Cabling System

You have simulated a load on the network based on one type of user. You do not, however, know the exact impact the load has placed on the other users accessing the cable system. How much has performance degraded because of the added load?

The next example sets up a performance test measuring file transfer time under varying loads, as shown in Figure 2.17. First you will transfer a file while generating a 10% load and record the transfer time. Then you will increase the load and record the impact on the file transfer time.

For this test, you will need to use the LANalyzer and one client workstation (for the file transfer). This test uses the following steps:

1 · Edit the LANalyzer's default application.

2 · Set up a receive channel.

3 · Perform a file transfer.

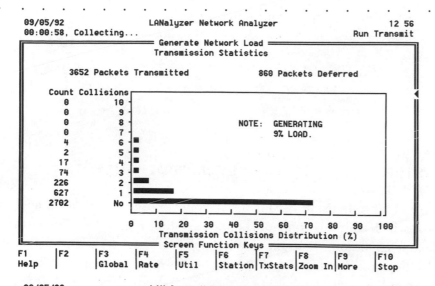

FIGURE 2.16

TxStats statistics display access to the medium.

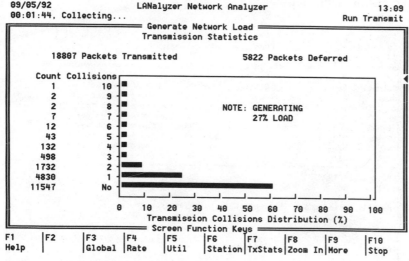

4 · Record the file transfer time.

5 · Increase the load; repeat the file transfer.

6 · Record the results.

FIGURE 2.17

Setting up the

performance test

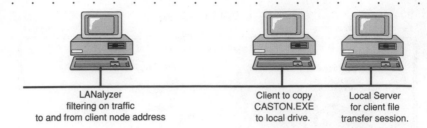

| LANalyzer filtering on traffic to and from client node address | Client to copy CASTON.EXE to local drive. | Local Server for client file transfer session. |

STEP 1: EDIT THE LANALYZER'S DEFAULT APPLICATION

In order to transmit varying loads, you will use the DEFAULT application, which is already configured for load-testing. Figure 2.18 illustrates the default application transmit channels. If your LANalyzer DEFAULT application is still configured as it was when installed, you can skip this step and continue with step 2.

FIGURE 2.18

DEFAULT application

transmit channels

```
09/05/92                  LANalyzer Network Analyzer                    13 11
Enter a name                                                      Edit Transmit
============== c:\xln\lanz\802.3\default ==============
TRANSMIT
Channel              Delay                    Preamble    Coll.
Name     Active  Count (100us)  CRC  Collide  Bytes       Backoff
tx_10%   Yes     Inf     100    Good  No      8 (normal)  Normal
tx_20%   Yes     Inf      47    Good  No      8 (normal)  Normal
tx_30%   Yes     Inf      28    Good  No      8 (normal)  Normal
tx_40%   Yes     Inf      18    Good  No      8 (normal)  Normal
tx_50%   Yes     Inf      12    Good  No      8 (normal)  Normal
tx_60%   Yes     Inf       6    Good  No      8 (normal)  Normal

MULTIPACKET TRANSMISSION
Txall    No        6       0    Good  No      8 (normal)  Normal

Transmit serially with the following relative frequencies:
         tx_10%    1        tx_20%   1        tx_30%    1
         tx_40%    1        tx_50%   1        tx_60%    1

Transmit after _    99:00:00 hours or  _


F1      |F2     |F3    |F4      |F5    |F6     |F7      |F8    |F9     |F10
Help    |Revert |Save  |Options |Mode  |Packet |Receive |Xmit  |Alarms |Back
```

This application is configured to transmit the following loads:

Channel 1—10% load   1518 byte packets every 100 microseconds

Channel 2—20% load   1518 byte packets every 47 microseconds

Channel 3—30% load   1518 byte packets every 28 microseconds

Channel 4—40% load   1518 byte packets every 18 microseconds

Channel 5—50% load   1518 byte packets every 12 microseconds

Channel 6—60% load   1518 byte packets every 6 microseconds

STEP 2: SET UP A RECEIVE CHANNEL

As shown in Figure 2.19, define one receive channel that will filter on packets to and from your client station. You will use this receive channel to capture and time-stamp packets while the station transfers files.

Run the application and begin transmitting a 10% load on the network.

STEP 3: PERFORM A FILE TRANSFER

In this example, you are copying the CASTON.EXE file from the PUBLIC directory to the local C drive. For this file transfer, you can use the DOS COPY command.

STEP 4: RECORD THE FILE TRANSFER TIME

Since the application captured only packets to and from the client workstation, all packets in the trace buffer are from the file transfer. To calculate the total required time for the file transfer, you can select the *relative*

FIGURE 2.19

Set up one receive channel to filter on traffic to and from your client station.

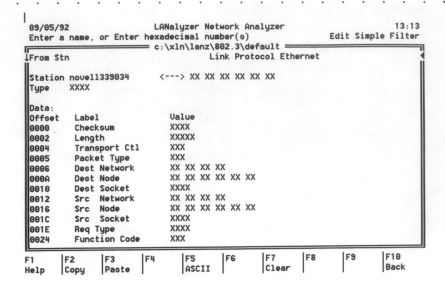

```
 09/05/92              LANalyzer Network Analyzer            13:13
 Enter a name, or Enter hexadecimal number(s)       Edit Simple Filter
========================= c:\xln\lanz\802.3\default =========================
↓From Stn                              Link Protocol Ethernet              ◄

Station novell339034      <---> XX XX XX XX XX XX
Type     XXXX

Data:
Offset   Label                 Value
0000     Checksum              XXXX
0002     Length                XXXXX
0004     Transport Ctl         XXX
0005     Packet Type           XXX
0006     Dest Network          XX XX XX XX
000A     Dest Node             XX XX XX XX XX XX
0010     Dest Socket           XXXX
0012     Src  Network          XX XX XX XX
0016     Src  Node             XX XX XX XX XX XX
001C     Src  Socket           XXXX
001E     Req Type              XXXX
0024     Function Code         XXX

F1      F2      F3      F4      F5      F6      F7      F8      F9      F10
Help    Copy    Paste           ASCII           Clear                   Back
```

time-stamp viewing option. Figure 2.20 depicts all packet arrival times required for the file transfer.

STEP 5: INCREASE THE LOAD; REPEAT THE FILE TRANSFER

Repeat steps 2 through 4 for each load and record the file transfer times.

STEP 6: RECORD THE RESULTS

As shown in Figure 2.21, file transfer time has increased dramatically under a load of greater than 30%.

You have now experienced the delay that users are subjected to when trying to work on a network segment that is heavily used.

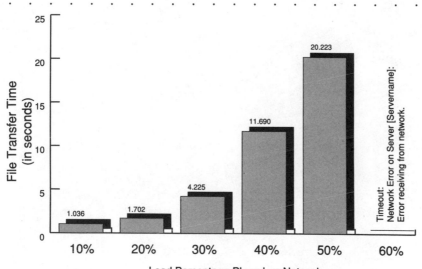

```
09/05/92              LANalyzer Network Analyzer              18:03
Press Alt-T to toggle between summary modes              Trace Summary
══════════════════════════ Trace Buffer ══════════════════════════
↑ Created on 09/05/92 18:02:21   Elapsed Time 00:00:30   Total Packets   999◀

  Pkt#  Source         Destination    Protocol  Size  Error  Channels  Rel Time
     1  novell339034   novell017181   NetWare    64          .......8   0.000 ms
     2  novell017181   novell339034   NetWare   308          .......8   8.264 ms
     3  novell339034   novell017181   NetWare    64          .......8   9.267 ms
     4  novell017181   novell339034   NetWare   464          .......8  19.857 ms
     5  novell339034   novell017181   NetWare    64          .......8  30.271 ms
     6  novell017181   novell339034   NetWare   304          .......8  31.018 ms
     7  novell339034   novell017181   NetWare    64          .......8  35.576 ms
     8  novell017181   novell339034   NetWare   308          .......8  43.250 ms
     9  novell339034   novell017181   NetWare    64          .......8  44.516 ms
    10  novell017181   novell339034   NetWare   308          .......8  47.345 ms
    11  novell339034   novell017181   NetWare    64          .......8  48.342 ms
    12  novell017181   novell339034   NetWare   308          .......8  56.723 ms
    13  novell339034   novell017181   NetWare    64          .......8  57.710 ms
    14  novell017181   novell339034   NetWare   348          .......8  67.222 ms
    15  novell339034   novell017181   NetWare    64          .......8  68.369 ms
    16  novell017181   novell339034   NetWare   348          .......8  72.116 ms

F1      F2      F3      F4        F5      F6       F7        F8      F9      F10
Help    Load    Print   Options   Save    Decode   Compare   Find    Go To   Back
```

F I G U R E 2.20

*Calculating the file
transfer time*

F I G U R E 2.21

*Network performance
during load test*

This chapter has examined bandwidth utilization and its effect on network efficiency. Using the LANalyzer, you have generated a load on the network and analyzed the responses. When you performed a load test and examined your transmit statistics, you determined how often packets were transmitted successfully on the first attempt. By timing a file transfer under various load conditions, you examined network performance degradation under higher utilization.

The next chapter deals with the wiring specifications and performance of Ethernet networks, including 10Base5, 10Base2, and 10BaseT. The chapter presents analysis and troubleshooting techniques using various cabling tests and watching for specific network errors.

CHAPTER 3

Wiring Specifications and Performance

Chapters 1 and 2 examined how CSMA/CD networks access the cabling system and how to analyze bandwidth utilization. However, what if the cabling system itself is not configured properly? Workstations may not be able to transmit or receive. Studying the utilization would be pointless since either there would be no traffic or the utilization statistics might be misleading.

The wiring system of an Ethernet network provides the communication medium upon which packets travel.

The 802.3 specification includes various CSMA/CD wiring configurations. This chapter begins with an overview of the most common wiring configurations for NetWare Ethernet LANs:

- ▶ 10Base5 (thicknet)

- ▶ 10Base2 (thinnet)

- ▶ 10BaseT (unshielded twisted-pair, or UTP)

You will use the LANalyzer to track and determine the causes of various errors that may be related to faulty wiring or may not follow recommended wiring specifications and limitations.

10Base5

10Base5 networks use thick Ethernet cable for the primary trunk and drop cables to the individual workstations, as shown in Figure 3.1. Although bulky and difficult to install, this cabling system allows greater distance on cable segments.

The following table lists 10Base5 cabling specifications:

Taps per segment	100
Maximum node separation	5 segments /4 repeaters

Maximum segment length	500 meters
Network span	2500 meters
Minimum length between transceivers	2.5 meters
Maximum transceiver cable length	50 meters

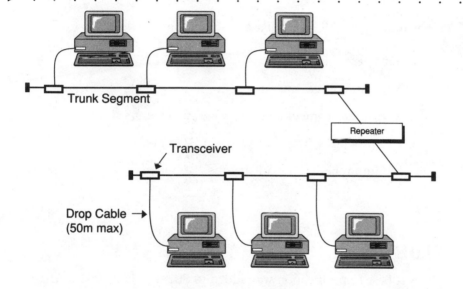

FIGURE 3.1

Thicknet cabling system

10Base2

10Base2 networks use thin coaxial cable, as shown in Figure 3.2. These systems are often referred to as "thinnet" or "cheapernet." This specification does not allow the use of drop cables to the workstation. Instead, workstations are attached directly to the primary trunk, using T-connectors.

FIGURE 3.2

Thinnet cabling system

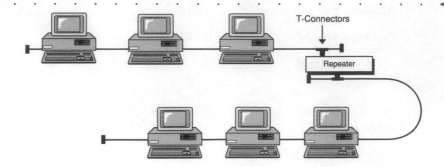

The following table lists 10Base2 cabling specifications:

Taps per segment	30
Maximum node separation	5 segments /4 repeaters
Maximum segment length	185 meters
Network span	925 meters
Minimum between workstations	.5 meters

10BaseT

The 10BaseT specification was added to 802.3 in late 1991. It defines a CSMA/CD network that uses unshielded twisted-pair (a common type of telephone wire) wiring in a star configuration, as shown in Figure 3.3. Because of its potentially low cabling costs and modular style, 10BaseT networks are becoming extremely popular for NetWare LANs.

The 10BaseT specification defines only unshielded twisted-pair wiring. It does not include shielded twisted-pair cabling. Proper operation is dependent upon an acceptable number of twists per foot. These twists prevent crosstalk. *Crosstalk* is caused when signals stray from one wiring pair to another, corrupting the signal.

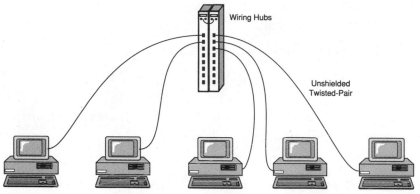

The following table lists 10BaseT cabling specifications:

Maximum nodes per segment	512
Concentrators in sequence	4 maximum
Maximum node separation	5 segments /4 repeaters
Maximum workstation-to-concentrator length	100 meters

Improper Cabling Problems

Improper cabling of networks can cause a variety of problems on NetWare LANs. Symptoms include slow performance, inability to establish or maintain a workstation connection, and corrupted transmissions.

Many of the symptoms presented in this chapter, such as CRC errors and collisions, are covered in detail in Chapter 5. Cabling problems that can affect network performance include

- ▶ Opens or shorts in the cable
- ▶ Noise or electromagnetic interference (EMI)

- ▶ Inadequate interspacing (spacing between taps or workstations)

- ▶ Improper termination

- ▶ Improper ground

- ▶ Segment too long

Using a protocol analyzer, you can determine whether or not a network has a possible cabling problem.

TESTING FOR SHORTS AND OPENS

The LANalyzer and many other protocol analyzers provide a cable-checking mechanism much like a TDR (time domain reflectometer). They transmit a series of bits down the cable, time the response, and examine the return signal (if there is one).

This function is also used to determine if the cable problem is a short or an open. Figure 3.4 shows how the LANalyzer indicates a short in the cable. A short may be caused by a slight break in the cable or poor connectors. Often, a short causes only intermittent network problems. To simulate a

F I G U R E 3.4

The LANalyzer indicates a short in the cable.

```
09/05/92              LANalyzer Network Analyzer              15 51
                                                          Cable Check

      Board set to baseband Ethernet mode.

    ♥ Continuously checking Transceiver and Ethernet cable.

      Short on Ethernet cable
      Distance to fault on Ethernet is 45 meters.
      Distance on Cheapernet is 22 meters.



   F1    |F2    |F3    |F4    |F5    |F6    |F7    |F8    |F9    |F10
   Help  |      |      |      |      |      |      |      |      |Back
```

short, unfold a metal paper clip and touch one end to the cable's center conductor and the other to the shield.

An open, however, causes the entire network segment to be unavailable for transmission. Figure 3.5 shows how the LANalyzer indicates an open cable segment. A segment that has only local collisions occuring on it must be open at one end. Removing the terminator from one end of a segment will simulate an open.

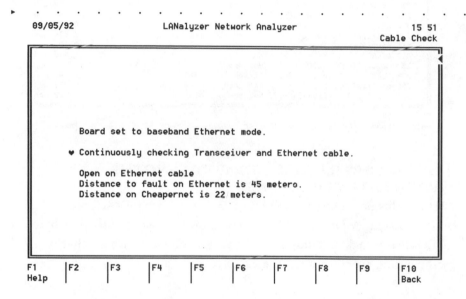

```
09/05/92                 LANalyzer Network Analyzer                    15 51
                                                                   Cable Check


         Board set to baseband Ethernet mode.

       ♥ Continuously checking Transceiver and Ethernet cable.

         Open on Ethernet cable
         Distance to fault on Ethernet is 45 meters.
         Distance on Cheapernet is 22 meters.




 F1      F2      F3      F4      F5      F6      F7      F8      F9      F10
 Help                                                                   Back
```

FIGURE 3.5

The LANalyzer indicates an open cable segment.

INDICATIONS OF IMPROPER GROUNDING

An excessive number of CRC errors, as shown in Figure 3.6, may be indicative of a network that has been improperly grounded and contains a distributed fault. A *distributed fault* is one that cannot be attributed to a single component on the network. If CRC errors are coming from multiple stations, check cable grounding. However, if you can attribute CRC errors to a single network interface card, replace the card.

Late collisions may also be caused by a deaf node, as covered in Chapter 5.

FIGURE 3.6

CRC errors from multiple stations indicate a cable grounding problem.

```
09/05/92                    LANalyzer Network Analyzer              21 24
Press ALT-T to toggle between summary modes                   Trace Summary
                             === b:\crc ===
Created On 09/05/92 20:15:32   Elapsed Time 00:00:19   Total Packets      2600

   Pkt# Source      Destination Protocol   Size  Error  Channels IntPkt Time
‡  344 novell1EF22C SJF-SALSA   NetWare      74  CRC    12......  0.403 ms◀
‡  345 novell1EF22C SJF-SALSA   NetWare      74         1.......  0.403 ms◀
   346 novell1187450 MKTG       NetWare      64  CRC    12......  0.475 ms
   347 MKTG        novell1EF22C NetWare     184  CRC    12......  0.770 ms
   348 MKTG        novell1EF22C NetWare     184         1.......  0.770 ms
   349 exos8e4501  SALES        NetWare      64  CRC    12......  0.561 ms
   350 SJF-SALSA   novell1EF22C NetWare      64         1.......  0.671 ms
   351 3com90d0b5  SALES        NetWare      64  CRC    12......  0.412 ms
   352 SALES       novell1EF22C NetWare     184         1.......  0.756 ms
   353 novell1897612 ADMIN1     NetWare      64  CRC    12......  0.559 ms
   354 novell1897612 ADMIN1     NetWare      64  CRC    12......  0.559 ms
   355 novell1EF22C SALES       NetWare      64         1.......  0.392 ms
   356 SALES       novell1EF22C NetWare      64         1.......  0.545 ms
   357 novell1EF22C BLDG4       NetWare     568         1.......  1.002 ms
   358 BLDG4       novell1EF22C NetWare     390         1.......  1.343 ms
   359 novell1674590 BLDG4      NetWare      64  CRC    12......  0.521 ms
   360 SJF-SALSA   novell1EF22C NetWare     184         1.......  0.733 ms

 F1    |F2    |F3    |F4      |F5     |F6     |F7      |F8   |F9     |F10
 Help  |Load  |Print |Options |Buffer |Decode |Compare |Find |Go To  |Back
```

DETECTING ILLEGAL SEGMENT LENGTHS WITH LATE COLLISIONS

Late collisions, illustrated in Figure 3.7, may also be a symptom of a cabling problem. A *late collision* is a collision that has occured 64 bytes or more into the packet. It indicates that a segment may be longer than allowed by the wiring specifications (see Chapter 3).

FIGURE 3.7

Late collisions may indicate that a segment is longer than specifications allow.

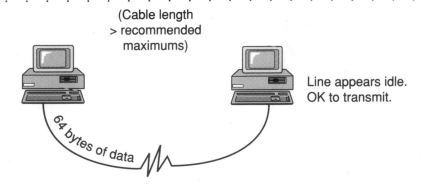

(Cable length > recommended maximums)

64 bytes of data

Line appears idle.
OK to transmit.

A station will believe it has control of the cable segment if it has already transmitted 64 bytes. If another node at the far end of the segment has not yet seen the packet and transmits, this packet will collide with the first transmission after the first 64 bytes have been sent.

TESTING STATION CONNECTIVITY

Using the LANalyzer, you can test a workstation's transceiver cable (the wire connecting a workstation to an external transceiver), as shown in Figure 3.8. Placing the LANalyzer on the transceiver cable that is in question, load the LANalyzer software and transmit a single packet on the network. (Try the NODEVIEW application.) An error message is displayed at the top of the screen if the LANalyzer cannot transmit.

The location of cabling problems can be very difficult to detect on an Ethernet network. When the network is down, how can one localize a fault? Many technicians recommend "shortening" an Ethernet segment until the problems are no longer seen and then beginning to expand the network

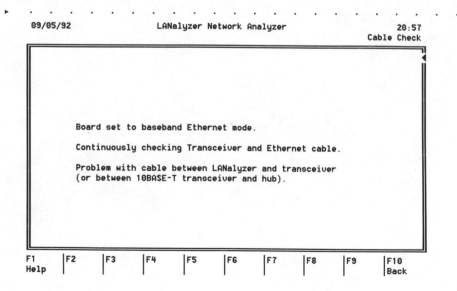

FIGURE 3.8

Testing the transceiver cable connection

until the problem recurs. Using the LANalyzer, you can detect errors that result from poor wiring, grounding, and not following defined specifications for Ethernet cabling systems.

This chapter has listed the specifications for the three most common Ethernet cabling systems: 10Base5, 10Base2, and 10BaseT. Using the specifications and analysis procedures defined, you should now be confident in testing and solving typical cabling problems such as cabling shorts, opens, and improper grounding.

The next chapter defines the four Ethernet frame types that can be found in the NetWare environment.

CHAPTER 4

Netware's Ethernet Frame Structure

In Chapters 1 through 3, you examined the medium access method (CSMA/CD), cabling utilization, and cabling specifications for 802.3/Ethernet LANs. When stations access the transmission medium, however, data must be encapsulated in a frame. *Frames* provide a method for synchronizing receiving stations, defining the sender and addressee, and defining the upper-layer protocol using the frame (such as NetWare's IPX Protocol or IP, the Internet Protocol).

Since the release of NetWare v3.0, the use of multiple frame types and multiple protocols has become quite common. This feature allows the interconnection of a variety of protocols, such as NetWare, AppleTalk Phase I and II, TCP/IP, and FTAM.

This flexibility has caused some confusion regarding frames, protocols, and their interoperability. This chapter first examines the NetWare operating system support for Ethernet frames, as well as the protocols that can be used with each frame type. Further in this chapter, you will view the structure of the four frame types that can be found on NetWare Ethernet LANs. Finally, you will use the frame structure information to analyze a LAN to determine what frames are in use by servers and clients and why a workstation may receive a "File server not found" message.

Frame Types on NetWare LANs

NetWare supports four different frame structures for Ethernet network cards. In the NetWare environment, they are called

NOTE
This book uses the frame type names defined by Novell and used within the AUTOEXEC.NCF and NET.CFG files.

Ethernet_802.3

Ethernet_II

Ethernet_802.2

Ethernet_SNAP

When NetWare v3.x is used, frame types are specified in the NET.CFG file for Open Data-Link Interface (ODI) workstation drivers. At the file server, the frame type is specified at the server console prompt or within the AUTOEXEC.NCF file. NetWare v3.11's ODI support allows multiple protocols and multiple frame types to use a single board, as you can see in Figure 4.1.

NOTE
Ethernet_802.3 is the default frame type for NetWare v2.x and v3.x networks.

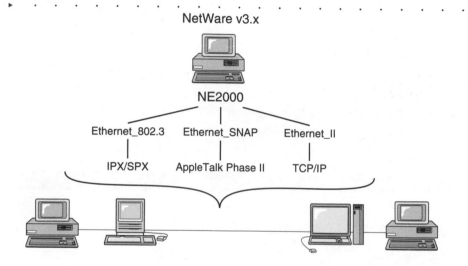

NetWare v3.x

NE2000

Ethernet_802.3   Ethernet_SNAP   Ethernet_II

IPX/SPX   AppleTalk Phase II   TCP/IP

FIGURE 4.1
NetWare LANs can use multiple frames and protocols.

NetWare v2.x, non-ODI drivers, and external routers (BRIDGE.EXE or ROUTER.EXE) may use only the Ethernet_802.3 and Ethernet_II frame types. These frame types can be specified using the ECONFIG utility. The ECONFIG utility is covered later in this chapter.

Table 4.1 lists the NetWare operating systems and the frame types they support.

With the release of NetWare v3.11, you can now have up to four frame types used by a single card in the server. For example, an NE2000 driver can be loaded using all four frame types listed in Table 4.1. This allows a single network interface card to support protocols that do not use the same frame type.

NOTE
Novell's Multi-Protocol Router is an external router that supports multiple frame types and multiple protocols.

TABLE 4.1

NetWare Operating System
Frame Support

NETWARE VERSION	FRAME TYPES SUPPORTED
NetWare v2.x	Ethernet_802.3 (802.3 Raw)
	Ethernet_II
NetWare v3.x	Ethernet_802.3 (802.3 Raw)
	Ethernet_II
	Ethernet_802.2
	Ethernet_SNAP

MATCHING PROTOCOLS WITH SUPPORTED FRAME TYPES

Not all protocols can be used with each frame type available. Refer to Table 4.2 for a quick reference listing of frames and protocols.

TABLE 4.2

Protocols and Associated
Frame Types

PROTOCOLS	FRAME TYPES
Ethernet_II	IPX/SPX, TCP/IP, and AppleTalk Phase I
Ethernet_802.2	IPX/SPX and FTAM
Ethernet_802.3	IPX/SPX
Ethernet_SNAP	IPX/SPX, TCP/IP, and AppleTalk Phase II

The Ethernet_802.3 frame type can be bound only to NetWare's IPX/SPX protocol. If you attempt to bind Ethernet_802.3 to another frame type, you will receive this error message: "Warning: [PROTOCOL] does not recognize the media 'ETHERNET_802.3'. Using defaults. Attempt to bind [PROTOCOL] LAN protocol to [LAN DRIVER/version/date] failed."

If this command was in an AUTOEXEC.NCF file, the error message may scroll past on the console screen when you boot the server. To check the frame types bound to the protocols, type CONFIG at the server, as shown in Figure 4.2.

NOTE
**Chapter 5 examines
various frame errors
and their causes.**

```
:CONFIG

File server name: SALES1
IPX internal network number: A9990001

NetWare NE3200 v3.18 (920115)
     Hardware setting: Slot 5, I/O Port 5C80h to 5CAFh, Interrupt 5h
     Node address: 00001B0945D4
     Frame type: ETHERNET_802.3
     Board name: IPXNET
     LAN protocol: IPX network B4440101

NetWare NE3200 v3.18 (920115)
     Hardware setting: Slot 5, I/O Port 5C80h to 5CAFh, Interrupt 5h
     Node address: 00001B0945D4
     Frame type: ETHERNET_802.2
     Board name: TEMP
     No LAN protocols are bound to this LAN board.
```

FIGURE 4.2

*Typing **CONFIG** shows no
protocol bound to an
Ethernet_802.2 frame.*

The following sections review the structure of each Ethernet frame type. By understanding a properly formed frame, you should be able to determine when a frame is corrupted or malformed.

Ethernet_802.3

With NetWare versions up to and including v3.11, Ethernet_802.3 is the default frame type. This frame type is often referred to as "802.3 raw."

PROTOCOLS SUPPORTED

The Ethernet_802.3 frame type, shown in Figure 4.3, is exclusive to Novell's IPX/SPX Protocol. Only Novell's IPX/SPX Protocol can be bound to this frame type.

"802.3 raw" is similar to a true 802.3-compliant frame but does not contain the LLC (Logical Link Control) information in the packet (hence, the "raw" designator).

FIGURE 4.3

Ethernet_802.3 frame

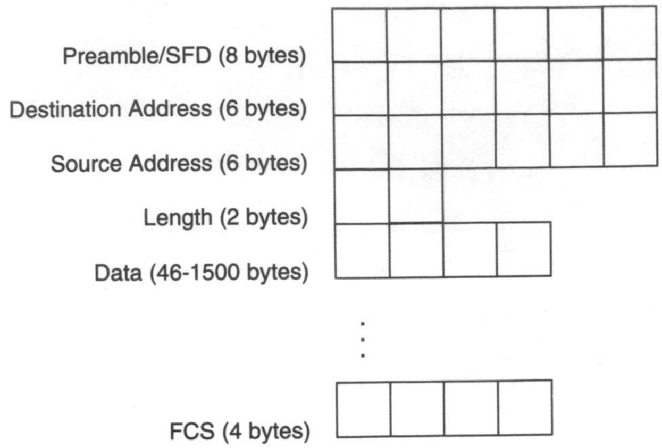

Preamble/SFD (8 bytes)

Destination Address (6 bytes)

Source Address (6 bytes)

Length (2 bytes)

Data (46-1500 bytes)

FCS (4 bytes)

ETHERNET_802.3 FRAME STRUCTURE

The following sections define the fields shown in Figure 4.3.

Preamble and Start Frame Delimiter

The preamble is a 7-byte field used to synchronize the receiving stations. It contains alternating 1's and 0's. The start frame delimiter (SFD) is 1 byte and trails the preamble. The SFD also contains alternating 1's and 0's. The SFD, however, ends with two consecutive 1's. The two 1's signify the beginning of the frame.

The preamble and start frame delimiters are shown in Figure 4.4.

Destination Address

The destination address, shown in Figure 4.5, is a 6-byte field that contains the hardware (or node) address of the station on the local segment to which the packet is addressed. The address FF-FF-FF-FF-FF-FF denotes a broadcast address.

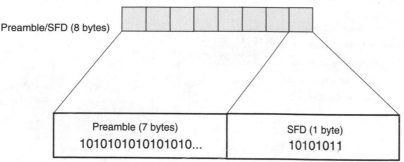

Preamble/SFD (8 bytes)

Preamble (7 bytes)	SFD (1 byte)
1010101010101010...	10101011

The preamble is used for synchronization.

The Start Frame Delimiter indicates data is about to begin.

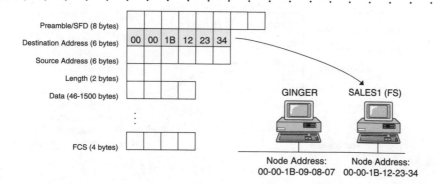

Preamble/SFD (8 bytes)
Destination Address (6 bytes)
Source Address (6 bytes)
Length (2 bytes)
Data (46-1500 bytes)
FCS (4 bytes)

00 00 1B 12 23 34

GINGER   SALES1 (FS)

Node Address: Node Address:
00-00-1B-09-08-07   00-00-1B-12-23-34

Source Address

The source address, shown in Figure 4.6, contains the node address of the station on the local segment that sent the packet. The source address contains the hardware (or node) address of a local workstation, server, or router. The source address cannot be broadcast (FF-FF-FF-FF-FF-FF).

Length Field

The length field, shown in Figure 4.7, is a 2-byte field that defines the length of upper-layer data contained in the data portion of the frame. This value must be 1500 (decimal) or less in a valid Ethernet_802.3 frame.

NOTE
If the frame is valid and the length value is greater than 1500 (decimal), it is an Ethernet_II frame and this is a type field.

FIGURE 4.6

*The source address
contains the node number
of the transmitting station
on the local segment.*

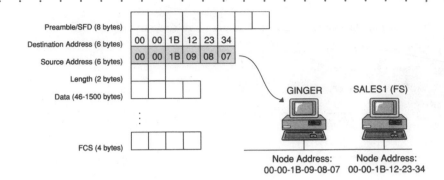

FIGURE 4.7

*The length field denotes the
length of the data portion
of the frame.*

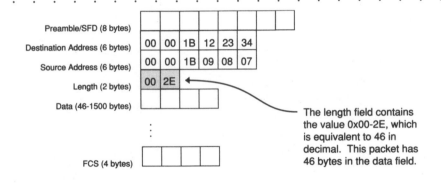

Data Field

The data field, shown in Figure 4.8, is where NetWare's IPX header will begin. The length of the data field must be between 46 and 1500 bytes.

NOTE
**The IPX header format
is defined in Chapter 6.**

Padding

In order to achieve the Ethernet minimum of 64 bytes for a frame, the data field must be a minimum of 46 bytes. The 46-byte data field, added to the 18-byte frame fields, totals the required 64-byte frame size.

However, if the data to be transmitted in the packet does not meet the 46-byte minimum length, it will be padded with bytes, as shown in Figure 4.9, to ensure that the data portion of the frame is least 46 bytes in length.

Preamble/SFD (8 bytes)

Destination Address (6 bytes) | 00 | 00 | 1B | 12 | 23 | 34

Source Address (6 bytes) | 00 | 00 | 1B | 09 | 08 | 07

Length (2 bytes) | 00 | 2E

Data (46-1500 bytes) | FF | FF

FCS (4 bytes)

Since Novell's IPX/SPX is the only protocol that may be bound to the Ethernet_802.3 frame, the data portion will always start with the IPX header -- the IPX header begins with 0xFF-FF.

Preamble/SFD (8 bytes)

Destination Address (6 bytes) | 00 | 00 | 1B | 12 | 23 | 34

Source Address (6 bytes) | 00 | 00 | 1B | 09 | 08 | 07

Length (2 bytes) | 00 | 2E

Data (46-1500 bytes) | FF | FF

Padding | AB | CD | EF | 34

FCS (4 bytes)

The data portion can be padded to ensure that the entire frame meets the minimum requirement of 64 bytes in length.

Frame Check Sequence (FCS)

Error-checking is built into each Ethernet frame to ensure that only valid frames are processed by the receiving station. The FCS field contains a 4-byte CRC (Cyclic Redundancy Check) value. A CRC check is performed by the transmitting station before sending the packet. The CRC value is placed in the FCS field, as you can see in Figure 4.10. The receiving station will

FIGURE 4.10

*CRC values are placed in
the FCS field.*

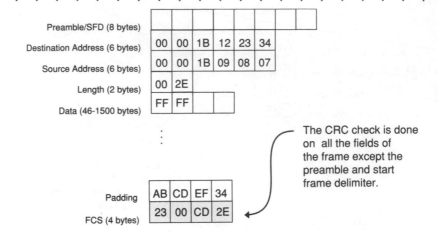

perform the same CRC check and match the resulting value against the contents of the FCS field. If the numbers match, the frame is assumed to be valid. The Ethernet chipset will check this field and determine whether or not a packet is valid. As shown in Chapter 1, an alignment test will also be performed on any packet with an invalid CRC value.

The CRC value is calculated based upon the contents of the destination address, source address, length, data, and pad.

Total Ethernet_802.3 Frame Length

When defining the total frame length, the preamble and start frame delimiter are not counted. Based on the preceding information, minimum and maximum lengths are defined by adding all the frame field lengths:

Destination address	6 bytes
Source address	6 bytes
Length	2 bytes
Data and padding	46–1500 bytes

FCS   4 bytes

Minimum frame size   64 bytes

Maximum frame size   1518 bytes

Figure 4.11 shows a decode of the Ethernet_802.3 frame.

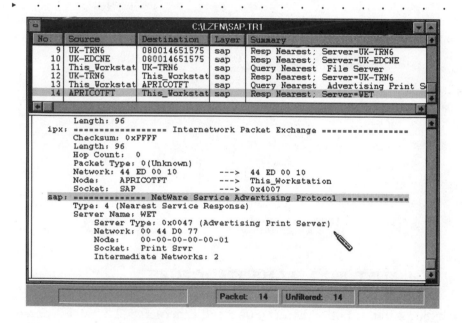

FIGURE 4.11

Decode of Ethernet_802.3

Ethernet_802.2

The Ethernet_802.2 frame type is considered IEEE-compliant because it contains both the 802.3 fields and the 802.2 fields. The 802.2 fields are also referred to as the LLC (Logical Link Control) layer within the frame.

PROTOCOLS SUPPORTED

The Ethernet_802.2 frame, shown in Figure 4.12, can be linked with Novell's IPX/SPX Protocol and the FTAM (File Transfer, Access, and Management) Protocol.

FIGURE 4.12

802.2 frame structure

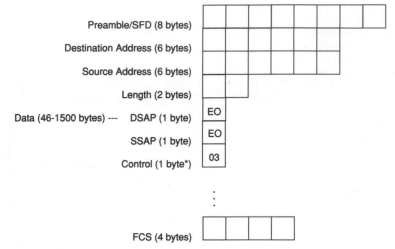

Preamble/SFD (8 bytes)

Destination Address (6 bytes)

Source Address (6 bytes)

Length (2 bytes)

Data (46-1500 bytes) --- DSAP (1 byte)   EO

SSAP (1 byte)   EO

Control (1 byte*)   03

FCS (4 bytes)

* NetWare's IPX/SPX will always use a 1-byte control field containing
the value 0x03, that denotes an unnumbered format for the Ethernet_802.2 layer.

ETHERNET_802.2 FRAME STRUCTURE

The Ethernet_802.2 frame contains common fields with the Ethernet_802.3 frame. Both Ethernet_802.2 and Ethernet_802.3 frames contain

- ▸ The preamble and start frame delimiter (8 bytes)
- ▸ The destination address (6 bytes)
- ▸ The source address (6 bytes)
- ▸ The length (2 bytes)
- ▸ The data and padding (46–1500 bytes)
- ▸ The FCS field (4 bytes)

In the Ethernet_802.2 frame, the 802.2 (or LLC) fields begin immediately after the length field of the 802.3 header. Figure 4.13 details the 802.2 (LLC) fields.

Preamble/SFD (8 bytes)

Destination Address (6 bytes)

Source Address (6 bytes)

Length (2 bytes)

Data (46-1500 bytes) --- DSAP (1 byte) EO

SSAP (1 byte) EO

Control (1 byte) 03

The 802.2 fields for NetWare's IPX/SPX always include the values shown here.

FCS (4 bytes)

Destination Service Access Point

The Destination Service Access Point (DSAP) field denotes the destination upper-layer (or network-layer) protocol type of the packet. NetWare IPX/SPX packets will contain the hexadecimal value 0xE0 in the DSAP field.

Source Service Access Point

The Source Service Access Point (SSAP) field (1 byte) denotes the upper-layer (or network-layer) protocol type of the packet, as does the DSAP. NetWare IPX/SPX packets will contain the hexadecimal value 0xE0 in the SSAP field.

Control Field

When NetWare's IPX/SPX is used, the control field will contain the value 0x03, which denotes the 802.2 unnumbered format. The unnumbered

NOTE
Values represented in hexadecimal format may be preceded by "0x" in this book.

format indicates that the LLC layer will provide connectionless services. Currently, NetWare's IPX/SPX Protocols do not rely on the LLC layer for connection-oriented services. Figure 4.14 shows a NetWare IPX/SPX packet using the Ethernet_802.2 frame format.

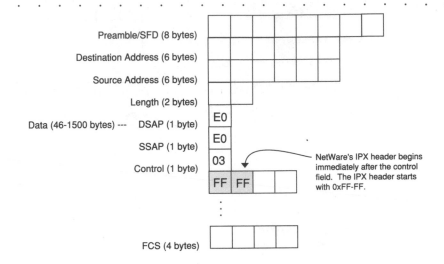

FIGURE 4.14

NetWare IPX using the
Ethernet_802.2 frame

TOTAL ETHERNET_802.2 FRAME LENGTH

When the total frame length is defined, the preamble and start frame delimiter are not counted. Based on the preceding information, minimum and maximum lengths are defined by adding all the frame field lengths:

Destination address	6 bytes
Source address	6 bytes
Length	2 bytes
Data and padding	46–1500 bytes

LLC fields include
DSAP	1 byte
SSAP	1 byte
Control	1 byte

FCS   4 bytes

Minimum frame size   64 bytes

Maximum frame size   1518 bytes

Figure 4.15 shows a decode of the Ethernet_802.2 frame.

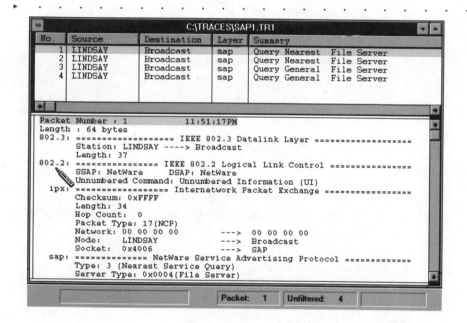

FIGURE 4.15

Decode of the
Ethernet_802.2 frame

Ethernet_SNAP

SNAP stands for Sub-Network Access Protocol. This frame type is derived from the Ethernet_802.2 structure. It is illustrated in Figure 4.16.

PROTOCOLS SUPPORTED

Protocols that can use the Ethernet_SNAP frame type include IPX/SPX, TCP/IP, and AppleTalk Phase II.

FIGURE 4.16

Ethernet_SNAP frame

structure

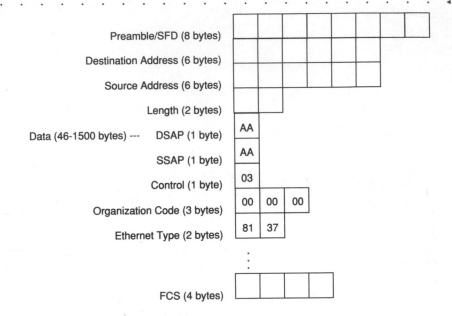

ETHERNET_SNAP FRAME STRUCTURE

As you can see, the following fields are the same as the Ethernet_802.2 frame:

- ► Preamble and start frame delimiter (8 bytes)

- ► Destination address (6 bytes)

- ► Source address (6 bytes)

- ► Length (2 bytes)

- ► Data and padding (46–1500 bytes)

- ► LLC 802.2 (DSAP, SSAP, and control fields)

- ► FCS (4 bytes)

DSAP, SSAP, and Control Fields

In Ethernet_SNAP frames, the value of the DSAP and SSAP fields will always be 0xAA. The value 0xAA indicates that the frame is a SNAP format frame.

The control field of SNAP frames is always 1 byte in length and contains the value 0x03 (unnumbered). It is followed by the organization code and Ethernet type fields, as shown in Figure 4.17.

<table>
<tr><td>Preamble/SFD (8 bytes)</td><td></td></tr>
<tr><td>Destination Address (6 bytes)</td><td></td></tr>
<tr><td>Source Address (6 bytes)</td><td></td></tr>
<tr><td>Length (2 bytes)</td><td></td></tr>
<tr><td>Data (46-1500 bytes) --- DSAP (1 byte)</td><td>AA</td></tr>
<tr><td>SSAP (1 byte)</td><td>AA</td></tr>
<tr><td>Control (1 byte)</td><td>03</td></tr>
<tr><td>Organization Code (3 bytes)</td><td>00 00 00</td></tr>
<tr><td>Ethernet Type (2 bytes)</td><td>81 37</td></tr>
<tr><td></td><td>FF FF</td></tr>
<tr><td>FCS (4 bytes)</td><td></td></tr>
</table>

The type field is used to define which upper-layer protocol the frame is being used by. The number 0x81-37 was assigned to Novell. The IPX header begins immediately following the Ethernet type field.

Ethernet_SNAP
organization code and
Ethernet type fields

Organization Code

The organization code field denotes the organization that assigned the Ethernet type field to follow. NetWare's IPX/SPX packets contain 0x00-00-00 in the organization code field.

Ethernet Type Field

The Ethernet type field is used to define the upper-layer protocol. NetWare's Ethernet type number is 0x8137.

The following is a list of values for the Ethernet type field for various network protocols:

IP (Internet Protocol)	0x0800
ARP (Address Resolution Protocol)	0x0806
Reverse ARP	0x8035
AppleTalk	0x809B
AppleTalk ARP	0x80F3
NetWare IPX/SPX	0x8137

TOTAL FRAME LENGTH

When defining the total frame length, the preamble and start frame delimiter are not counted. Based on the preceding information, minimum and maximum lengths are defined by adding all the frame field lengths:

Destination address	6 bytes
Source address	6 bytes
Length	2 bytes
Data and padding	46–1500 bytes

The data field includes

DSAP	1 byte
SSAP	1 byte
Control	1 byte
Organization code	3 bytes
Ethernet type	2 bytes
FCS field	4 bytes

Minimum frame size   64 bytes

Maximum frame size   1518 bytes

Figure 4.18 shows a sample of an IPX/SPX packet using the Ethernet_SNAP frame format.

```
┌──────────────────────────────────────────────────────────────────┐
│ ▭                          C:\TRACES\SAP3.TR1                  ▼ ▲ │
│ No.  Source      Destination   Layer  Summary                   ▲ │
│    1 SALES1      LINDSAY        wdog   Poll inactive station; Conn=2 │
│    2 LINDSAY     Broadcast      sap    Query Nearest  File Server │
│    3 LINDSAY     Broadcast      sap    Query Nearest  File Server │
│    4 LINDSAY     Broadcast      sap    Query General  File Server ▼ │
│ ◄                                                               ► │
│──────────────────────────────────────────────────────────────────│
│ Packet Number : 3            11:55:38PM                         ▲ │
│ Length : 64 bytes                                                 │
│ 802.3: ================= IEEE 802.3 Datalink Layer =============== │
│         Station: LINDSAY ----> Broadcast                          │
│         Length: 42                                                │
│ 802.2: ============= IEEE 802.2 Logical Link Control ============ │
│         SSAP: SNAP     DSAP: SNAP                                 │
│         Unnumbered Command: Unnumbered Information (UI)           │
│         SNAP Organization Code: 00 00 00                         │
│         SNAP Ethernet Type: 0x8137 (NetWare)                     │
│    ipx: ================= Internetwork Packet Exchange =========== │
│         Checksum: 0xFFFF                                          │
│         Length: 34                                               │
│         Hop Count:  0                                            │
│         Packet Type: 17(NCP)                                     │
│         Network: 00 00 00 00      --->  00 00 00 00              │
│         Node:    LINDSAY          --->  Broadcast               │
│         Socket:  0x4006           --->  SAP                     │
│    sap: ============= NetWare Service Advertising Protocol ======= │
│         Type: 3 (Nearest Service Query)                          │
│         Server Type: 0x0004(File Server)                       ▼ │
│──────────────────────────────────────────────────────────────────│
│                              │ Packet:  3 │ Unfiltered:  5 │       │
└──────────────────────────────────────────────────────────────────┘
```

F I G U R E 4.18

*Decode of Ethernet_SNAP
frame*

Ethernet_II

Ethernet_II frames are distinctive because of the type field that follows the source address. Ethernet_802.3, Ethernet_802.2, and Ethernet_SNAP frames contain a length field after the source address. The Ethernet_II frame structure is shown in Figure 4.19.

FIGURE 4.19

Ethernet_II frame structure

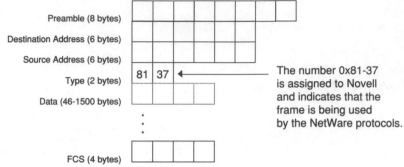

PROTOCOLS SUPPORTED

The Ethernet_II frame can be used with IPX/SPX, TCP/IP, and AppleTalk Phase I.

ETHERNET_II FRAME STRUCTURE

There are two areas that distinguish the Ethernet_II frame from the others listed previously: the preamble/start frame delimiter and the type field.

Preamble

The 8-byte preamble field contains alternating 1's and 0's just as the 7-byte preamble of the other frame structures; however, in an Ethernet_II frame the 1-byte start frame delimiter (10101011) is considered part of the preamble.

Type Field

Unlike all the other frames, Ethernet_II contains a type field instead of a length field. This field denotes the upper-layer protocol that is using the packet.

Following is a list of values that can be contained in the type field to identify the various protcols using the frame:

IP (Internet Protocol)	0x0800
ARP (Address Resolution Protocol)	0x0806
Reverse ARP	0x8035
AppleTalk	0x809B
AppleTalk ARP	0x80F3
NetWare IPX/SPX	0x8137

Note that these are the same as the values that can be used in the SNAP Ethernet type field.

Total Frame Length

When total frame length is defined, the preamble is not counted. Based on the preceding information, minimum and maximum lengths are defined by adding all the frame field lengths:

Destination address	6 bytes
Source address	6 bytes
Type	2 bytes
Data and padding	46–1500 hytes
FCS	4 bytes

| Minimum frame size | 64 bytes |
| Maximum frame size | 1518 bytes |

Figure 4.20 shows a decode of the Ethernet_II frame.

FIGURE 4.20

Decode of the Ethernet_II frame

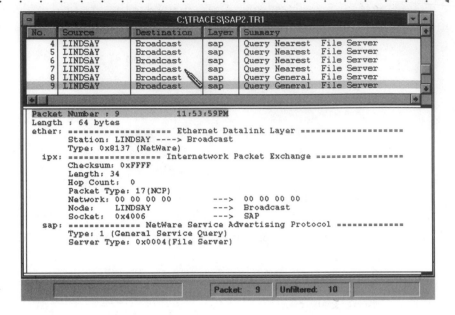

NOTE
Novell's Multi-Protocol Router (MPR) permits dynamic linking and unlinking of protocols and frame types while acting as an external router.

THE ECONFIG UTILITY

NetWare 2.x operating systems, non-ODI drivers, and the NetWare external router programs (BRIDGE.EXE and ROUTER.EXE) do not permit the dynamic linking and unlinking of protocols with frame types. They can support only the frame types Ethernet_802.3 and Ethernet_II.

If you wish to use the Ethernet_II frame type with NetWare 2.x servers, non-ODI client drivers, or the NetWare external router program, you must use the ECONFIG utility.

The ECONFIG utility can be run on the files listed in the following sections to configure them to use the Ethernet_II frame type:

▸ IPX.COM (non-ODI client IPX driver)

▸ NET$OS.EXE (NetWare OS)

▸ BRIDGE.EXE (external router program—old)

▸ ROUTER.EXE (external router program)

Ethernet_802.3 to Ethernet_II Frame Type

In order to configure these files to use the Ethernet_II frame format, you must use the defined ECONFIG command syntax.

For IPX.COM, at the DOS prompt, type

ECONFIG IPX.COM SHELL:E 8137

For NET$OS.EXE, log in to the server with supervisory privileges. You may ECONFIG the operating system, but the new configuration will not be in effect until you reboot the server. From within the SYSTEM directory, flag NET$OS.EXE as shareable, read-write, and type

ECONFIG NET$OS.EXE [LAN Designator]:E 8137

For the NetWare external router programs BRIDGE.EXE and ROUTER.EXE, access the directory containing BRIDGE.EXE or ROUTER.EXE and type

ECONFIG BRIDGE.EXE [LAN Designator]:E 8137

or

ECONFIG ROUTER.EXE [LAN Designator]:E 8137

Ethernet_II to Ethernet_802.3 Frame Type

In order to configure a non-ODI client IPX driver, NetWare 2.x operating system, or external router program to use the default Ethernet_802.3 frame format again, you may use the ECONFIG utility, specifying the type as "N." The "N" denotes that you are using the NetWare default frame type, Ethernet_802.3.

The following table shows you how to configure these programs back to the Ethernet_802 frame:

IPX.COM   Type **ECONFIG IPX.COM SHELL:N**

NET$OS.EXE   Type **ECONFIG NET$OS.EXE [LAN Designator]:N**

BRIDGE.EXE   Type **ECONFIG NET$OS.EXE [LAN Designator]:N**

ROUTER.EXE   Type **ECONFIG ROUTER.EXE [LAN Designator]:N**

Multiple Protocols/Multiple Frames

With the ODI capabilities of NetWare v3.x, it became possible to use a variety of frame types with server and workstation drivers. However, a server and a workstation must use the same frame type to communicate, as you can see in Figure 4.21.

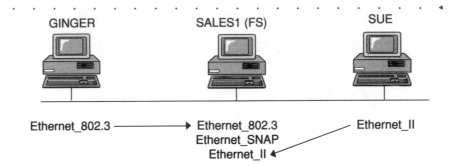

For example, if a NetWare v3.x server is using the Ethernet_802.3 frame type, workstations must use the Ethernet_802.3 frame in order to communicate with the server.

Differentiating between Frame Types

The simple flowchart presented in Figure 4.22 defines how to tell which frame type a packet is using.

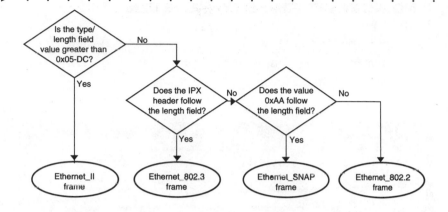

FIGURE 4.22

Frame type flowchart

"File Server Not Found"

Many times, the "File server not found" message is caused by not using the same frame type at the server and client. With a protocol analyzer, this situation is easy to spot.

FINDING WHAT FRAME TYPE THE SERVER IS RUNNING

By capturing a file server's Service Advertising Process (SAP) packets, you can tell which frame types the server is configured to use. NetWare servers will broadcast SAP packets every 60 seconds to announce the services that are available (file services, print services, remote console services, and so on).

A NetWare server will broadcast one SAP packet for each frame type loaded. If a server is using all four frame types defined, it will send out four SAP packets in a row—one for each frame type. View the packets to see the frame types in use by the server.

NOTE
For more information on the function and structure of SAP packets, refer to Chapter 9.

FINDING WHAT FRAME TYPE THE CLIENT IS RUNNING

By simply capturing and viewing packets from the workstation, you can view the frame type the client is using. In Figure 4.23, the client is using the Ethernet_SNAP frame format.

FIGURE 4.23

Capturing packets from a workstation that is using the Ethernet_SNAP format

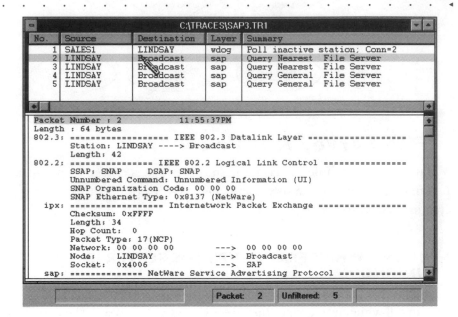

Configuring NetWare v3.x to Use Multiple Frame Types

If you are running multiple protocols from your NetWare server, you can also configure it to use multiple frame types.

For example, on a NetWare LAN with 100 workstations, if you load the TCP/IP stack at the server, you must load your LAN driver with either the Ethernet_II or Ethernet_SNAP frame type. The default frame type of Ethernet_802.3 does not support the TCP/IP Protocol.

You can use the following commands in the AUTOEXEC.NCF to bind NetWare's IPX/SPX to the default frame type and TCP/IP to the Ethernet_II frame type:

```
load NE2000 port=300 int=3 frame=ETHERNET_802.3
bind IPX to NE2000 net=BA5EBA11
load tcpip
load ne2000 port=300 int=3 frame=Ethernet_II
bind IP to NE2000 addr=130.50.20.31
```

Filtering on a Frame Type

Using the proper values in the correct fields, you can set up an analyzer to capture packets based on their frame types. Figure 4.24 highlights the fields that are unique to each of the frame types.

Understanding the structures of the various frame types and how to use each one will help troubleshoot the "File server not found" message and various configuration errors. Learning the difference between a properly formatted frame (as presented in this chapter) and an illegal or malformed frame will also assist in network troubleshooting.

In this chapter you have viewed the proper structure of the four frame types supported by Novell: Ethernet_II, Ethernet_802.2, Ethernet_802.3, and Ethernet_SNAP. You have also learned how to determine what frame types are in use by the servers and clients and how to use the ECONFIG utility and AUTOEXEC.CFG file to configure a system to use other frame types.

The next chapter examines the types and causes of Ethernet frame errors.

FIGURE 4.24

Fields unique to each
frame type

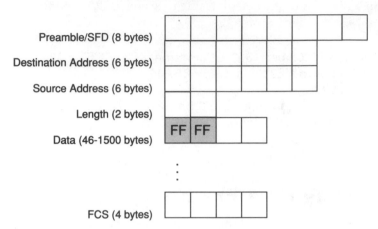

ETHERNET_802.3

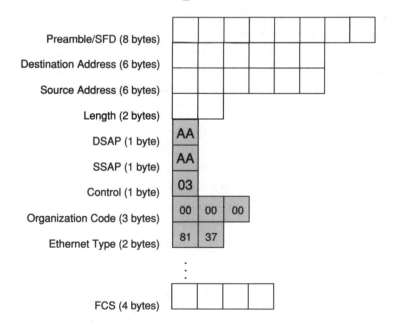

ETHERNET_SNAP

ETHERNET_802.2

Preamble/SFD (8 bytes)

Destination Address (6 bytes)

Source Address (6 bytes)

Length (2 bytes)

DSAP (1 byte)   EO

SSAP (1 byte)   EO

Control (1 byte)   03

FCS (4 bytes)

ETHERNET_II

Preamble (8 bytes)

Destination Address (6 bytes)

Source Address (6 bytes)

Type (2 bytes)   81 37

Data (46-1500 bytes)

FCS (4 bytes)

Troubleshooting at the Data Link Layer

If a station transmits a properly formed frame, as defined in Chapter 4, and the wiring system does not cause corruption of the frame, the receiving station should detect a legal frame and process the data contained therein. Unfortunately, not all stations transmit properly formed frames; faulty transceivers, network interface cards, and LAN drivers may cause malformed frames to be transmitted. The cabling system, as well, may cause the corruption of frames on the wire.

In this chapter you will use the LANalyzer and LANalyzer for NetWare to track, capture, and view illegal or corrupt frames. The chapter focuses on frames that do not meet the defined frame specifications. By analyzing and interpreting these frame errors, you can determine if a network is overloaded or if the cabling system, network interface card, LAN driver, or transceiver is faulty.

There are four types of errors examined in this chapter:

► Local and remote collisions

► CRC/alignment errors and late collisions

► Frame size errors

► Jabber

Monitoring Local and Remote Collisions

Although collisions are normal for CSMA/CD LANs, when the number of collisions becomes excessive, network performance is degraded. By viewing related information you can determine if a collision is due to an overloaded network segment or a faulty component. Network administrators should monitor their network to observe what a typical number of local and remote collisions is for their installation. Figure 5.1 illustrates local and remote collisions. The following table compares local and remote collision statistics:

COLLISION TYPE	< 64 BYTES	BAD CRC	CD PAIR TRIGGERED
Local	Yes	Yes	Yes
Remote	Yes	Yes	No

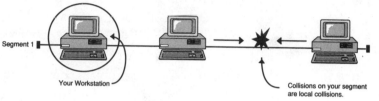

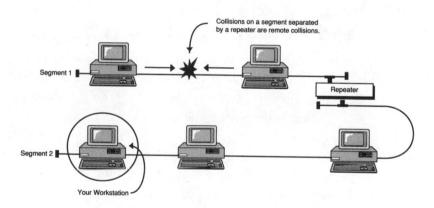

FIGURE 5.1
Local/remote collisions

LOCAL COLLISIONS

Local collisions are collisions that occur on the local segment. A *collision fragment* is less than 64 bytes in length, with a bad CRC. Local collisions are detected by the collision-detection circuitry on the network interface card or transceiver. The detection of a collision by the collision detection circuitry differentiates local collisions from remote collisions, which are not noticed by the receive pair.

REMOTE COLLISIONS

Remote collisions occur on the other side of a repeater separating network segments. A remote collision is assumed when a packet that is less than 64 bytes and has an invalid CRC is observed. Repeaters will pass on collision fragments to all connected segments, whereas bridges and routers will not. If you are experiencing excessive remote collisions, you may wish to install a bridge between the segments to filter out collisions. Ideally, however, you would reduce the load on the segment where the excessive collisions occur by reconfiguring the cabling system or fixing a problem component.

Determining the Cause of Excessive Local and Remote Collisions

How many collisions are too many? Each network can withstand different amounts of collisions before noticeable performance degradation. When the collisions begin to impact your network to the point that users begin complaining about performance, the collisions are excessive.

When you view collision statistics, it is also important to view the utilization statistics. This information will help determine whether excessive collisions are due to an overloaded segment or a faulty component. Whether caused by hardware problems or excessive traffic, this rise in collisions is generally rapid and easily identified by comparison to historical collision statistics.

OVERLOADED SEGMENT

If both utilization and the number of collisions are high, it is likely that the collisions are a result of increased traffic on the network segment.

In Figure 5.2, on the first screen you are viewing a network segment that is experiencing high utilization. On the second screen, you can see the number of collisions displayed. The number of collisions displayed in the errors table has also increased dramatically.

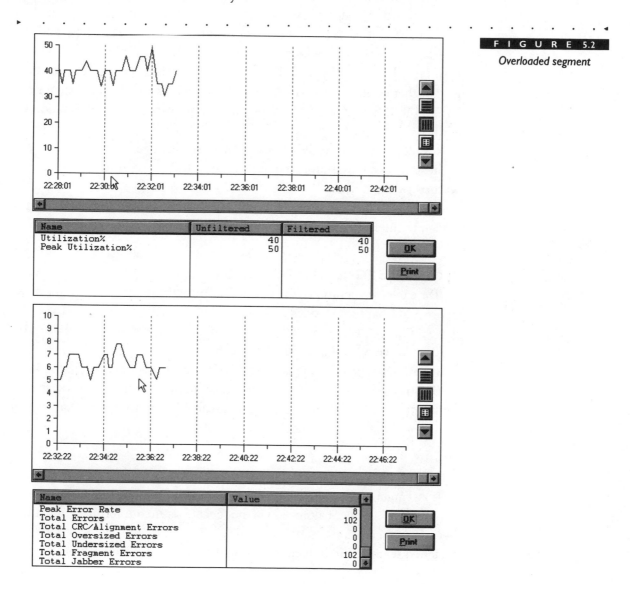

FIGURE 5.2

Overloaded segment

One possible solution for this situation involves the reconfiguration (load balancing) of the network cabling system using bridges and/or routers. (Repeaters do not filter traffic.) Bridges and routers will filter out remote collisions and keep locally addressed traffic on a single segment.

As defined in Chapter 3, when a bridge connecting two or more segments sees a packet, it records the source hardware (or physical) address and the interface number from which the packet arrived. This information will be maintained and used by the bridge to determine which packets are destined for another segment and which should not be forwarded. True bridges examine the Ethernet address only—not the network (IPX) information or addressing.

Routers will forward only packets that are destined to another network address. Packets that are destined for the local network will not be forwarded by the routers.

Figure 5.3 illustrates segment utilization before and after installing a bridge to filter traffic.

CABLE SEGMENT TOO LONG

If a cable segment exceeds the maximum allowed by specification (as defined in Chapter 3), nodes at the far end of the cable may believe the cable is free when, in fact, a packet is on the wire. Since the packet on the wire may not have propagated throughout the cabling system, nodes at the far end may transmit, thereby causing a collision. In this case, since the local collisions are not due to an extremely busy network, utilization will not be higher than normal. Check the segment cable length to ensure that it does not exceed the maximum length allowed.

REMOTE SEGMENT OVERLOADED

If a segment is experiencing a high number of remote collisions, it indicates that the segment attached via the repeater is encountering a high number of local collisions. Determine the cause of the local collisions on the attached segment. To reduce the number of remote collisions crossing onto

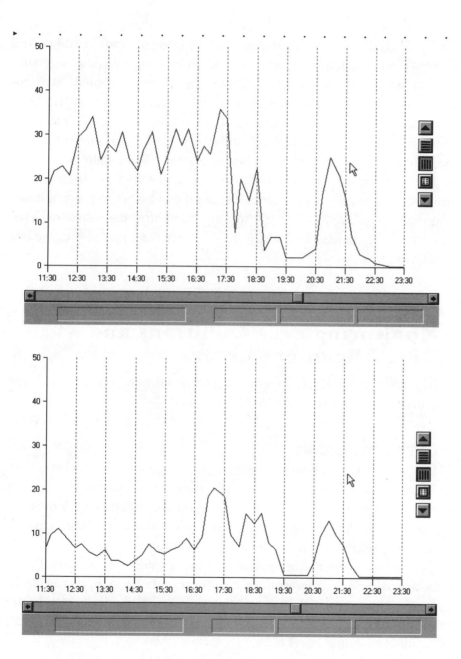

FIGURE 5.3

Before and after installing a
bridge/router

the local segment, replace the repeater with a bridge or router. Bridges and routers filter out collisions to prevent them from crossing onto other segments.

A network with segments connected by repeaters should have approximately the same traffic (load) on all segments since all traffic is "repeated" and not filtered. If one segment seems to have significantly more collisions, it may be the result of bad hardware, such as a nonfunctional carrier sense, or one of the network boards or transceivers. Since stations involved in a collision will try to retransmit right away (within the backoff constraints), monitor several collisions and see if you can identify a single station that always seems to be transmitting soon after the collisions. That station is likely to have bad hardware. This situation may also cause late collisions.

Monitoring Late Collisions and CRC/Alignment Errors

Late collisions and CRC/alignment errors indicate problems with the network cabling or components.

LATE COLLISIONS

Late collisions are defined as packets that are greater than 64 bytes with an invalid CRC. They also trigger the station's collision-detection pair if they occur on a local segment. Late collisions are counted only for the local segment; if the late collision packet is being transmitted from across a router, the packet is seen as a CRC/alignment error.

Late collisions are not normal on an Ethernet network. A late collision indicates that a station transmitted a sufficient number of bytes (64) to be considered in control of the transmission medium. All stations should defer to the packet on the wire. If all nodes follow the defined rules of CSMA/CD, late collisions should never occur.

CRC/ALIGNMENT ERRORS

Packets that do not contain the proper CRC (cyclical redundancy check) value in the frame check sequence field are considered "errored." Upon transmitting a frame on the medium, a station will append a CRC value to the end of the frame. This value is the remainder of a mathematical equation that the source station performs on the contents of the frame. The destination station must perform the same equation and compare the results to the value in the FCS field. If the values do not match, the frame is counted as a CRC error.

If the frame does not end on an 8-bit boundary, it is considered an alignment error. Both types of errors are grouped and counted as CRC/alignment errors. The following table compares late collision and CRC/alignment errors:

ERROR TYPE	< 64 BYTES	BAD CRC	CD PAIR TRIGGERED
Late collision	No	Yes	Yes
CRC/alignment	No	Yes	No

Determining the Cause of Late Collisions and CRC/Alignment Errors

Late collisions and CRC/alignment errors are not considered "normal" for an Ethernet LAN. These types of errors should be tracked and resolved to ensure that they do not affect network performance. There are two primary causes of these errors: cabling problems and component problems.

CABLING PROBLEMS

Cabling problems such as shorts or noise caused by electromagnetic interference are most likely to blame for CRC/alignment errors. Improper cabling (not following specifications) is the most likely cause for late collisions. If a network is experiencing an increasing number of late collisions or CRC/alignment errors, check the following potential cabling problems:

▸ **Segment too long:** Nodes at the far end of the cabling system transmit, unaware that a station at the other end has already gained control of the medium by transmitting the first 64 bytes of a frame.

▸ **Failing cable:** Packet data traveling through shorted or damaged cabling may become corrupt before reaching the destination station.

▸ **Segment not grounded properly:** Improper grounding of a segment may allow ground-induced noise to corrupt data flow.

▸ **Improper termination:** If a cable segment is not properly terminated, allowing the signal to be absorbed upon reaching the end of the segment, a partial signal will bounce back and collide with existing signals.

▸ **Taps too close:** Follow the minimum recommended spacing between cable taps to ensure minimal reflection buildup and data distortion.

▸ **Noisy cable:** Interference or noise (electromagnetic interference produced by motors or other devices) can distort the signals and cause CRC/alignment errors.

COMPONENT PROBLEMS

Faulty components can cause either late collisions or CRC/alignment errors. The following is a list of some common component problems:

▸ **Deaf/partially deaf node:** A faulty station that cannot hear the activity is considered a *deaf node*. If a station is suspected of being a deaf node, the network interface card or transceiver should be replaced.

▸ **Failing repeater, transceiver, or controller card:** Repeaters, transceivers, and controller cards can disrupt the network signal, transmit erroneous signals on the wire (jabber), or ignore incoming packets. The malfunctioning component should be replaced.

Monitoring Frame-Length Errors

As defined in Chapter 4, Ethernet frames must be between 64 and 1518 bytes in length (including the header and FCS). Frames that are less than 64 bytes or greater than 1518 bytes but have a valid CRC field are considered frame-length errors.

SHORT FRAMES

Short frames (also called "runts") are less than 64 bytes in length but have a valid CRC value.

LONG FRAMES

Frames that are longer than 1518 bytes yet have a valid CRC value are *long frames.*

Determining the Cause of Illegal-Length Frames

Illegal-length frames are credited to the transmitting station. Finding the node responsible for sending illegal-length frames is easy since the frame is well formed and contains the source address in the header.

Generally, illegal-length frames are caused by a faulty LAN driver. Check the revision of the LAN driver and replace it if it is old. If the LAN driver is current, the file may be corrupt. Reload it from the original disk or copy a LAN driver file from another station that is transmitting properly sized frames.

Routers may also be the cause of illegal-length frames. If a router connects two dissimilar network types and does not enforce the proper frame size restrictions on either side, it may transmit illegal-length frames. If a router is continuously transmitting illegal-length frames, notify the manufacturer.

Monitoring Jabber

Jabber is defined as a frame that is greater than 1518 bytes and has a bad CRC. Jabber is associated with a malfunctioning transceiver. By specification, a transceiver may only transmit for 150 milliseconds. This is sufficient time to transmit 1518 bytes. If a transceiver does not halt transmission after 1518 bytes, it is called a *jabbering transceiver*. If you suspect a transceiver is jabbering, check the transmit light on the outside to see if it is continuously transmitting. Replace a jabbering transceiver to ensure that network performance is not affected.

This chapter defined numerous frame errors that can occur on an Ethernet segment. Monitoring your network and setting alarms will help catch errors before they affect your network communications. Table 5.1 summarizes the characteristics of each error condition.

Now that you've completed Part I of this book, you should have a good feel for the Ethernet access method, cabling system, and errors associated with improper cabling, faulty components, and high utilization.

Part II examines the NetWare protocols, including IPX, SPX, Burst Mode, NCP, SAP, and RIP.

TABLE 5.1

Error Conditions

ERROR	TRIGGERING CONDITION	POSSIBLE CAUSE
Local collisions	Less than 64 bytes	Overloaded segment
	Bad CRC	Cable segment too long
	CD triggered	
Remote collisions	Less than 64 bytes	Remote segment overload
	Bad CRC	Remote cable segment too long
Late collisions	Equal to or greater than 64 bytes	Deaf node
	Bad CRC	Segment too long
	CD triggered	Component problem
CRC/alignment	From 64 to 1518 bytes long	Failing cable
	Bad CRC	Noisy cable
	Doesn't end on 8-bit boundary	Component problem
Short frames	Less than 64 bytes	Faulty LAN driver
	Good CRC	
Long frames	Greater than 1518 bytes	Faulty LAN driver
	Good CRC	
Jabber	Greater than 1518 bytes	Faulty transceiver
	Bad CRC	

Netware Protocols

Part II concentrates on the NetWare protocols. Each chapter details a specific NetWare protocol and presents analysis techniques for monitoring, troubleshooting, and optimizing your NetWare LAN.

Chapter 6 details Novell's Internetwork Packet Exchange (IPX) and Sequenced Packet Exchange (SPX) Protocols, including how to resolve IPX timeout problems and check an SPX session for proper establishment.

Chapter 7 defines the NetWare Core Protocol (NCP) structure and purpose and presents several "conversations" between client and server using the NCP protocol.

Chapter 8 introduces Burst Mode and describes the steps for installing and configuring Burst Mode at the server and client.

Chapter 9 explores Novell's Service Advertising Protocol (SAP). You examine a SAP packet decode to determine which services are available to the local segment.

Chapter 10 defines NetWare's Routing Information Protocol (RIP). You view RIP packets on a segment to learn about remote networks and examine methods for measuring router throughput performance.

In Chapter 11 you will work with NetWare's Diagnostic Responder, which can be used to "ping" workstations anywhere on an IPX internet.

Chapter 12 defines some miscellaneous NetWare protocols, including Watchdog packets, registration packets, and messaging packets.

Netware's IPX/SPX Protocols

This chapter examines Novell's IPX and SPX Protocols. The chapter first defines the IPX packet structure and functionality. By examining the fields in the IPX header, you will determine how far the packet has traveled to arrive at the local network. Once you have examined the SPX header structure, you will see an SPX communication between a client and server.

When stations transmit data, they place a frame around the data (encapsulation) to determine where the data should be sent, who sent the data, and what the upper-layer protocol is. The upper-layer protocols examined in this book are NetWare specific.

When a NetWare client and server are communicating, they may be using either connection-oriented or connectionless services. Connection-oriented communications use Novell's Sequenced Packet Exchange (SPX) Protocol. Connectionless communications use Novell's Internetwork Packet Exchange (IPX) Protocol.

IPX and SPX communications require an additional header to be placed in front of the data, before the frame, as shown in Figure 6.1. These headers include routing data, sequencing information, and upper-layer protocol identification (such as NCP, SAP, RIP).

FIGURE 6.1
IPX header placed before request

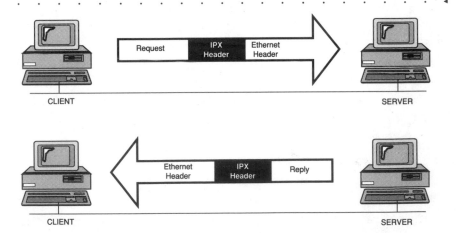

Most of NetWare's client/server communications use the IPX Protocol for transport. Developers must compare the advantages and disadvantages of each protocol to determine if their application requires IPX or SPX.

Advantages and Disadvantages of IPX and SPX

NetWare's IPX and SPX offer two distinctly different network communications protocols. IPX is connectionless. SPX is connection oriented. Many application programmers need to weigh the low overhead of IPX against the guaranteed delivery of SPX.

IPX is a connectionless (or datagram) protocol. (Connectionless protocols are often compared to regular mail. You drop a letter in the mailbox and trust that it will be delivered.) No connection "handshake" is required prior to communicating with an IPX partner. There is no guarantee of delivery, however, and packets can arrive in any sequence. IPX supports broadcast of packets, whereas SPX communications must be established with each station individually before data can be sent.

SPX is connection oriented and requires the SPX partner to be available before data can be sent. (Connection-oriented protocols are often compared to sending a registered letter. Information regarding the delivery, such as acceptance of the letter, is returned to the sender.) SPX packets are sequenced, so they arrive in proper order, whereas IPX packets can arrive in any order. SPX is a slower communication protocol because of the packet overhead (12 bytes per packet) and the acknowledgment required for each packet of data sent.

The first part of this chapter discusses the IPX packet structure, how to interpret field values, and how to optimize the network configuration based on the information contained therein. The second part of this chapter defines the functionality and structure of Novell's SPX Protocol.

The IPX Header

The IPX header is always 30 bytes in length and begins with the hexadecimal value 0xFFFF. IPX headers are transmitted after the media access control frame but before the packet data. Figure 6.2 defines the IPX header format.

FIGURE 6.2

IPX header format

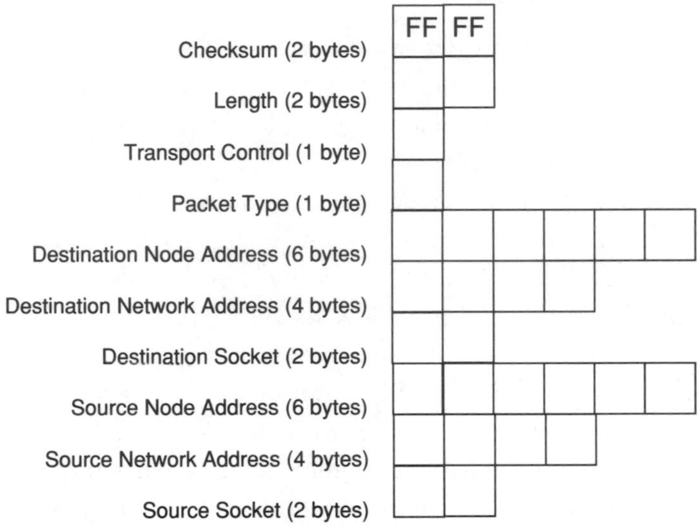

Checksum (2 bytes)	FF	FF			
Length (2 bytes)					
Transport Control (1 byte)					
Packet Type (1 byte)					
Destination Node Address (6 bytes)					
Destination Network Address (4 bytes)					
Destination Socket (2 bytes)					
Source Node Address (6 bytes)					
Source Network Address (4 bytes)					
Source Socket (2 bytes)					

CHECKSUM

The checksum field in the IPX header is not used. The value 0xFFFF is placed in the checksum field, which is 2 bytes long. Novell intentionally did not use the checksum field in the IPX header because a CRC check is already done on the entire frame and data. In the future, Novell plans to allow users to implement the IPX checksum if desired.

Contrary to popular belief, the maximum length of an IPX header and data on Ethernet is currently 1518 bytes. If, however, an IPX packet will cross a router without using the Large Internet Packet (LIP) Protocol, the maximum of 576 bytes is applicable. Novell has created the Large Internet Packet (LIP) Protocol to allow stations to transmit larger frame sizes across IPX routers. The Burst Mode Protocol (which supports the larger packets) is covered in Chapter 8.

LENGTH

The length field contains the length of the internetwork packet. This includes the IPX header and the data that follows. It does not include the Ethernet frame fields.

NOTE
Packets that contain an uneven number of bytes in the data portion will have one additional byte of random data placed at the end in order to "evenize" the packet. Some routers generate errors as the result of an uneven amount of data; therefore, all packets are evenized.

TRANSPORT CONTROL

The transport control field is used by IPX routers and denotes the number of routers that an IPX packet has crossed (hops used). This field is set to 0 by the originating station. Packets may cross up to 15 routers. The packet will be discarded by the 16th router.

PACKET TYPE

The packet type field indicates the type of service that a packet will use, as shown in the following table. For IPX-based communications, this value will be 0, 4, 5, or 17.

IPX-based communications	0 or 4
SPX-based communications	5
NCP communications	17

DESTINATION NETWORK

The destination network field contains the 4-byte network address on which the destination node resides. If this field contains 0x-00-00-00-00,

▸ ▪ ▪ ▪ ▪ ▪ ▪ ▪ ▪ ▪ ▪ ▪ ▪ ▪ ▪ ▪ ▪ ▪ ▪ ◂

> NetWare's IPX header structure is similar to the XNS (Xerox Networking System) IDP (Internet Datagram Packet) header structure. An IPX header, however, contains the value 0xFF-FF in the checksum field. XNS packets will contain a checksum value in the checksum field.

the packet is destined for the same network as the source station. It will not be passed on by a router.

DESTINATION NODE

The destination node address is a 6-byte field that contains the node address of the destination station or 0xFF-FF-FF-FF-FF-FF (broadcast).

Packets addressed to a NetWare 3.x server will contain the value 0x00-00-00-00-00-01 in the destination node address within the IPX header. This is the node address automatically assigned to the NetWare protocol stack on the internal IPX network. The destination address in the Ethernet frame, however, will show the actual hardware address of the server if it is on the local network.

DESTINATION SOCKET

The destination socket is a 2-byte field that contains the socket number of the intranode process to which the packet is addressed. Common socket numbers include

0x451	NetWare core protocol (see Chapter 7)
0x452	Service advertising packet (see Chapter 9)
0x453	Routing information packet (see Chapter 10)
0x455	NetBIOS packet
0x456	Diagnostic packet (see Chapter 11)
0x457	Serialization packet (see Chapter 11)

At the workstation, socket numbers are dynamically assigned. These dynamic socket numbers range from 0x4000 to 0x8000. Figure 6.3 shows a packet that is destined for a NetWare routing information socket.

Checksum (2 bytes)	FF	FF				
Length (2 bytes)	00	28				
Transport Control (1 byte)	00					
Packet Type (1 byte)	01					
Destination Node Address (6 bytes)	FF	FF	FF	FF	FF	FF
Destination Network Address (4 bytes)	00	00	00	00		
Destination Socket (2 bytes)	04	53				
Source Node Address (6 bytes)	00	00	1B	09	08	07
Source Network Address (4 bytes)	AB	01	01	01		
Source Socket (2 bytes)	40	03				

Network AB-01-01-01

CLIENT
Node: 00-00-1B-09-08-07

SERVER

FIGURE 6.3

IPX header addressed to the RIP socket

SOURCE NETWORK

The source network number is the network address to which the source node belongs. If the source node is a NetWare v3.x server, the source network in the IPX header will be the internal IPX address.

SOURCE NODE

The source node field contains the 6-byte node address of the transmitting station. If the packet is transmitted by a NetWare v3.x server, this field will contain the value 0x00-00-00-00-00-01. Unlike the destination address field, this field cannot contain a broadcast address (0xFF-FF-FF-FF-FF-FF).

SOURCE SOCKET

The source socket field contains the socket number of the process that is transmitting the packet. Workstations may use dynamically assigned socket numbers ranging from 0x4000 to 0x8000, while servers reply from defined socket numbers, as described earlier.

Packets That Have Crossed Routers

Many large internetworks are connected with routers. When a packet crosses a router, as shown in Figure 6.4, it undergoes several changes. These changes include the following:

▸ The transport control field will be incremented by 1.

▸ The existing media access frame (Ethernet, TokenRing, etc.) will be stripped off.

▸ A new frame will be placed on the packet.

After a router strips off the frame, it places a new Ethernet (or Token Ring or ARCnet) frame on the data. The new frame contains the hardware address of the destination (if it is on a network attached to the router) or the next router in the path to the destination network.

FIGURE 6.4

Viewing a packet that has crossed a router

```
Packet Number : 12            6:24:24PM
Length : 64 bytes
802.3: ==================== IEEE 802.3 Datalink Layer ====================
        Station: FS-BLDG2 ----> NW386-1
        Length: 36
  ipx: ==================== Internetwork Packet Exchange ====================
        Checksum: 0xFFFF
        Length: 36
        Hop Count:  1
        Packet Type: 0(Unknown)
        Network: C9 13 86 38      ---> 00 04 44 67
        Node:    00-00-00-00-00-01 ---> 00-00-00-00-00-01
        Socket:  0x0000           ---> Serialize
  ser: ========= Novell Serialization (Copy Protection) Packet =========
        Serialization Data: 0 4 0 153 0 1
```

By examining the transport control field, you can determine how many routers a packet has crossed to reach the local network, as shown in Figure 6.5.

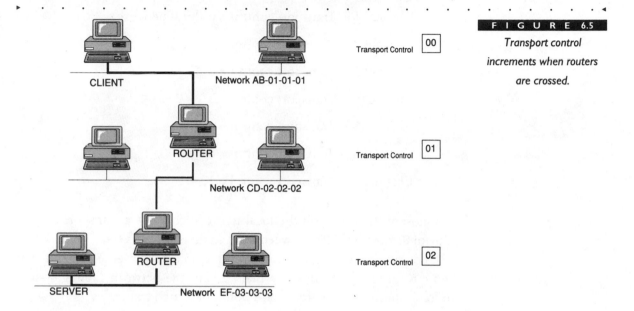

FIGURE 6.5

Transport control increments when routers are crossed.

Using the Transport Control Information to Optimize the LAN

You can use the transport control field information to determine if a network can be reconfigured for optimal performance. If a workstation communicates only with servers located on another network, perhaps the workstation should be placed directly on that network rather than routing all its packets through the local network and attached router.

For example, you can use a protocol analyzer to track packets that have crossed one or more routers.

The HOPCOUNT application listed in Figure 6.6 was defined with the following criteria:

Channel 1   Transport control = 0 (local network)

Channel 2   Transport control = 1

Channel 3   Transport control = 2

Channel 4   Transport control = 3

Channel 5   Transport control = 4–7

Channel 6   Transport control = 8–11

Channel 7   Transport control = 12–15

If most of the traffic on the local network contains a transport control value of 0, most traffic is between local stations and servers.

If, however, much of the traffic is from remote networks, as illustrated in Figure 6.7, this is an indication that perhaps the network cabling system could be optimized to reduce the amount of routed traffic.

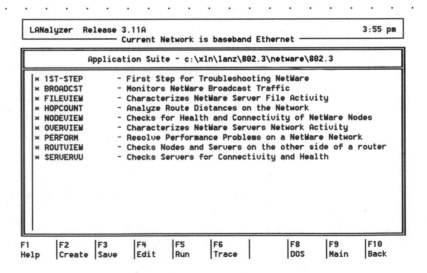

```
LANalyzer   Release 3.11A                                        3:55 pm
                  ── Current Network is baseband Ethernet ──

┌─────────────────────────────────────────────────────────────────────┐
│        Application Suite - c:\xln\lanz\802.3\netware\802.3            │
│ ┌───────────────────────────────────────────────────────────────────│
│ │ ⨯ 1ST-STEP     - First Step for Troubleshooting NetWare            │
│ │ ⨯ BROADCST     - Monitors NetWare Broadcast Traffic                │
│ │ ⨯ FILEVIEW     - Characterizes NetWare Server File Activity        │
│ │ ⨯ HOPCOUNT     - Analyze Route Distances on the Network            │
│ │ ⨯ NODEVIEW     - Checks for Health and Connectivity of NetWare Nodes│
│ │ ⨯ OVERVIEW     - Characterizes NetWare Servers Network Activity     │
│ │ ⨯ PERFORM      - Resolve Performance Problems on a NetWare Network   │
│ │ ⨯ ROUTVIEW     - Checks Nodes and Servers on the other side of a router│
│ │ ⨯ SERVERVU     - Checks Servers for Connectivity and Health         │
│ │                                                                     │
│ └───────────────────────────────────────────────────────────────────│
└─────────────────────────────────────────────────────────────────────┘
F1     F2     F3    F4    F5    F6          F8    F9     F10
Help   Create Save  Edit  Run   Trace       DOS   Main   Back
```

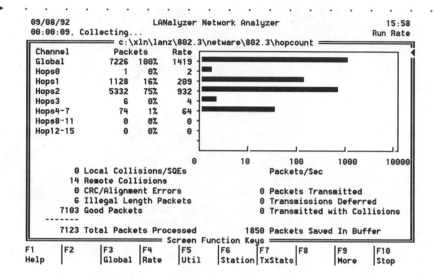

FIGURE 6.7

*Most traffic from remote
networks*

Using the flowchart shown in Figure 6.8 for guidance, you can determine whether or not the LAN needs reconfiguration.

As shown in Figure 6.9, you can move a station to the local network to reduce the traffic on intermediate networks. However, since recabling or moving users between networks is not always a practical solution, you can explore moving applications and/or data from remote to local segments.

If a workstation's requests are being routed excessively, the communications are being slowed down as they pass through each router. Stations may be experiencing IPX timeouts because of poorly configured routes.

IPX Timeouts

The NetWare shell (NETX.COM) uses IPX to transport requests to a file server. IPX, however, is not a connection-oriented service and does not guarantee delivery of packets. The request-response nature of NetWare's NCP and workstation shell (except Burst Mode technology, covered in Chapter 8) is used to guarantee that packets have arrived at the destination. For example, if a workstation transmits an NCP request to open a file using

Flowchart on segment

balancing

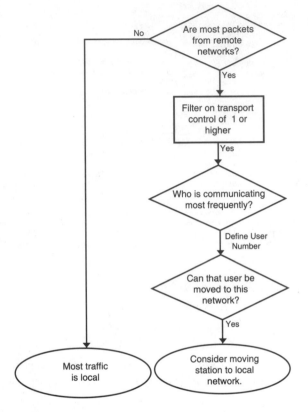

IPX for transport, the NCP reply from the server is an indication that the request arrived successfully.

However, some conditions may exist on the LAN that prevent a request from arriving or the response from returning. The NetWare shell maintains a receive timeout timer. If a response is not received within the receive timeout value, the shell will use IPX again to send another NCP request, as shown in Figure 6.10.

If a station is intermittently receiving a timeout message, it indicates a possible problem on the network. The LAN may have a cable problem (a short), or perhaps there is excessive traffic on the local segment. You can

FIGURE 6.9

Move to a local segment

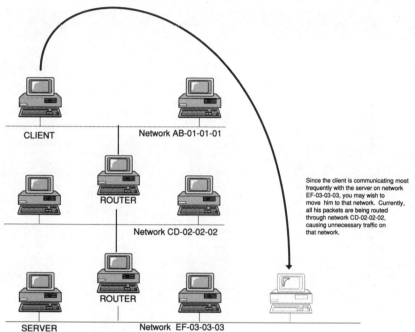

CLIENT   Network AB-01-01-01

ROUTER

Network CD-02-02-02

ROUTER

SERVER   Network EF-03-03-03

Since the client is communicating most frequently with the server on network EF-03-03-03, you may wish to move him to that network. Currently, all his packets are being routed through network CD-02-02-02, causing unnecessary traffic on that network.

check each of these conditions by using the methods defined in Chapters 2 and 3.

Until the problem is fixed, however, you may wish to increase the number of attempts that the workstation will make before displaying the time-out message to the user. The default retry count is 20. To increase the IPX retry count, place the following line in a workstation's SHELL.CFG or NET.CFG file:

```
IPX RETRY COUNT = 30
```

F I G U R E 6.10

Repeat request by NCP
using IPX for transport

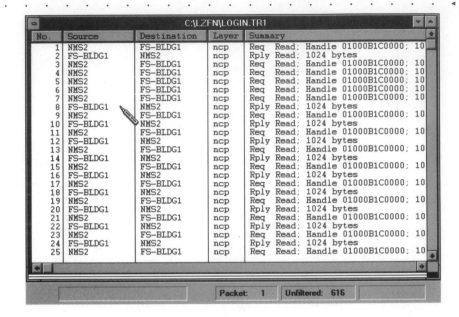

No.	Source	Destination	Layer	Summary
1	NMS2	FS-BLDG1	ncp	Req Read; Handle 01000B1C0000; 10
2	FS-BLDG1	NMS2	ncp	Rply Read; 1024 bytes
3	NMS2	FS-BLDG1	ncp	Req Read; Handle 01000B1C0000; 10
4	NMS2	FS-BLDG1	ncp	Req Read; Handle 01000B1C0000; 10
5	NMS2	FS-BLDG1	ncp	Req Read; Handle 01000B1C0000; 10
6	NMS2	FS-BLDG1	ncp	Req Read; Handle 01000B1C0000; 10
7	NMS2	FS-BLDG1	ncp	Req Read; Handle 01000B1C0000; 10
8	FS-BLDG1	NMS2	ncp	Rply Read; 1024 bytes
9	NMS2	FS-BLDG1	ncp	Req Read; Handle 01000B1C0000; 10
10	FS-BLDG1	NMS2	ncp	Rply Read; 1024 bytes
11	NMS2	FS-BLDG1	ncp	Req Read; Handle 01000B1C0000; 10
12	FS-BLDG1	NMS2	ncp	Rply Read; 1024 bytes
13	NMS2	FS-BLDG1	ncp	Req Read; Handle 01000B1C0000; 10
14	FS-BLDG1	NMS2	ncp	Rply Read; 1024 bytes
15	NMS2	FS-BLDG1	ncp	Req Read; Handle 01000B1C0000; 10
16	FS-BLDG1	NMS2	ncp	Rply Read; 1024 bytes
17	NMS2	FS-BLDG1	ncp	Req Read; Handle 01000B1C0000; 10
18	FS-BLDG1	NMS2	ncp	Rply Read; 1024 bytes
19	NMS2	FS-BLDG1	ncp	Req Read; Handle 01000B1C0000; 10
20	FS-BLDG1	NMS2	ncp	Rply Read; 1024 bytes
21	NMS2	FS-BLDG1	ncp	Req Read; Handle 01000B1C0000; 10
22	FS-BLDG1	NMS2	ncp	Rply Read; 1024 bytes
23	NMS2	FS-BLDG1	ncp	Req Read; Handle 01000B1C0000; 10
24	FS-BLDG1	NMS2	ncp	Rply Read; 1024 bytes
25	NMS2	FS-BLDG1	ncp	Req Read; Handle 01000B1C0000; 10

C:\LZFN\LOGIN.TR1

Packet: 1   Unfiltered: 616

NOTE
Chapters 7, 9, 10, and
11 define how to use
the IPX header values
to filter for NCP, SAP,
RIP, and Diagnostic
Services packets.

NetWare v3.x Server Considerations

NetWare v3.x servers send packets from node address 0x00-00-00-00-00-01. This is the node address automatically assigned to the NetWare protocol stack on the IPX internal network.

When filtering on packets being sent to a NetWare server, be certain to use this node address in the IPX header. The network address will contain the internal IPX network address assigned when the server is first brought up.

Figure 6.11 shows communication between a workstation and a NetWare v3.x server.

NetWare v2.x servers, however, do not have an internal IPX network. Communications between a workstation and a NetWare v2.x server are shown in Figure 6.12.

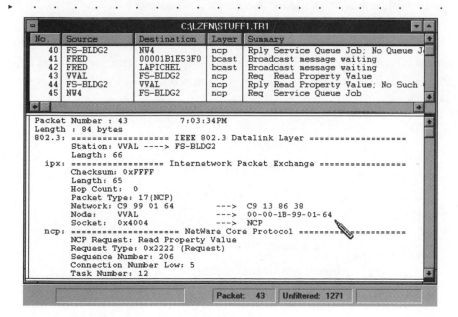

FIGURE 6.11

IPX header to NetWare

v3.x server

```
─ C:\LZFN\LOGIN.TR1 ▼ ▲
Packet Number : 3          6:35:50PM
Length : 68 bytes
802.3: =================== IEEE 802.3 Datalink Layer ==================
       Station: NMS2 ----> FS-BLDG1
       Length: 50
  ipx: ================== Internetwork Packet Exchange ===============
       Checksum: 0xFFFF
       Length: 50
       Hop Count:  0
       Packet Type: 17(NCP)
       Network: 01 CA FF 03      --->  0A BA DA BA
       Node:    NMS2             --->  00-00-00-00-00-01
       Socket:  0x4003           --->  NCP
  ncp: ================== NetWare Core Protocol ====================
       NCP Request: Read
       Request Type: 0x2222 (Request)
       Sequence Number: 18
       Connection Number Low: 2
       Task Number: 2
       Connection Number High: 0
       Function Code: 72
       File Handle: 0x01 0x00 0x0B 0x1C 0x00 0x00
       Starting Byte Offset: 9216
       Bytes to Read: 1024



                        Packet:  3    Unfiltered: 616
```

FIGURE 6.12

IPX header to NetWare

v2.x server

```
─ C:\LZFN\STUFF1.TR1 ▼ ▲
No.  Source      Destination   Layer  Summary
 40  FS-BLDG2    NW4           ncp    Rply Service Queue Job; No Queue J
 41  FRED        00001B1E53F0  bcast  Broadcast message waiting
 42  FRED        LAPICHEL      bcast  Broadcast message waiting
 43  VVAL        FS-BLDG2      ncp    Req  Read Property Value
 44  FS-BLDG2    VVAL          ncp    Rply Read Property Value; No Such
 45  NW4         FS-BLDG2      ncp    Req  Service Queue Job

Packet Number : 43          7:03:34PM
Length : 84 bytes
802.3: =================== IEEE 802.3 Datalink Layer ==================
       Station: VVAL ----> FS-BLDG2
       Length: 66
  ipx: ================== Internetwork Packet Exchange ===============
       Checksum: 0xFFFF
       Length: 65
       Hop Count:  0
       Packet Type: 17(NCP)
       Network: C9 99 01 64      --->  C9 13 86 38
       Node:    VVAL             --->  00-00-1B-99-01-64
       Socket:  0x4004           --->  NCP
  ncp: ================== NetWare Core Protocol =============
       NCP Request: Read Property Value
       Request Type: 0x2222 (Request)
       Sequence Number: 206
       Connection Number Low: 5
       Task Number: 12

                        Packet:  43   Unfiltered: 1271
```

Sequenced Packet Exchange (SPX)

NOTE
SPX provides sequenced and ac-knowledged com-munications. It does not, however, provide sliding window functionality.

When a communication is dependent upon receipt of each packet in sequence, Novell's IPX Protocol may not be adequate since it is a connection-less, nonguaranteed delivery protocol. The SPX Protocol can be used to provide guaranteed packet delivery.

SPX communications are used for programs such as Novell's Print Server (PSERVER) and Remote Printer (RPRINTER), as well as Remote Console (RCONSOLE). If programmers require their application to use guaranteed packet delivery, they can design the program to use SPX. An SPX header contains all the fields defined in the IPX header and an additional 12 bytes. The additional 12 bytes provide sequence and acknowledgment fields.

The SPX Header

NOTE
The length field value includes the data field length and 42 bytes for the SPX header.

An SPX header, as shown in Figure 6.13, is always 42 bytes long and begins with the same initial fields as an IPX header.

Earlier in this chapter, field definitions were given for checksum; length; transport control; packet type; destination network; node and socket; and source network, node, and socket. In an SPX header, the packet type field will contain the value 0x05, indicating that the packet uses SPX for transport.

FIGURE 6.13

SPX header format

| Connection Control (1 byte) |
| Datastream Type (1 byte) |
| Source Connection ID (2 bytes) |
| Destination Connection ID (2 bytes) |
| Sequence Number (2 bytes) |
| Acknowledgement Number (2 bytes) |
| Allocation Number (2 bytes) |

The fields described in the following sections are unique to the SPX header.

CONNECTION CONTROL

The connection control field controls the bidirectional flow of data. Values can include the following:

0x10	End-of-Message	Symbolizes that the client wishes to end the connection
0x20	Attention	This field is not implemented yet
0x40	Acknowledgment Required	Data has been sent, and acknowledgment is required
0x80	System Packet	Acknowledgment packet; SPX uses this internally; it is not delivered to the shell of the destination station.

DATASTREAM TYPE

The datastream type is a 1-byte field that indicates the type of data contained within the packet. This field can contain a client-defined number or one of the following values:

0xFE	End-of-Connection	Generated to indicate that a client wishes to terminate a communication
0xFF	End-of-Connection Acknowledgment	Transmitted upon receipt of an End-of-Connection request

SOURCE CONNECTION ID

The source connection ID is a 2-byte number assigned by the source SPX station; it is used for demultiplexing SPX communications. Since concurrently active connections on a machine can use the same socket number, this field is necessary to distinguish each virtual connection. This number will be used in the destination connection ID field by an SPX partner when responding to an originator.

DESTINATION CONNECTION ID

The destination connection ID is a 2-byte field that contains the connection ID number of the destination station. During the initial connection establishment, this field will be set to 0xFFFF since the sender does not yet know the destination connection ID that the receiver will use.

SEQUENCE NUMBER

The sequence number is a 2-byte field that contains the count of data packets transmitted from a station. This number will increment only after receiving an acknowledgment for a data packet transmitted. A station will not increment this counter when it transmits an acknowledgment packet.

ACKNOWLEDGE NUMBER

During an SPX connection, it is possible for packets to be lost. The acknowledge number field contains the value of the sequence number expected in the next SPX packet from the SPX partner. If the sequence number is not correct, the receiving station assumes an error in communications has occurred.

ALLOCATION NUMBER

The allocation number field indicates the number of receive buffers available at a workstation. This value begins with 0 for the first buffer available; therefore, the value 6 in this field indicates that seven packet receive buffers are available. When the receiving station's application processes information received, it frees up a buffer. If the station is busy and cannot clear the packets from the buffers, the number of available buffers will decrease each time a data packet is received by a station.

Establishing and Terminating an SPX Connection

SPX connections must be established before data packets can be exchanged. This is often referred to as an *SPX handshake*. Figure 6.14 shows the SPX headers used to establish a connection between systems.

Monitoring an SPX Connection

In an SPX connection, various values within the header will be used for sequencing and acknowledgment of packets. Figure 6.15 illustrates an SPX conversation progressing normally.

In the example, the client has established an SPX connection with the file server. In packet number 1, the client is sending data to the server. Packet number 2 shows the server acknowledging receipt of the data. Packets 3 and 5 show that the server is transmitting data to the client now. Packets 4 and 6 are the acknowledgment packets from the client. Remember that the acknowledgment number field increments to indicate the next sequence number expected. The sequence number field increments only for data that is sent.

When an SPX client has completed the communication, it will transmit an SPX Close Connection request to the SPX partner. The partner, in turn, will respond with an End of Connection reply with a closing acknowledgment, thereby terminating the connection.

Figure 6.16 shows an SPX session being terminated by the client.

FIGURE 6.14

SPX header during

handshake

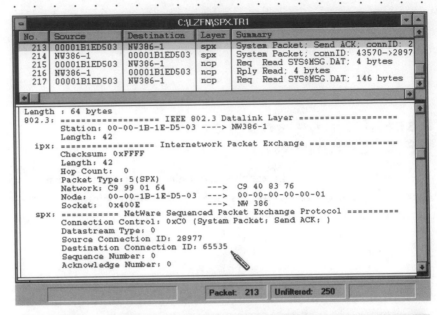

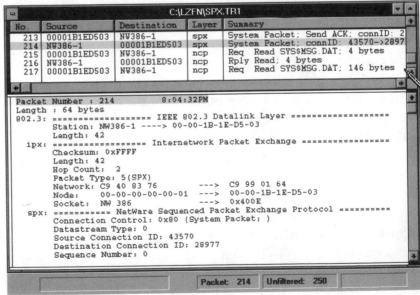

FIGURE 6.14

SPX header during

handshake (continued)

```
┌─────────────────────────────────────────────────────────────────────┐
│ □                          C:\LZFN\SPX.TR1                      ▼ ▲  │
├──────┬───────────────┬─────────────┬───────┬────────────────────────┤
│ No.  │ Source        │ Destination │ Layer │ Summary                 │
├──────┼───────────────┼─────────────┼───────┼────────────────────────┤
│ 221  │ 00001B1ED503  │ NW386-1     │ spx   │ Send ACK; connID: 28977->43570 │
│ 222  │ NW386-1       │ 00001B1ED503│ spx   │ System Packet; connID: 43570->2897 │
└──────┴───────────────┴─────────────┴───────┴────────────────────────┘

  ipx: ================= Internetwork Packet Exchange =================
        Checksum: 0xFFFF
        Length: 172
        Hop Count:  0
        Packet Type: 5(SPX)
        Network: C9 99 01 64      --->  C9 40 83 76
        Node:    00-00-1B-1E-D5-03 --->  00-00-00-00-00-01
        Socket:  0x400E           --->  NW 386
  spx: =========== NetWare Sequenced Packet Exchange Protocol ==========
        Connection Control: 0x40 (Send ACK; )
        Datastream Type: 0
        Source Connection ID: 28977
        Destination Connection ID: 43570
        Sequence Number: 0
        Acknowledge Number: 0
        Allocation Number 6
 Data:
   0: FE FF 9D CB 40 2D 4E 50 5A 4D 86 03 DC AE 11 79  |....@-NPZM.....y
  10: 1B 41 F5 33 EB 18 B5 C3 98 EC 91 0A 8E 2F C1 42  |.A.3........./.B
  20: 15 D8 8B C4 82 3F 6E 0C 1D 42 1C ED E5 D7 2F 56  |.....?n..B..../V
  30: 77 72 38 57 0C 07 D7 4A A2 0E 3B 87 29 3D 46 17  |wr8W..J..;.)=F.
  40: 6E E2 BE 11 AF 96 45 CE 54 2C 8B F7 77 80 13 36  |n.....E.T,..w..6
  50: 79 96 51 BE 65 AD A6 5F 6F FB 07 58 7E CF 18 8E  |y.Q.e.._o..X~...

                         ┌──────────────┬─────────────────┐
                         │ Packet: 221  │ Unfiltered: 250 │
                         └──────────────┴─────────────────┘
```

```
┌─────────────────────────────────────────────────────────────────────┐
│ □                          C:\LZFN\SPX.TR1                      ▼ ▲  │
├──────┬───────────────┬─────────────┬───────┬────────────────────────┤
│ No   │ Source        │ Destination │ Layer │ Summary                 │
├──────┼───────────────┼─────────────┼───────┼────────────────────────┤
│ 221  │ 00001B1ED503  │ NW386-1     │ spx   │ Send ACK; connID: 28977->43570 │
│ 222  │ NW386-1       │ 00001B1ED503│ spx   │ System Packet; connID: 43570->2897 │
└──────┴───────────────┴─────────────┴───────┴────────────────────────┘

 Packet Number : 222           8:04:32PM
 Length : 64 bytes
 802.3: ==================== IEEE 802.3 Datalink Layer ==================
        Station: NW386-1 ----> 00-00-1B-1E-D5-03
        Length: 42
  ipx: ================= Internetwork Packet Exchange =================
        Checksum: 0xFFFF
        Length: 42
        Hop Count:  2
        Packet Type: 5(SPX)
        Network: C9 40 83 76      --->  C9 99 01 64
        Node:    00-00-00-00-00-01 --->  00-00-1B-1E-D5-03
        Socket:  NW 386           --->  0x400E
  spx: =========== NetWare Sequenced Packet Exchange Protocol ==========
        Connection Control: 0x80 (System Packet; )
        Datastream Type: 0
        Source Connection ID: 43570
        Destination Connection ID: 28977
        Sequence Number: 0
        Acknowledge Number: 1
        Allocation Number 1

                         ┌──────────────┬─────────────────┐
                         │ Packet: 222  │ Unfiltered: 250 │
                         └──────────────┴─────────────────┘
```

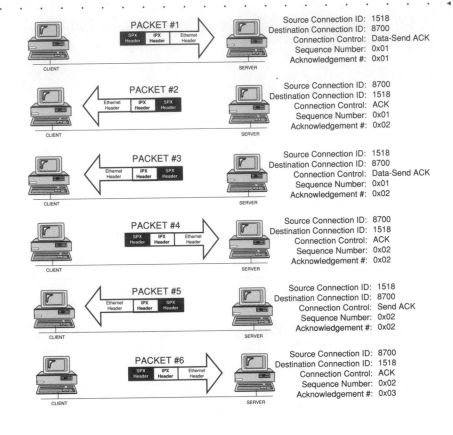

FIGURE 6.15

SPX communication

PACKET #1

Source Connection ID:	1518
Destination Connection ID:	8700
Connection Control:	Data-Send ACK
Sequence Number:	0x01
Acknowledgement #:	0x01

PACKET #2

Source Connection ID:	8700
Destination Connection ID:	1518
Connection Control:	ACK
Sequence Number:	0x01
Acknowledgement #:	0x02

PACKET #3

Source Connection ID:	1518
Destination Connection ID:	8700
Connection Control:	Data-Send ACK
Sequence Number:	0x01
Acknowledgement #:	0x02

PACKET #4

Source Connection ID:	8700
Destination Connection ID:	1518
Connection Control:	ACK
Sequence Number:	0x02
Acknowledgement #:	0x02

PACKET #5

Source Connection ID:	1518
Destination Connection ID:	8700
Connection Control:	Send ACK
Sequence Number:	0x02
Acknowledgement #:	0x02

PACKET #6

Source Connection ID:	8700
Destination Connection ID:	1518
Connection Control:	ACK
Sequence Number:	0x02
Acknowledgement #:	0x03

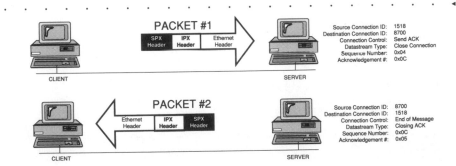

FIGURE 6.16

SPX session being terminated

PACKET #1

Source Connection ID:	1518
Destination Connection ID:	8700
Connection Control:	Send ACK
Datastream Type:	Close Connection
Sequence Number:	0x04
Acknowledgement #:	0x0C

PACKET #2

Source Connection ID:	8700
Destination Connection ID:	1518
Connection Control:	End of Message
Datastream Type:	Closing ACK
Sequence Number:	0x0C
Acknowledgement #:	0x05

SPX Timeout Monitoring/Configuring

There are several configurable parameters that can be customized for SPX connections on NetWare v3.x networks. If a network has a heavy bandwidth utilization or poor wiring, SPX connections may timeout.

To configure SPX parameters at a NetWare v3.x file server, use the SPXCONFG utility.

- **SPX Watchdog Abort Timeout (in ticks):** Available values for this setting are between 540 and 5400 ticks. The default is 540 ticks.

- **SPX Watchdog Verify Timeout (in ticks):** Available values for this setting are from 10 ticks to 255 ticks. The default is 54 ticks.

- **SPX Ack Wait Timeout (in ticks):** Available values range from 10 to 3240 ticks. The default value is 108 ticks.

- **SPX Default Retry Count:** Available values for this setting range from 1 to 255 attempts. The default is 10.

- **Maximum Concurrent SPX Connections:** Available values for this setting range from 100 to 2000. The default is 1000.

There are several parameters you can use with SPXCONFG. To view available parameters, at the server console prompt type

LOAD SPXCONFG H

At the workstation, specific SPX parameters can be defined in the SHELL.CFG or NET.CFG file.

- **SPX Abort Timeout (in ticks):** This parameter defines how long an SPX partner will wait before terminating a session. The default is 540 ticks.

NOTE
A tick is approximately 1/18th of a second.

▸ **SPX Listen Timeout**: This SPX parameter adjusts the amount of time SPX will wait before requesting the other side to verify the connection. The default is 108 ticks.

▸ **SPX Verify Timeout**: This parameter adjusts the interval between SPX packets sent to the SPX partner to inform the partner that the connection is valid even though no data is being sent at this moment. The default is 54 ticks.

As defined in this chapter, Novell's IPX and SPX header will follow the type or length field of the Ethernet frame. The IPX header is always 30 bytes long and contains information for routing and upper-layer protocol identification. The SPX header includes all the fields of the IPX header and an additional 12 bytes that contain sequencing and acknowledgment fields.

Analyzing information contained in the IPX and SPX headers, you can determine if most communications are local or remote and whether the network is subjected to routing inefficiencies.

So far, you have looked at how packets are framed and routed and how connection-oriented services are tracked. The next chapter examines Novell's NetWare Core Protocol (NCP), which defines the structure of client requests and server responses.

CHAPTER 7

The Network Core Protocol

So far, this book has discussed the method for transmitting packets using a frame (Ethernet) and network header (IPX/SPX). You know that data transmitted across the network must have a frame for local transmission and an IPX or IPX/SPX header for routing and sequencing. Inside these packets, however, some standardized language for requests and replies must be defined.

NCP messages are prepared and sent using the formats and conventions specified by Novell's defined NCP standards. This chapter examines NCP functions and message formats, including Request and Reply header formats.

NCP is the language that NetWare servers and clients speak. Clients make requests of servers using the NetWare Core Protocol (NCP). An NCP header follows the frame and IPX/SPX header, as you can see in Figure 7.1.

Workstations transmit NCP messages to request file reads and writes, create queue jobs, determine drive mappings set, search through directories, and so on. Servers answer NCP requests with NCP replies.

By understanding the NCP communications, you can determine the types of requests being made by NetWare clients. You can use this information to determine the types of operations a server is most commonly asked for (such as file reads and writes, queue requests, and so on).

Protocol analyzers that decode NetWare protocols display the NCP request or reply in plain English instead of code.

FIGURE 7.1

*The NCP header follows
the IPX/SPX header.*

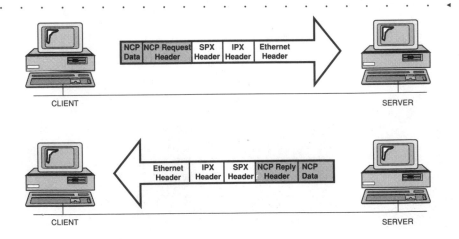

Establishing an NCP Connection

Before a client is permitted to make NCP requests of a server, it must attach to a server and request an NCP connection. The server, in turn, executes the request and transmits an NCP reply, granting the connection if possible. Each client NCP request solicits a server NCP reply, as shown in Figure 7.2. This one-request, one-response communication has given NCP the nickname "ping-pong" protocol.

NOTE
Chapter 8 focuses on the Burst Mode Protocol, which you can use to increase the efficiency of NetWare file reads and writes.

The NCP Request and Reply Header Formats

NCP requests and replies each contain a unique header that is of fixed length and followed by a variable data portion. The NCP Request header contains five fields, and the NCP Reply header contains seven fields.

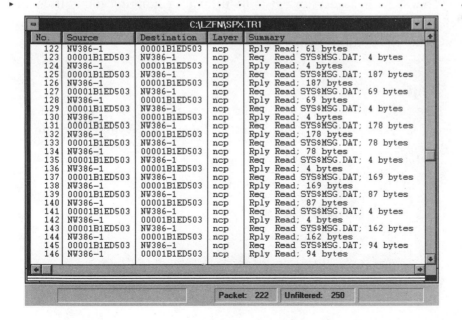

NCP requests and replies

NCP REQUEST HEADER

Clients must identify themselves and the purpose of their NCP message to the server. There are five fields of an NCP Request header that contain information used by the receiving server to determine the type of NCP message (request, reply, establish connection, destroy connection, and so on), check to see if the client is communicating in a proper sequence, determine which client is sending the NCP message, and track the task that the client has requested. The NCP Request header is shown in Figure 7.3.

Request Type (2 bytes)

Sequence Number (1 byte)

Connection Number Low (1 byte)

Task Number (1 byte)

Connection Number High (1 byte)

The Request header format is used for all communications from the client to the server. This header is 6 bytes long and is followed by additional NCP information that defines the client's request.

Request Type

The first field, request type, indicates the type of NCP request that is being sent from the client to the server. Request type values include the following:

1111	Create a service connection
2222	Service request
5555	Destroy service connection
7777	Burst Mode transfer (covered in Chapter 8)

When a client wishes to connect to a server, it issues a Create Service Connection NCP request and specifies type 1111 in the request type field. When a station wishes to detach from a server, it issues a Destroy Service Connection request, specifying type 5555 in the request type field.

Client requests use 2222 in the request type field to specify a general service request. This may be a request for a file, a query of the bindery, a submission of a queue job, and so on.

When using the Burst Mode Protocol for file reads and writes, the client will use 7777 in the type field.

NOTE
The Burst Mode
Protocol is discussed
in detail in Chapter 8.

Sequence Number

You use the sequence number to track the sequence of the communication between the server and client. Clients will place the last sequence number plus 1 in this field.

Connection Number Low

The connection number low field contains the service connection number assigned to the client upon logging into the server. You can observe this number in the NetWare Monitor screen under "Connection Information" and by typing USERLIST at a workstation.

Task Number

The task number indicates which client task is making the request. The server will track these tasks and automaticallly deallocate resources when a task ends. Task number 0 is used to signal to the server that all tasks have ceased execution and resources may be deallocated.

Connection Number High

The connection number high field should (at this time) be set to 0x00. It is not currently used.

NCP REPLY HEADER

When the server answers a client's request, it has special considerations that must be addressed in the header format. The server must tell the client if the request received was completed successfully and whether the NCP connection is still valid. The server will use an NCP Reply header, as shown in Figure 7.4, after the IPX/SPX header and before the additional NCP information.

FIGURE 7.4

NCP Reply header

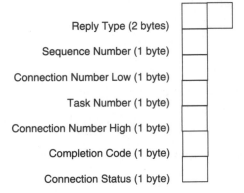

Reply Type (2 bytes)

Sequence Number (1 byte)

Connection Number Low (1 byte)

Task Number (1 byte)

Connection Number High (1 byte)

Completion Code (1 byte)

Connection Status (1 byte)

The NCP Reply header has two more fields than the Request header. These are the completion code and connection status fields.

NCP Reply Types

NCP reply type values include the following:

3333	Service reply
7777	Burst Mode Connection
9999	Request Being Processed

Servers answer most NCP requests with a service reply, specifying type 3333 in the reply type field. If a server has a client's request queued for execution and the client reexecutes a request because it has not received a reply from the server, the server responds with a Request Being Processed NCP reply. This causes the workstation to reset its shell timeout, increment its retry counters, and continue to wait. If the reply is not received by the client before the timeout counter expires, the client repeats the request. The default number of retries is 20; however, the client can increase this number, as described in Chapter 6.

When using Burst Mode to transfer files to and from workstations, the server uses NCP reply type 7777.

Completion Code

The completion code indicates whether or not the client's request was successful. A 0 in the completion code field indicates that the request was successful. Any other value in the completion code field indicates that an error occurred while processing the client's request.

Connection Status Flags

NetWare clients must check the connection status flags field in all incoming NCP replies from a server. If **DOWN** is typed at the console prompt to bring the server down, the fourth bit in this byte will be set to 1.

NCP Function Codes and Subfunction Codes

Besides the standard Request or Reply headers discussed above, each NCP message must contain an NCP function code identifying the service being requested or replied to.

For example, if a workstation requests to open a file, as shown in Figure 7.5, it transmits an NCP message type 2222 (request) with a function code of 76. This function code is defined by Novell as Open File. Upon

NCP request to open a file

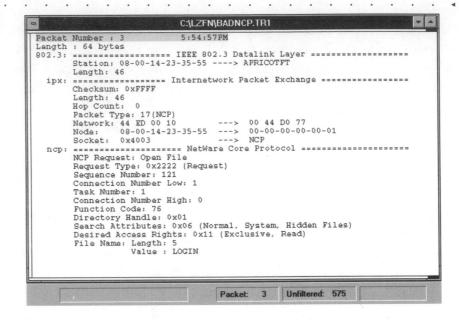

```
┌─────────────────────────────────────────────────────────────────────┐
│ ▭                          C:\LZFN\BADNCP.TR1                     ▼ ▲ │
├─────────────────────────────────────────────────────────────────────┤
│ Packet Number : 3               5:54:57PM                             │
│ Length : 64 bytes                                                     │
│ 802.3: ==================== IEEE 802.3 Datalink Layer ============    │
│         Station: 08-00-14-23-35-55 ----> APRICOTFT                    │
│         Length: 46                                                    │
│    ipx: =================== Internetwork Packet Exchange ========     │
│         Checksum: 0xFFFF                                              │
│         Length: 46                                                    │
│         Hop Count: 0                                                  │
│         Packet Type: 17(NCP)                                          │
│         Network: 44 ED 00 10        --->  00 44 D0 77                 │
│         Node:    08-00-14-23-35-55  --->  00-00-00-00-00-01           │
│         Socket:  0x4003             --->  NCP                         │
│    ncp: =================== NetWare Core Protocol ==============      │
│         NCP Request: Open File                                        │
│         Request Type: 0x2222 (Request)                                │
│         Sequence Number: 121                                          │
│         Connection Number Low: 1                                      │
│         Task Number: 1                                                │
│         Connection Number High: 0                                     │
│         Function Code: 76                                             │
│         Directory Handle: 0x01                                        │
│         Search Attributes: 0x06 (Normal, System, Hidden Files)        │
│         Desired Access Rights: 0x11 (Exclusive, Read)                 │
│         File Name: Length: 5                                          │
│                    Value : LOGIN                                      │
│                                                                       │
│                                                                       │
├─────────────────────────────────────────────────────────────────────┤
│             │    │              │ Packet:  3 │ Unfiltered:  575 │      │
└─────────────────────────────────────────────────────────────────────┘
```

receipt of an NCP message containing the type 2222 and the function code 76, the server knows the client is requesting to open a file. The file name and access level requested appear later in the NCP packet.

Many NCP function codes require a subfunction code as well. For example, many NCP messages dealing with the bindery use function code 23. To differentiate among the various types of bindery requests, NCP messages must specify a subfunction code. For example, Get Bindery Access Level is function code 23 and subfunction code 70, as you can see in Figure 7.6, while Get Internet Address is function code 23 and subfunction code 19, as shown in Figure 7.7.

Typical NCP function and subfunction codes that are seen on NetWare LANs include the ones shown in Table 7.1.

```
┌─────────────────────────────────────────────────────────────────────┐
│ ▢              C:\TRACES\LOGIN.TR1                            ▼ ▲      │
├─────────────────────────────────────────────────────────────────────┤
│ Packet Number : 257              11:39:16PM                           │
│ Length : 64 bytes                                                     │
│ 802.3: =================== IEEE 802.3 Datalink Layer ================ │
│         Station: LINDSAY ----> MKTG-45                                │
│         Length: 40                                                    │
│   ipx: =================== Internetwork Packet Exchange ============= │
│         Checksum: 0xFFFF                                              │
│         Length: 40                                                    │
│         Hop Count:  0                                                 │
│         Packet Type: 17(NCP)                                          │
│         Network: C9 99 00 06        --->  00 00 11 62                 │
│         Node:    LINDSAY            --->  00-00-00-00-00-01           │
│         Socket:  0x4003             --->  NCP                         │
│   ncp: =================== NetWare Core Protocol =================    │
│         NCP Request: Get Bindery Access Level                         │
│         Request Type: 0x2222 (Request)                                │
│         Sequence Number: 136                                          │
│         Connection Number Low: 1                                      │
│         Task Number: 3                                                │
│         Connection Number High: 0                                     │
│         Function Code: 23                                             │
│         Subfunction Length: 1 bytes                                   │
│         Subfunction Code: 70                                          │
│                                                                       │
├─────────────────────────────────────────────────────────────────────┤
│           │        │  Packet:  257  │ Unfiltered:  981  │            │
└─────────────────────────────────────────────────────────────────────┘
```

F I G U R E 7.6

Request for Get Bindery Access Level uses function code 23 and subfunction code 70.

```
┌─────────────────────────────────────────────────────────────────────┐
│ ▢              C:\LZFN\BADNCP.TR1                             ▼ ▲      │
├─────────────────────────────────────────────────────────────────────┤
│ Packet Number : 325              5:55:17PM                            │
│ Length : 64 bytes                                                     │
│ 802.3: =================== IEEE 802.3 Datalink Layer ================ │
│         Station: APRICOTFT ----> FS-BLDG4                             │
│         Length: 42                                                    │
│   ipx: =================== Internetwork Packet Exchange ============= │
│         Checksum: 0xFFFF                                              │
│         Length: 41                                                    │
│         Hop Count:  1                                                 │
│         Packet Type: 17(NCP)                                          │
│         Network: 00 44 D0 77        --->  44 ED EE E0                 │
│         Node:    00-00-00-00-00-01  --->  00-00-00-00-00-01           │
│         Socket:  0x5123             --->  NCP                         │
│   ncp: =================== NetWare Core Protocol =================    │
│         NCP Request: Get Internet Address                             │
│         Request Type: 0x2222 (Request)                                │
│         Sequence Number: 2                                            │
│         Connection Number Low: 1                                      │
│         Task Number: 1                                                │
│         Connection Number High: 0                                     │
│         Function Code: 23                                             │
│         Subfunction Length: 2 bytes                                   │
│         Subfunction Code: 19                                          │
│         Target Connection: 1                                          │
│                                                                       │
├─────────────────────────────────────────────────────────────────────┤
│           │        │  Packet:  325  │ Unfiltered:  575  │            │
└─────────────────────────────────────────────────────────────────────┘
```

F I G U R E 7.7

Get Internet Address uses function code 23 and subfunction code 19.

TABLE 7.1

NCP Function Codes

SERVICE	REQUEST TYPE	FUNCTION CODE	SUBFUNCTION CODE
Accounting Services			
Get Current Account Status	2222	23	150
Submit Account Charge	2222	23	151
Submit Account Hold	2222	23	152
Submit Account Note	2222	23	153
Bindery Services			
Add Bindery Object to Set	2222	23	65
Change Bindery Object Password	2222	23	64
Change Bindery Object Security	2222	23	56
Change Bindery Security	2222	23	59
Close Bindery	2222	23	68
Create Bindery Object	2222	23	50
Create Property	2222	23	57
Delete Bindery Object	2222	23	51
Delete Bindery Object from Set	2222	23	66
Delete Property	2222	23	58
Get Bindery Access Level	2222	23	70
Get Bindery Object Access Level	2222	23	72
Get Bindery Object ID	2222	23	53

SERVICE	REQUEST TYPE	FUNCTION CODE	SUBFUNCTION CODE
Get Bindery Object in Set	2222	23	54
Is Bindery Object in Set?	2222	23	67
Is Calling Station a Manager?	2222	23	73
Keyed Change Password	2222	23	75
Keyed Verify Password	2222	23	74
List Relations of an Object	2222	23	76
Open Bindery	2222	23	69
Read Property Value	2222	23	61
Rename Object	2222	23	52
Scan Bindery Object	2222	23	55
Scan Bindery Object Trustee Paths	2222	23	71
Scan Property	2222	23	60
Verify Bindery Object Password	2222	23	63
Write Property Value	2222	23	62
Connection Services			
Create Service Connection	1111	—	—
Destroy Service Connection	5555	—	—
End of Job	2222	24	—
Get Internet Address	2222	23	19

TABLE 7.1

NCP Function Codes

(continued)

SERVICE	REQUEST TYPE	FUNCTION CODE	SUBFUNCTION CODE
Get Login Key	2222	23	23
Get Object Connection List	2222	23	21
Get Station Number	2222	19	—
Get Station's Logged Information	2222	23	22
Keyed Object Login	2222	23	24
Login Object	2222	23	20
Logout	2222	25	—
Negotiate Buffer Size	2222	33	—
Request Being Processed	9999	—	—
Request Processed	3333	—	—
Directory Services			
Add Extended Trustee to Directory or File	2222	22	39
Add Trustee to Directory	2222	22	13
Add User Disk Space Restriction	2222	22	33
Allocate Permanent Directory Handle	2222	22	18
Allocate Special Temporary Directory Handle	2222	22	22
Allocate Temporary Directory Handle	2222	22	19
Create Directory	2222	22	10

SERVICE	REQUEST TYPE	FUNCTION CODE	SUBFUNCTION CODE
Deallocate Directory Handle	2222	22	20
Delete Directory	2222	22	11
Delete Trustee from Directory	2222	22	14
Get Directory Disk Space Restriction	2222	22	35
Get Directory Entry	2222	22	31
Get Directory Information	2222	22	45
Get Directory Path	2222	22	1
Get Effective Directory Rights	2222	22	3
Get Effective Rights for Directory Entry	2222	22	42
Get Name Space Directory Entry	2222	22	48
Get Name Space Information	2222	22	47
Get Object Disk Usage and Restrictions	2222	22	41
Get Volume Info with Handle	2222	22	21
Get Volume Info with Number	2222	18	—
Get Volume Information	2222	22	44
Get Volume Name	2222	22	6
Get Volume Number	2222	22	5

T A B L E 7.1

NCP Function Codes

(continued)

SERVICE	REQUEST TYPE	FUNCTION CODE	SUBFUNCTION CODE
Map Directory Number to Path	2222	22	243
Modify Maximum Rights Mask	2222	22	4
Open Data Stream	2222	22	49
Purge Salvagable File	2222	22	29
Recover Salvagable File	2222	22	28
Remove Extended Trustee from Directory or File	2222	22	43
Remove User Disk Space Restriction	2222	22	34
Rename Directory	2222	22	15
Rename or Move	2222	22	46
Scan a Directory	2222	22	30
Scan Directory Disk Space	2222	22	40
Scan Directory for Trustees	2222	22	12
Scan Directory Information	2222	22	2
Scan File or Directory for Extended Trustees	2222	22	38
Scan Salvagable Files	2222	22	27
Scan Volume's User Disk Restrictions	2222	22	32
Set Directory Disk Space Restrictions	2222	22	36

SERVICE	REQUEST TYPE	FUNCTION CODE	SUBFUNCTION CODE
Set Directory Entry Information	2222	22	37
Set Directory Handle	2222	22	0
Set Directory Information	2222	22	25
File Services			
Allow Task to Access File	2222	78	—
Close File	2222	66	—
Commit File	2222	61	—
Copy from One File to Another	2222	74	—
Create File	2222	67	—
Create New File	2222	77	—
Erase File	2222	68	—
File Search Continue	2222	63	—
File Search Initialize	2222	62	—
Get Current Size of File	2222	71	—
Get Sparse File Data Block Bit Map	2222	85	—
Open File	2222	76	—
Rename File	2222	69	—
Scan File Information	2222	23	15
Search for a File	2222	64	—
Set File Attributes	2222	70	—
Set File Extended Attributes	2222	79	—

TABLE 7.1

NCP Function Codes

(continued)

SERVICE	REQUEST TYPE	FUNCTION CODE	SUBFUNCTION CODE
Set File Information	2222	23	16
Set File Time and Date Stamp	2222	75	—
File Server Environment			
Allocate a Resource	2222	15	—
Check Console Privileges	2222	23	200
Clear Connection Number	2222	23	210
Deallocate a Resource	2222	16	—
Disable File Server Login	2222	23	203
Disable Transaction Tracking	2222	23	207
Down File Server	2222	23	211
Enable File Server Login	2222	23	204
Enable Transaction Tracking	2222	23	208
Get Disk Utilization	2222	23	14
Get File Server Date and Time	2222	20	—
Get File Server Description Strings	2222	23	201
Get File Server Information	2222	23	17
Get File Server Login Status	2222	23	205

SERVICE	REQUEST TYPE	FUNCTION CODE	SUBFUNCTION CODE
Get Network Serial Number	2222	23	18
Get Object's Remaining Disk Space	2222	23	230
Send Console Broadcast	2222	23	209
Set File Server Date and Time	2222	23	202
Verify Serialization	2222	23	12
Message Services			
Broadcast to Console	2222	21	9
Disable Broadcasts	2222	21	2
Enable Broadcasts	2222	21	3
Get Broadcast Message	2222	21	1
Send Broadcast Message	2222	21	0
Print Services			
Close Spool File	2222	17	1
Create Spool File	2222	17	9
Get Printer's Queue	2222	17	10
Set Spool File Flags	2222	17	2
Spool a Disk File	2222	17	3
Write to Spool File	2222	17	0
Queue Services			
Abort Servicing Queue Job	2222	23	115
Attach Queue Server to Queue	2222	23	111

SERVICE	REQUEST TYPE	FUNCTION CODE	SUBFUNCTION CODE
Change Queue Job Entry	2222	23	109
Change Queue Job Position	2222	23	110
Change to Client's Rights	2222	23	116
Close a File and Start Queue Job	2222	23	105
Create Queue	2222	23	100
Create Queue Job and File	2222	23	104
Destroy Queue	2222	23	101
Detach Queue Server from Queue	2222	23	112
Finish Servicing Queue Job	2222	23	114
Get Queue Job File Size	2222	23	120
Get Queue Job List	2222	23	107
Read Queue Current Status	2222	23	102
Read Queue Job Entry	2222	23	108
Read Queue Server Current Status	2222	23	118
Remove Job From Queue	2222	23	106
Restore Queue Server Rights	2222	23	117
Service Queue Job	2222	23	113

SERVICE	REQUEST TYPE	FUNCTION CODE	SUBFUNCTION CODE
Set Queue Current Status	2222	23	103
Set Queue Server Current Status	2222	23	119
Synchronization Services			
Clear File	2222	7	—
Clear File Set	2222	8	—
Clear Logical Record	2222	11	—
Clear Logical Record Set	2222	14	—
Clear Physical Record	2222	30	—
Clear Physical Record Set	2222	31	—
Close Semaphore	2222	32	4
Examine Semaphore	2222	32	1
File Set Lock	2222	1	—
File Release Lock	2222	2	—
Lock File Set	2222	4	—
Lock Logical Record Set	2222	10	—
Lock Physical Record Set	2222	27	—
Log File	2222	3	—
Log Logical Record	2222	9	—
Log Physical Record	2222	26	—
Open Semaphore	2222	32	0
Release File	2222	5	—

TABLE 7.1
NCP Function Codes
(continued)

TABLE 7.1

NCP Function Codes

(continued)

SERVICE	REQUEST TYPE	FUNCTION CODE	SUBFUNCTION CODE
Release File Set	2222	6	—
Release Logical Record	2222	12	—
Release Logical Record Set	2222	13	—
Release Physical Record	2222	28	—
Release Physical Record Set	2222	29	—
Signal Semaphore	2222	32	3
Wait on Semaphore	2222	32	2
Transaction Tracking Services			
TTS Abort Transaction	2222	34	3
TTS Begin Transaction	2222	34	1
TTS End Transaction	2222	34	2
TTS Get Application Thresholds	2222	34	5
TTS Get Transaction Bits	2222	34	9
TTS Get Workstation Thresholds	2222	34	7
TTS Is Available	2222	34	0
TTS Set Application Thresholds	2222	34	6
TTS Set Transaction Bits	2222	34	10
TTS Set Workstation Thresholds	2222	34	8
TTS Transaction Status	2222	34	4

Sample NCP Communications

The remainder of this chapter depicts a NetWare client and server communicating by using NCP requests and replies.

ATTACHING TO A NETWARE SERVER

When a NetWare client loads the shell (NETX.COM), the first NCP call the client sends is a Create Service Connection, as shown in Figure 7.8. This NCP type number is 1111. The server replies, granting a connection if possible.

Packets 11 and 12 are the Negotiate Buffer Size NCP calls. In these packets, the client and server are exchanging the maximum packet size they may use. The client then issues a Logout NCP call to ensure that any previous connection it may have held open is closed. Finally, the client requests the file server information through a Get File Server Date and Time NCP.

No.	Source	Destination	Layer	Summary
1	LINDSAY	Broadcast	sap	Query Nearest File Server
2	MKTG-45	LINDSAY	sap	Resp Nearest; Server=SJF-AHUEY
3	LINDSAY	Broadcast	rip	Req network=00 00 11 62
4	MKTG-45	LINDSAY	rip	Resp network=00 00 11 62; 1 hops
5	LINDSAY	MKTG-45	ncp	Req Create Service Connection
6	00001B1EF36B	LINDSAY	sap	Resp Nearest; Server=SJF-CARLW
7	MKTG-45	LINDSAY	ncp	Rply Create Service Connection
8	LINDSAY	MKTG-45	ncp	Req Get File Server Information
9	00001B110014	LINDSAY	sap	Resp Nearest; Server=SJF-RUNTIME
10	MKTG-45	LINDSAY	ncp	Rply Get File Server Information
11	LINDSAY	MKTG-45	ncp	Req Negotiate Buffer Size
12	MKTG-45	LINDSAY	ncp	Rply Negotiate Buffer Size
13	LINDSAY	MKTG-45	ncp	Req Logout
14	MKTG-45	LINDSAY	ncp	Rply Logout
15	LINDSAY	MKTG-45	ncp	Req Get File Server Date and Time
16	MKTG-45	LINDSAY	ncp	Rply Get File Server Date and Time
17	00001B15089F	LINDSAY	sap	Resp Nearest; Server=SJF-COMPAQ
18	00001B03F363	LINDSAY	sap	Resp Nearest; Server=SJF-NMPD1
19	00001B1E5CD8	LINDSAY	sap	Resp Nearest; Server=SJF-NM3
20	00001B1E4C00	LINDSAY	sap	Resp Nearest; Server=SJF-NM14
21	00001B1E5CCD	LINDSAY	sap	Resp Nearest; Server=NMRENT2
22	00001B3321C3	LINDSAY	sap	Resp Nearest; Server=SJF-IMSP-LAB
23	00001B32EE91	LINDSAY	sap	Resp Nearest; Server=SJF-IMSP
24	FS2	LINDSAY	sap	Resp Nearest; Server=SJF-TLAU
25	FS2	LINDSAY	sap	Resp Nearest; Server=SJF-RUNTIME

C:\TRACES\NETX.TR1

Packet: 1   Unfiltered: 35

F I G U R E 7.8

The NetWare client launches NETX.COM.

LOGGING OUT OF A NETWARE SERVER

Figure 7.9 shows a portion of the logout procedure. After typing LOGOUT, the server copies the contents of the LOGOUT.EXE file to the client. Packet 101 shows the Close File NCP request from the client. This indicates that the client has received the entire file.

F I G U R E 7.9

The client issues the
LOGOUT command.

No.	Source	Destination	Layer	Summary
101	LINDSAY	SALES1	ncp	Req Close File LOGOUT.EXE
102	SALES1	LINDSAY	ncp	Rply Close File
103	LINDSAY	SALES1	ncp	Req Get Bindery Access Level
104	SALES1	LINDSAY	ncp	Rply Get Bindery Access Level
105	LINDSAY	SALES1	ncp	Req Get Bindery Object Name
106	SALES1	LINDSAY	ncp	Rply Get Bindery Object Name
107	LINDSAY	SALES1	ncp	Req Scan Bindery Object
108	SALES1	LINDSAY	ncp	Rply Scan Bindery Object
109	LINDSAY	SALES1	ncp	Req Get File Server Date and Time
110	SALES1	LINDSAY	ncp	Rply Get File Server Date and Time
111	LINDSAY	SALES1	ncp	Req Get Station's Logged Informat
112	SALES1	LINDSAY	ncp	Rply Get Station's Logged Informat
113	FS2	LINDSAY	ncp	Rply Read; 1024 bytes
114	LINDSAY	SALES1	ncp	Req Logout
115	FS2	LINDSAY	ncp	Rply Read; 1024 bytes
116	SALES1	LINDSAY	ncp	Rply Logout
117	FS2	LINDSAY	ncp	Rply Read; 1024 bytes
118	FS2	LINDSAY	ncp	Rply Read; 1024 bytes
119	LINDSAY	SALES1	ncp	Req Get Bindery Access Level
120	SALES1	LINDSAY	ncp	Rply Get Bindery Access Level
121	LINDSAY	SALES1	ncp	Req End Of Job
122	SALES1	LINDSAY	ncp	Rply End Of Job
123	LINDSAY	SALES1	ncp	Req End Of Job
124	SALES1	LINDSAY	ncp	Rply End Of Job
125	LINDSAY	SALES1	ncp	Req Get Directory Path

C:\TRACES\LOGOUT.TR1

Packet: 1   Unfiltered: 143

In packets 103, 105, 107, and 111, the client issues NCPs requesting information regarding the station's bindery access level (privileges), object name (login name), and logged information. The station's logged information includes the object name (username) and the time and date the user logged into the server.

MAPPING A NETWORK DRIVE LETTER

When issuing the MAP command, the server downloads the entire MAP.EXE file to the local workstation's memory. In Figure 7.10 you can see a portion of the NCP calls that occur when you map a directory. Packet 176 shows the directory that is being mapped. The directory name is

```
┌─────────────────────────────────────────────────────────────────┐
│ ⊟                    C:\TRACES\MAP.TR1                      ▼ ▲   │
├───────┬──────────────┬──────────────┬───────┬─────────────────────┤
│ No.   │ Source       │ Destination  │ Layer │ Summary          ↕  │
├───────┼──────────────┼──────────────┼───────┼─────────────────────┤
│   163 │ SALES1       │ LINDSAY      │ ncp   │ Rply Get Bindery Access Level    │
│   164 │ LINDSAY      │ SALES1       │ ncp   │ Req  Get Bindery Object Name     │
│   165 │ SALES1       │ LINDSAY      │ ncp   │ Rply Get Bindery Object Name     │
│   166 │ LINDSAY      │ SALES1       │ ncp   │ Req  Scan Bindery Object         │
│   167 │ SALES1       │ LINDSAY      │ ncp   │ Rply Scan Bindery Object         │
│   168 │ LINDSAY      │ SALES1       │ ncp   │ Req  Alloc Temporary Directory Han│
│   169 │ SALES1       │ LINDSAY      │ ncp   │ Rply Alloc Temporary Directory Han│
│   170 │ LINDSAY      │ SALES1       │ ncp   │ Req  Scan Directory Information Sc│
│   171 │ SALES1       │ LINDSAY      │ ncp   │ Rply Scan Directory Information Sc│
│   172 │ LINDSAY      │ SALES1       │ ncp   │ Req  Deallocate Directory Handle  │
│   173 │ SALES1       │ LINDSAY      │ ncp   │ Rply Deallocate Directory Handle  │
│   174 │ LINDSAY      │ SALES1       │ ncp   │ Req  Alloc Permanent Directory Han│
│   175 │ SALES1       │ LINDSAY      │ ncp   │ Rply Alloc Permanent Directory Han│
│   176 │ LINDSAY      │ SALES1       │ ncp   │ Req  Set Directory Handle HOME/LCH│
│   177 │ SALES1       │ LINDSAY      │ ncp   │ Rply Set Directory Handle         │
│   178 │ LINDSAY      │ SALES1       │ ncp   │ Req  Get Directory Path           │
│   179 │ SALES1       │ LINDSAY      │ ncp   │ Rply Get Directory Path VOL1:HOME/│
│   180 │ LINDSAY      │ SALES1       │ ncp   │ Req  Get Directory Path           │
│   181 │ SALES1       │ LINDSAY      │ ncp   │ Rply Get Directory Path VOL1:HOME/│
│   182 │ LINDSAY      │ SALES1       │ ncp   │ Req  End Of Job                   │
│   183 │ SALES1       │ LINDSAY      │ ncp   │ Rply End Of Job                   │
│   184 │ LINDSAY      │ SALES1       │ ncp   │ Req  End Of Job                   │
│   185 │ SALES1       │ LINDSAY      │ ncp   │ Rply End Of Job                   │
│   186 │ LINDSAY      │ SALES1       │ ncp   │ Req  Get Directory Path           │
│   187 │ SALES1       │ LINDSAY      │ ncp   │ Rply Get Directory Path VOL1:HOME/│
├───────┴──────────────┴──────────────┴───────┴─────────────────────┤
│ ◄                                                               ►  │
├─────────────────────────────┬─────────────┬───────────────────────┤
│                             │ Packet:   1 │ Unfiltered:  187      │
└─────────────────────────────┴─────────────┴───────────────────────┘
```

HOME/LCHAPPEL. When the client issues the Scan Directory Information request, the server returns information regarding the directory's creation date and time, the owner, and the access rights mask.

LAUNCHING A PROGRAM ON THE SERVER

When the client types a command to load an application that resides on the server, the communication follows three primary steps to download the application to the client:

1 · Search for the file.

2 · Download the file.

3 · Download any supplementary files.

In Figure 7.11, the client has typed **WP** to launch WordPerfect at her workstation. The Open File failures are because the file named WP is not located in the directory that the client is presently in. As seen in packet

FIGURE 7.11

The shell searches for the
file named WP.

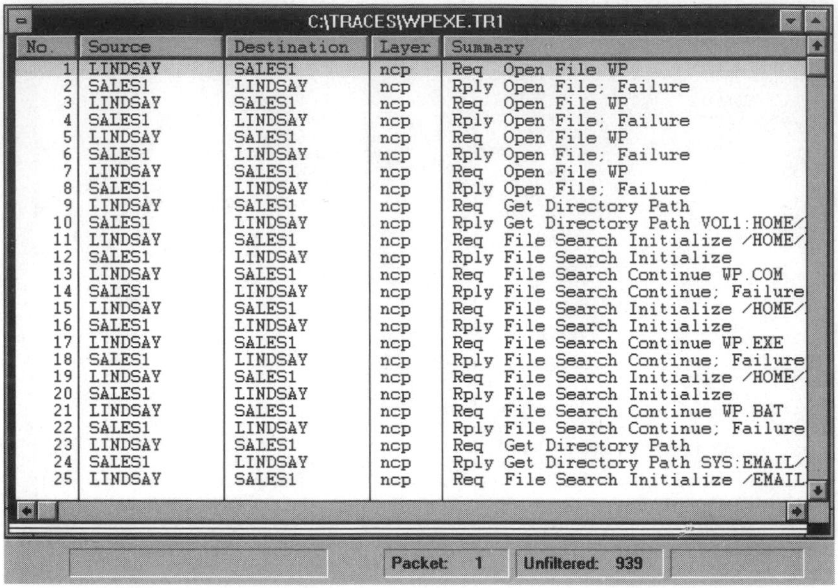

```
┌─────────────────────────────────────────────────────────────────┐
│ ▭                    C:\TRACES\WPEXE.TR1                      ▾ ▴ │
├──────┬───────────┬─────────────┬───────┬─────────────────────────┤
│ No.  │ Source    │ Destination │ Layer │ Summary                 │
├──────┼───────────┼─────────────┼───────┼─────────────────────────┤
│    1 │ LINDSAY   │ SALES1      │ ncp   │ Req  Open File WP       │
│    2 │ SALES1    │ LINDSAY     │ ncp   │ Rply Open File; Failure │
│    3 │ LINDSAY   │ SALES1      │ ncp   │ Req  Open File WP       │
│    4 │ SALES1    │ LINDSAY     │ ncp   │ Rply Open File; Failure │
│    5 │ LINDSAY   │ SALES1      │ ncp   │ Req  Open File WP       │
│    6 │ SALES1    │ LINDSAY     │ ncp   │ Rply Open File; Failure │
│    7 │ LINDSAY   │ SALES1      │ ncp   │ Req  Open File WP       │
│    8 │ SALES1    │ LINDSAY     │ ncp   │ Rply Open File; Failure │
│    9 │ LINDSAY   │ SALES1      │ ncp   │ Req  Get Directory Path │
│   10 │ SALES1    │ LINDSAY     │ ncp   │ Rply Get Directory Path VOL1:HOME/ │
│   11 │ LINDSAY   │ SALES1      │ ncp   │ Req  File Search Initialize /HOME/ │
│   12 │ SALES1    │ LINDSAY     │ ncp   │ Rply File Search Initialize │
│   13 │ LINDSAY   │ SALES1      │ ncp   │ Req  File Search Continue WP.COM │
│   14 │ SALES1    │ LINDSAY     │ ncp   │ Rply File Search Continue; Failure │
│   15 │ LINDSAY   │ SALES1      │ ncp   │ Req  File Search Initialize /HOME/ │
│   16 │ SALES1    │ LINDSAY     │ ncp   │ Rply File Search Initialize │
│   17 │ LINDSAY   │ SALES1      │ ncp   │ Req  File Search Continue WP.EXE │
│   18 │ SALES1    │ LINDSAY     │ ncp   │ Rply File Search Continue; Failure │
│   19 │ LINDSAY   │ SALES1      │ ncp   │ Req  File Search Initialize /HOME/ │
│   20 │ SALES1    │ LINDSAY     │ ncp   │ Rply File Search Initialize │
│   21 │ LINDSAY   │ SALES1      │ ncp   │ Req  File Search Continue WP.BAT │
│   22 │ SALES1    │ LINDSAY     │ ncp   │ Rply File Search Continue; Failure │
│   23 │ LINDSAY   │ SALES1      │ ncp   │ Req  Get Directory Path │
│   24 │ SALES1    │ LINDSAY     │ ncp   │ Rply Get Directory Path SYS:EMAIL/ │
│   25 │ LINDSAY   │ SALES1      │ ncp   │ Req  File Search Initialize /EMAIL │
├──────┴───────────┴─────────────┴───────┴─────────────────────────┤
│ ◄│                                                              │ ►│
├──────────────────┬────────────┬──────────────────┐              │
│                  │ Packet:  1 │ Unfiltered:  939 │              │
└──────────────────┴────────────┴──────────────────┘
```

number 13, the shell next searches for the file WP.COM. Since this failed, it then searches for WP.EXE and, finally, WP.BAT. If Lindsay had executed the file by typing the entire file name, she would have made only one request—asking for the file by its full name.

Since the file is not located in the directory that the user is in, the shell begins looking for the file through assigned search drives. In packet 25 you can see the shell searching in the EMAIL directory. The shell looks through all the search drives in order until it either finds the file and begins copying it to the local drive or cannot find the file and issues a "File Not Found" message.

In Figure 7.12, the shell has found the file in the HOME /LCHAPPEL /APPS directory. Once the file has been found, the shell begins copying the file to the local workstation's memory.

In Figure 7.13 you can see supplemental files being copied to the workstation. Packets 934 and 936 depict the client reading the WPLAC}.SET file. This file contains the preferences for the user's WordPerfect environment.

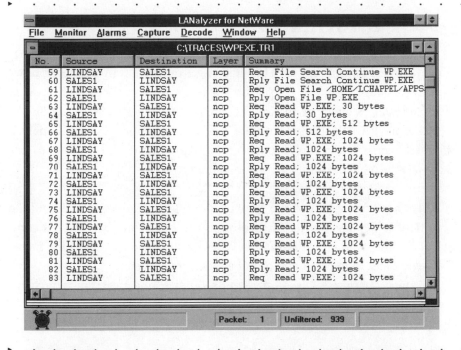

FIGURE 7.12

The file is copied to the client.

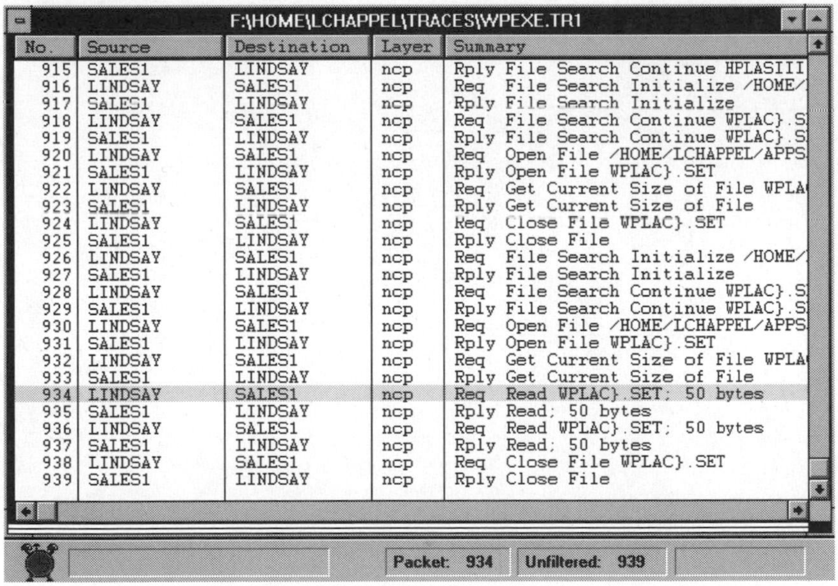

FIGURE 7.13

Any required supplemental files are also downloaded.

NCP Information

Novell does not publish details regarding its NCPs because the information is "Novell Confidential." The NCP codes defined in this chapter, however, were taken from the LANalyzer for NetWare screens, which provide clear, accurate decodes of all NetWare NCP functions and subfunctions.

Using the LANalyzer for NetWare, you can examine, read, and analyze the NCP requests and replies between NetWare clients and servers to understand the NetWare communications better.

This chapter has defined the NCP header types, Read and Reply, and the type field values used with NCP communications. You have viewed common NCP function and subfunction types for operations such as file reads, file writes, and logging in and out of a NetWare server.

The next chapter focuses on Novell's Burst Mode Protocol, which increases the efficiency of file reads and writes.

Burst Mode
Protocol

In Chapter 7, you learned that for every NCP request made by a workstation, an NCP reply is expected. This single-request, single-response (ping-pong) type of communication does not permit a multiple packet response from a single request from the client.

For example, if you requested a large file from the server, you must submit a request for the first part of the file and wait for the response. After receiving the first response, you can ask for the second part of the file. Once you've received the second part, you request the third, and so on. It would be much more efficient if you could make your request once and receive a response of multiple packets in sequence without making another request.

The Burst Mode Protocol was designed to make file reads and file writes more efficient.

This chapter discusses the key benefits of Burst Mode and defines how to implement it. It also examines the Burst Mode frame formats and analyzes a Burst Mode communication.

Burst Mode Features

The Burst Mode Protocol was designed to allow multiple responses to a single request for file reads and writes. Burst Mode increases the efficiency of client/server communications by allowing workstations to submit a single file read or write request and receive up to 64 kilobytes of data without submitting another request. The primary advantages of Burst Mode include the following:

▸ Large amounts of data can be transferred from a single request.

▸ Applications do not need to be "burst aware."

▸ A Burst window is configured based on transmission success.

TRANSFERRING LARGE AMOUNTS OF DATA FROM A SINGLE REQUEST

Using Burst Mode, a client makes a single file request of the server and can receive up to 64K of data back from that single request. This value is dependent upon the capability of the client and network to support this large file transfer without receive congestion or lost packets.

APPLICATIONS DO NOT NEED TO BE BURST AWARE

When a Burst Mode connection is established between a client and server, the workstation shell will automatically use the Burst Mode service whenever an application requests a read or write. Applications do not need to be adjusted to support Burst Mode.

THE BURST MODE WINDOW IS BASED ON SUCCESSFUL TRANSACTIONS

The *Burst Mode window* is the the number of unacknowledged bytes of data outstanding from a file read or write. The minimum window size is based on the maximum packet size allowed and the number of workstation packet burst buffers. In Figure 8.1, you are viewing a Burst Mode transaction where the window size is increasing from 7600 bytes to 7900 bytes per burst.

Implementing the Packet Burst Protocol

Now let's look at how Burst Mode is implemented, beginning with the use of special client and server software.

FIGURE 8.1

The Burst Mode window size increases based upon successful transactions.

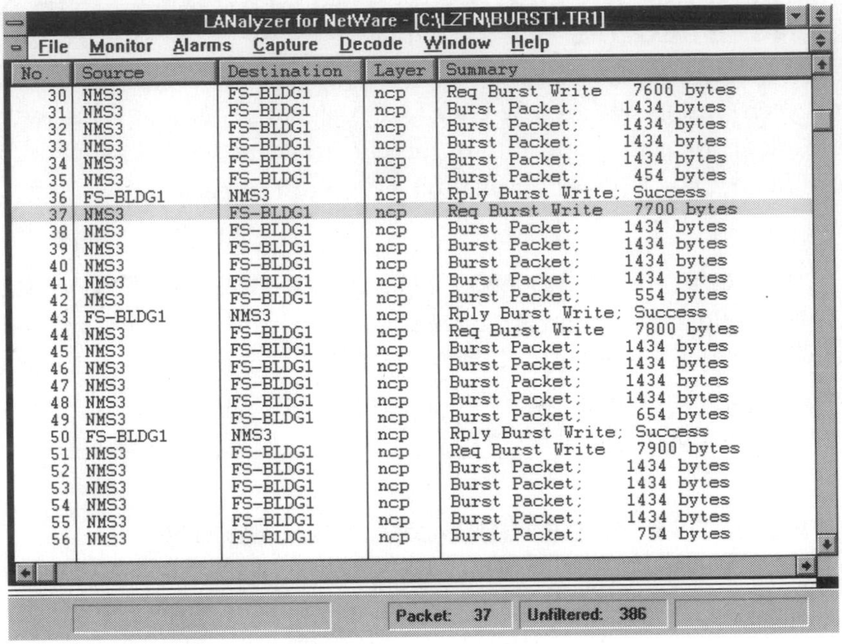

```
═  LANalyzer for NetWare - [C:\LZFN\BURST1.TR1]           ▼ ▲
═  File   Monitor  Alarms  Capture  Decode  Window  Help      ▲
                                                              ▼
  No.  Source      Destination   Layer  Summary                 ▲
    30 NMS3         FS-BLDG1       ncp   Req Burst Write    7600 bytes
    31 NMS3         FS-BLDG1       ncp   Burst Packet;      1434 bytes
    32 NMS3         FS-BLDG1       ncp   Burst Packet;      1434 bytes
    33 NMS3         FS-BLDG1       ncp   Burst Packet;      1434 bytes
    34 NMS3         FS-BLDG1       ncp   Burst Packet;      1434 bytes
    35 NMS3         FS-BLDG1       ncp   Burst Packet;       454 bytes
    36 FS-BLDG1     NMS3           ncp   Rply Burst Write; Success
    37 NMS3         FS-BLDG1       ncp   Req Burst Write    7700 bytes
    38 NMS3         FS-BLDG1       ncp   Burst Packet;      1434 bytes
    39 NMS3         FS-BLDG1       ncp   Burst Packet;      1434 bytes
    40 NMS3         FS-BLDG1       ncp   Burst Packet;      1434 bytes
    41 NMS3         FS-BLDG1       ncp   Burst Packet;      1434 bytes
    42 NMS3         FS-BLDG1       ncp   Burst Packet;       554 bytes
    43 FS-BLDG1     NMS3           ncp   Rply Burst Write; Success
    44 NMS3         FS-BLDG1       ncp   Req Burst Write    7800 bytes
    45 NMS3         FS-BLDG1       ncp   Burst Packet;      1434 bytes
    46 NMS3         FS-BLDG1       ncp   Burst Packet;      1434 bytes
    47 NMS3         FS-BLDG1       ncp   Burst Packet;      1434 bytes
    48 NMS3         FS-BLDG1       ncp   Burst Packet;      1434 bytes
    49 NMS3         FS-BLDG1       ncp   Burst Packet;       654 bytes
    50 FS-BLDG1     NMS3           ncp   Rply Burst Write; Success
    51 NMS3         FS-BLDG1       ncp   Req Burst Write    7900 bytes
    52 NMS3         FS-BLDG1       ncp   Burst Packet;      1434 bytes
    53 NMS3         FS-BLDG1       ncp   Burst Packet;      1434 bytes
    54 NMS3         FS-BLDG1       ncp   Burst Packet;      1434 bytes
    55 NMS3         FS-BLDG1       ncp   Burst Packet;      1434 bytes
    56 NMS3         FS-BLDG1       ncp   Burst Packet;       754 bytes  ▼
 ◄                                                             ►

                              Packet:  37    Unfiltered:  386
```

In order to use Burst Mode Protocol, both the client and server must be "burst enabled" using the Burst Mode NLM at the server and Burst Mode shell at the workstation. In addition, clients must include a Burst Mode parameter in the NET.CFG file indicating the number of packet burst buffers available at the client:

pb buffers = <n>

This NET.CFG parameter denotes the number of packet receive buffers that the workstation will allot to the packet burst. The variable n is a number between 0 and 10. If n is set to 0, Burst Mode is disabled.

Currently, packet burst buffers are kept in conventional memory even if the expanded or extended shell is loaded.

The packet size is negotiated when the Burst Mode shell requests a connection from a server. For example, on an Ethernet NetWare LAN, the client may negotiate a packet size of 1024 bytes. Therefore, each Burst Mode buffer requires 1126 bytes (the packet size plus the 102-byte Burst Mode header).

Initiating a Burst Mode Connection

When a client using the Burst Mode shell requests a connection to a Burst Mode enabled server, it negotiates the buffer size as usual and then requests a Packet Burst connection.

The Burst Mode connection NCP function number is 101 and does not require or use a subfunction code, as shown in Figure 8.2. When requesting the Burst Mode connection, the client states its maximum packet size as well as the maximum send and receive size. If the server is Burst Mode enabled, it will respond with a Burst Mode Connection reply, as shown in Figure 8.3.

If, however, a client attempts to establish a Burst Mode connection with a server that is not Burst Mode enabled, the server will answer back with an indication that "No Such Property" exists, as shown in Figure 8.4.

If the server does not allow Burst Mode file transfers, the communications will use the standard request-response method of NCP.

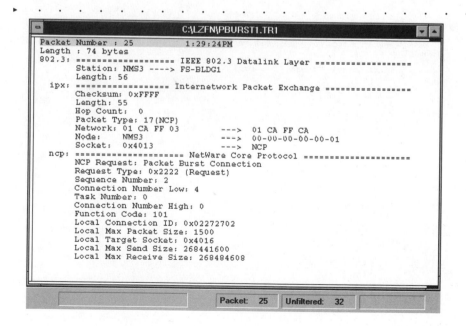

```
                              C:\LZFN\PBURST1.TR1
Packet Number : 25              1:29:24PM
Length : 74 bytes
802.3: ==================== IEEE 802.3 Datalink Layer ====================
        Station: NMS3 ----> FS-BLDG1
        Length: 56
  ipx:  ================= Internetwork Packet Exchange =================
        Checksum: 0xFFFF
        Length: 55
        Hop Count:  0
        Packet Type: 17(NCP)
        Network: 01 CA FF 03        --->  01 CA FF CA
        Node:    NMS3               --->  00-00-00-00-00-01
        Socket:  0x4013             --->  NCP
  ncp:  ==================== NetWare Core Protocol ====================
        NCP Request: Packet Burst Connection
        Request Type: 0x2222 (Request)
        Sequence Number: 2
        Connection Number Low: 4
        Task Number: 0
        Connection Number High: 0
        Function Code: 101
        Local Connection ID: 0x02272702
        Local Max Packet Size: 1500
        Local Target Socket: 0x4016
        Local Max Send Size: 268441600
        Local Max Receive Size: 268484608



                     Packet:   25   Unfiltered:   32
```

FIGURE 8.2

Burst Mode Connection

request

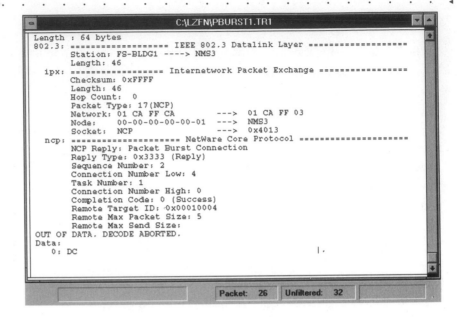

```
                                    C:\LZFN\PBURST1.TR1
Length : 64 bytes
802.3: ==================== IEEE 802.3 Datalink Layer ====================
        Station: FS-BLDG1 ----> NMS3
        Length: 46
   ipx: ================== Internetwork Packet Exchange ==================
        Checksum: 0xFFFF
        Length: 46
        Hop Count: 0
        Packet Type: 17(NCP)
        Network: 01 CA FF CA         --->  01 CA FF 03
        Node:    00-00-00-00-00-01  --->  NMS3
        Socket:  NCP                 --->  0x4013
   ncp: ==================== NetWare Core Protocol ====================
        NCP Reply: Packet Burst Connection
        Reply Type: 0x3333 (Reply)
        Sequence Number: 2
        Connection Number Low: 4
        Task Number: 1
        Connection Number High: 0
        Completion Code: 0 (Success)
        Remote Target ID: 0x00010004
        Remote Max Packet Size: 5
        Remote Max Send Size:
OUT OF DATA. DECODE ABORTED.
Data:
   0: DC                                                     |.
```
```
                                   Packet:  26   Unfiltered:  32
```

```
                                    C:\LZFN\PBURST1.TR1
Packet Number : 15              1:29:24PM
Length : 64 bytes
802.3: ==================== IEEE 802.3 Datalink Layer ====================
        Station: 386-CLASS3A ----> NMS3
        Length: 38
   ipx: ================== Internetwork Packet Exchange ==================
        Checksum: 0xFFFF
        Length: 38
        Hop Count: 0
        Packet Type: 17(NCP)
        Network: 01 CA FF CB         --->  01 CA FF 03
        Node:    00-00-00-00-00-01  --->  NMS3
        Socket:  NCP                 --->  0x4013
   ncp: ==================== NetWare Core Protocol ====================
        NCP Reply: Packet Burst Connection
        Reply Type: 0x3333 (Reply)
        Sequence Number: 2
        Connection Number Low: 5
        Task Number: 1
        Connection Number High: 0
        Completion Code: 251 (No Such Property)
Data:
   0: 00                                                     |.
```
```
                                   Packet:  15   Unfiltered:  32
```

Burst Mode Frame Format

As mentioned earlier, when a Burst Mode client wishes to perform file reads or writes, the shell will automatically use Burst Mode services.

Burst Mode communications require an NCP Burst header after the IPX header and before the burst data, as shown in Figure 8.5.

The fields of the Burst Mode header are detailed in the following sections.

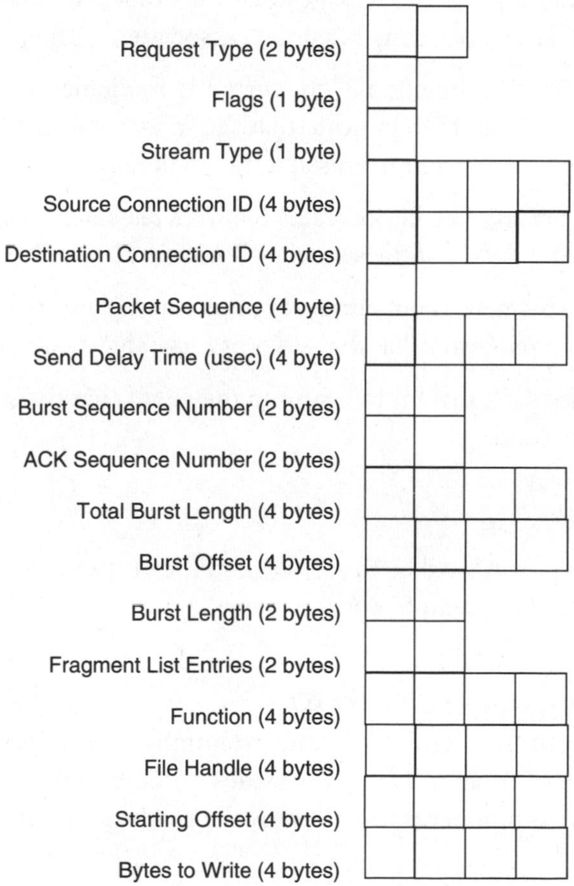

Request Type (2 bytes)
Flags (1 byte)
Stream Type (1 byte)
Source Connection ID (4 bytes)
Destination Connection ID (4 bytes)
Packet Sequence (4 byte)
Send Delay Time (usec) (4 byte)
Burst Sequence Number (2 bytes)
ACK Sequence Number (2 bytes)
Total Burst Length (4 bytes)
Burst Offset (4 bytes)
Burst Length (2 bytes)
Fragment List Entries (2 bytes)
Function (4 bytes)
File Handle (4 bytes)
Starting Offset (4 bytes)
Bytes to Write (4 bytes)

FIGURE 8.5

The Burst Mode header follows the IPX header.

TYPE FIELD

The type field is the NCP request/reply type field. When using Burst Mode, the type field will contain the value 0x7777, indicating that the packet is a burst packet.

FLAGS

The flags available include the following:

- ▸ **SYS:** Setting this bit indicates that the burst is a system packet and does not have any burst data associated with it.

- ▸ **SAK:** This bit function is not currently implemented but will eventually be set to indicate that the sender would like the receiver to transmit its missing fragment list.

- ▸ **EOB:** Setting this bit indicates that this packet contains the last of the burst data that the sender will transmit.

- ▸ **BSY:** This field is not currently implemented but will eventually notify a requester that the server is busy and it should wait.

- ▸ **ABT:** Setting this bit indicates to the client that the session is no longer valid.

STREAM TYPE

The stream type is used by the server, and the only current value is 0x02, which indicates "Big send burst."

SOURCE CONNECTION ID

The source connection ID is a random number that is generally formed from the current time of day and provides a unique identifier for a burst connection. This number is generated by the sender and cannot contain the value 0.

DESTINATION CONNECTION ID

The destination connection ID is a random number that is similar to the source connection ID, but it is defined by the receiver. The value cannot be 0.

PACKET SEQUENCE NUMBER

The packet sequence number tracks the current burst transaction and is incremented by 1 for every new packet a node transmits in each service transaction.

SEND DELAY TIME

The send delay time field identifies the delay time between each of the sender's packet transmissions and is specified in units of approximately 100 microseconds.

BURST SEQUENCE NUMBER

All replies in response to a single request are members of a burst set. Each packet in the set contains the same burst sequence number. Upon setting up the burst connection, this sequence number is 0 and will increment with each successive burst sent.

ACK SEQUENCE NUMBER

The ACK sequence number is the burst sequence number that the node expects to receive next and is used to determine if the last burst transmitted was successfully received.

All packets of a burst set will have the same burst sequence and ACK sequence number until the last packet of the burst set. The last packet will contain an ACK sequence number equal to the current burst sequence number plus 1. This indicates the number of the next burst sequence expected.

TOTAL BURST LENGTH

The total burst length field specifies the total length of the burst being transmitted (in bytes).

BURST OFFSET

The burst offset field defines where in the burst this packet's data will fit. If the offset is 0, this is the first packet of the burst transaction.

BURST LENGTH

The burst length field defines the length of the entire burst transaction. This will be the sum of all burst sets.

FRAGMENT LIST ENTRIES

The fragment list entries field defines the number of elements that are missing from the burst transaction. The missing fragment list will follow this number, if applicable. The value 0 indicates that there are no missing fragments.

FUNCTION

The function field defines whether the current burst transaction is a read or write.

Analyzing the Benefits of Burst Mode

The following session was captured using the LANalyzer for NetWare. In this example, a workstation using the Burst Mode shell has connected to a server that has Burst Mode enabled.

In this example, a large file write has been requested, copying the contents of the local drive, C, up to the file server. This is illustrated in Figure 8.6.

```
                          C:\LZFN\BURST1.TR1

802.3:  ═══════════════════ IEEE 002.3 Datalink Layer ═══════════════════
        Station: NMS3 ----> FS-BLDG1
        Length: 1500
 ipx:   ═══════════════════ Internetwork Packet Exchange ═══════════════════
        Checksum: 0xFFFF
        Length: 1500
        Hop Count:  0
        Packet Type: 17(NCP)
        Network: 01 CA FF 03       --->  01 CA FF CA
        Node:    NMS3              --->  00-00-00-00-00-01
        Socket:  0x4016            --->  NCP
 ncp:   ═══════════════════ NetWare Core Protocol ═══════════════════
        Type: 0x7777 (Burst Packet)
        Flags: 0x00
        Stream Type: 2 (Big Send Burst)
        Source Connection ID: 0x02272702
        Destination Connection ID: 0x01000400
        Packet Sequence Number: 251
        Send Delay Time (usec): 200
        Burst Sequence Number: 92
        ACK Sequence Number: 92
        Total Burst Length: 8324
        Burst Offset: 0
        Burst Length: 1434
        Fragment List Entries: 0
        Function: 2 (Write Request)
        File Handle: 0x49230000
        Starting Offset: 59400

                            Packet  83    Unfiltered  386
```

FIGURE 8.6

Burst Mode file write session

Figure 8.7 shows a Burst Mode Write request from the workstation labeled NMS3 to the server named FS-BLDG1.

The first packet in this trace is a request from the workstation, NMS3, to the server, FS-BLDG1, to create a file named DISKMAP.DAT. This is the file that will be copied up to the server next—you are viewing the 28th packet in the trace. After the server replies that the file has been created successfully, the workstation begins the file transfer.

The workstation will begin the transfer, allowing a total of 7600 bytes transmitted to be outstanding (without acknowledgment). As each transfer proceeds successfully, the number of outstanding bytes will increment by 100 throughout the burst transaction.

▶ · ◀

FIGURE 8.7

Burst Mode Write request

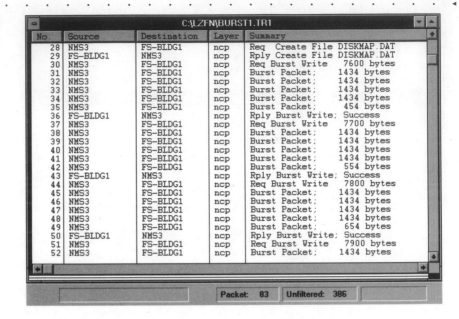

This chapter has defined the key benefits of the Burst Mode Protocol and examined a Burst Mode Connection request, Burst Mode Connection reply, and Burst Mode file write session. You have also examined the response received when a Burst Mode client attempts to make a Burst Mode connection to a server that does not have Burst Mode enabled.

The next chapter examines NetWare's Service Advertising Protocol (SAP).

CHAPTER 9

Service
Advertising
Protocol

NOTE
Throughout this chap-
ter, the term "server"
is used to identify ser-
vice-oriented processes
that may be running on
a NetWare server,
router, or workstation.

Up to this point, this book has discussed how clients transmit NCP re-quests to servers on a network. Before a client can communicate with a serv-er, however, it must know what servers are available on the network. This information is made available through Novell's Service Advertising Protocol (SAP). This chapter discusses how servers are advertised throughout the network and how clients acquire this information. Finally, the chapter ex-amines SAP packets that indicate which servers are not available to clients on the local network.

SAP Functionality

Novell's SAP services provide information on all the known servers throughout the entire network. These servers can include file servers, print servers, NetWare access servers, remote console servers, and so on. Each server type is assigned a number by Novell. Many servers also have a name that is assigned by the person installing or configuring the network. The server name and type number are advertised throughout the network and stored in each server's bindery. The *bindery* is a database of resources and clients on the network.

When a client requests information about available services, servers use the information stored in their binderies to reply to the client, as shown in Figure 9.1.

The SAP packets use IPX for transport and are defined by the value 0x0452 in the destination and source socket fields of the IPX header. As shown in Figure 9.2, you can find SAP information directly after the IPX header.

There are three types of SAP packets that may be seen on a NetWare LAN:

▸ Periodic SAP information broadcasts

▸ SAP service queries

▸ SAP service responses

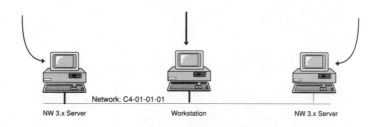

Server Name: SALES1
Server Type: 0x0004 (File Server)
Network: 0x99-00-00-01 (Internal IPX)
Node: 0x00-00-00-00-00-01

Server Name: MKTG-45
Server Type: 0x0004 (File Server)
Network: 0x88-00-00-01 (Internal IPX)
Node: 0x00-00-00-00-00-01

Server Name: PS01
Server Type: 0x0047 (Advertising Print Server)
Network: 0x99-00-00-01
Node: 0x00-00-00-00-00-01

Server Name: PS02
Server Type: 0x0047 (Advertising Print Server)
Network: C4-01-01-01
Node: 0x00-00-1B-09-81-3E

Server Name: MKTG-45
Server Type: 0x000107 (NetWare 386)
Network: 0x88-00-00-01
Node: 0x00-00-00-00-00-01

Network: C4-01-01-01

NW 3.x Server   Workstation   NW 3.x Server

F I G U R E   9.1

Servers maintain a list of services in their binderies.

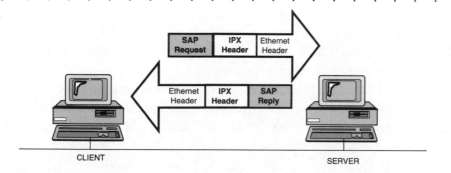

SAP Request | IPX Header | Ethernet Header

Ethernet Header | IPX Header | SAP Reply

CLIENT   SERVER

F I G U R E   9.2

SAP packets use IPX for transport.

These three types of SAP packets enable up-to-date service information to be distributed throughout the network, as well as specific service address information.

Periodic SAP Information Broadcasts

As mentioned earlier, all servers maintain a list of available network services in their binderies. As shown in Figure 9.3, this list of services is broadcast onto locally attached networks to inform other servers and routers of

F I G U R E 9.3

Servers broadcast SAP packets onto all locally attached networks.

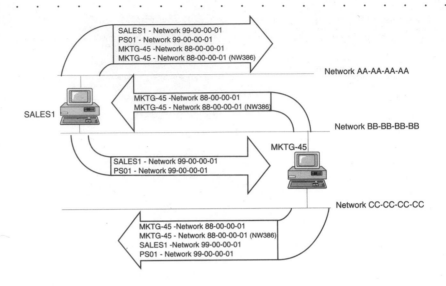

SALES1 - Network 99-00-00-01
PS01 - Network 99-00-00-01
MKTG-45 -Network 88-00-00-01
MKTG-45 - Network 88-00-00-01 (NW386)

Network AA-AA-AA-AA

MKTG-45 -Network 88-00-00-01
MKTG-45 - Network 88-00-00-01 (NW386)

SALES1

Network BB-BB-BB-BB

MKTG-45

SALES1 - Network 99-00-00-01
PS01 - Network 99-00-00-01

Network CC-CC-CC-CC

MKTG-45 -Network 88-00-00-01
MKTG-45 - Network 88-00-00-01 (NW386)
SALES1 -Network 99-00-00-01
PS01 - Network 99-00-00-01

network services available. Using this method, routers and servers maintain current information about network services.

These SAP information packets are broadcast on the network every 60 seconds. These packets do not require a request packet before being transmitted. This differentiates the SAP information broadcast packets from SAP Service Reply packets. Upon receipt of these information packets, servers update the service information contained in their binderies.

Figure 9.3 depicts how server information is propagated through an internetwork containing three separate Ethernet LANs. Server SALES1 is a file server with PSERVER.NLM loaded. This server will broadcast its services, NCP and print, on network AA-AA-AA-AA and network BB-BB-BB-BB every 60 seconds. Upon receipt of the packets, the server MKTG-45 will update its bindery information and broadcast all known services onto network CC-CC-CC-CC. In that SAP broadcast, MKTG-45 will include services provided by SALES1 and its own available services, file and remote console (NetWare 386).

If several minutes pass and a server fails to broadcast SAP information, all routers and servers will assume the server is not available and remove the server from their binderies.

Each SAP information broadcast packet can contain information about up to seven servers. As shown in Figure 9.4, packets that contain information about more than one server repeat the server type, server name, network address, node, socket, and intermediate networks fields.

NOTE
SAP information broadcast packets use the same structure as SAP Response packets and are defined later in this chapter.

SAP Service Query

When a workstation wishes to know about services available on the internetwork, it transmits a server query SAP. For example, a workstation transmits this packet when the shell (NETX.COM) is loaded in order to learn of available servers. There is currently only one type of service query implemented by Novell: the Nearest Service query.

The Nearest Service query is used to find a particular server type on the network. For example, as shown in Figure 9.5, to find the nearest (most quickly responding) file server, a Nearest Service query for server type 0x0004 is used.

Contrary to popular belief, when a Nearest Service Query packet is transmitted, the station will receive responses from *each* server that provides the service type requested by the client, not just the nearest one. As shown later in this chapter, you can use the Nearest Service query to build a list of available servers on the network.

The Nearest Service Query packet format is shown in Figure 9.6.

NOTE
Although contained in various technical documents, the General Service query is not currently implemented by Novell and is not discussed in detail in this chapter. The format for General Service Query packets is identical to that of the Nearest Service Query packets except that the service type field contains the value 0x0001.

PACKET TYPE

The packet type field defines whether the packet is a General Service query (not currently implemented) or Nearest Service query. The packet type for the Nearest Service query is 0x0003. The packet type for the General Service query is 0x0001.

FIGURE 9.4

SAP broadcasts can

advertise up to seven

servers per packet.

```
Packet Number : 151        11:48:28AM
Length : 498 bytes
802.3: ==================== IEEE 802.3 Datalink Layer ====================
      Station: 00-00-0C-01-60-5E ——> FF-FF-FF-FF-FF-FF
      Length: 480
ipx: ================== Internetwork Packet Exchange ==================
      Checksum: 0xFFFF
      Length: 480
      Hop Count:  0
      Packet Type: 4(IPX)
      Network: DE AD BE EF      —> DE AD BE EF
      Node:   00-00-1B-00-14-5E  —> FF-FF-FF-FF-FF-FF
      Socket:  SAP            —> SAP
sap: ============== NetWare Service Advertising Protocol ============
      Type: 2 (General Service Response)
      Server Name: IBM95
         Server Type: 0x0004 (File Server)
         Network: 84 07 00 95
         Node:    00-00-00-00-00-01
         Socket:  NCP
         Intermediate Networks: 2
      Server Name: MKTG-45
         Server Type: 0x0004 (File Server)
         Network: 88-00-00-01
         Node:    00-00-00-00-00-01
         Socket:  NCP
         Intermediate Networks: 2
      Server Name: SALES1
         Server Type: 0x0004 (File Server)
         Network: 99-00-00-01
         Node:    00-00-00-00-00-01
         Socket:  NCP
         Intermediate Networks: 2
      Server Name: ADMIN1
         Server Type: 0x0004 (File Server)
         Network: 00 20 82 73
         Node:    00-00-00-00-00-01
         Socket:  NCP
         Intermediate Networks: 2
      Server Name: SALES2
         Server Type: 0x0004 (File Server)
         Network: 00 20 82 83
         Node:    00-00-00-00-00-01
         Socket:  NCP
         Intermediate Networks: 2
      Server Name: BACKUP1
         Server Type: 0x0004 (File Server)
         Network: 00 10 86 51
         Node:    00-00-00-00-00-01
         Socket:  NCP
         Intermediate Networks: 2
      Server Name: ADMIN2
         Server Type: 0x0004 (File Server)
         Network: 00 10 02 22
         Node:    00-00-00-00-00-01
         Socket:  NCP
         Intermediate Networks: 2
```

A station uses a Nearest Service query to determine the nearest file server.

```
—                        LANalyzer for NetWare                    ▼ ♦
File  Monitor  Alarms  Capture  Decode  Window  Help
▢                            C:\LZFN\SAP.TRI                         ▼ ▲
Packet Number : 3              6:08:37PM
Length : 64 bytes
802.3: =================== IEEE 802.3 Datalink Layer ==================
       Station: 08-00-14-65-15-75 ----> FF-FF-FF-FF-FF-FF
       Length: 34
  ipx: ================= Internetwork Packet Exchange =================
       Checksum: 0xFFFF
       Length: 34
       Hop Count:  0
       Packet Type: 17(NCP)
       Network: 00 00 00 00       --->  00 00 00 00
       Node:    08-00-14-65-15-75  --->  FF-FF-FF-FF-FF-FF
       Socket:  0x4006            --->  SAP
  sap: ============== NetWare Service Advertising Protocol =============
       Type: 3 (Nearest Service Query)
       Server Type: 0x0004(File Server)



                       Packet:  3    Unfiltered:  14
```

IPX Header (Socket 0x0452)

Packet Type (2 bytes)

Server Type (2 bytes)

Service Query packet format

SERVER TYPE

The server type field defines the type of service desired. The server types are defined by Novell and include the following:

Type 0x0004   File server

Type 0x0005   Job server

Type 0x0007   Print server

Type 0x0009   Archive server

Type 0x000A   Job queue

Type 0x0021   NAS SNA gateway

Type 0x002D   Time Synchronization VAP

Type 0x002E   Dynamic SAP

Type 0x0047   Advertising print server

Type 0x004B   Btrieve VAP 5.0

Type 0x004C   SQL VAP

Type 0x007A   TES—NetWare VMS

Type 0x0098   NetWare access server

Type 0x009A   Named Pipes server

Type 0x009E   Portable NetWare—UNIX

Type 0x0107   NetWare 386

Type 0x0111   Test server

Type 0x0166   NetWare management

Type 0x026A   NetWare management

So far, this chapter has described two of the three types of NetWare SAP packets that are available: SAP information broadcasts and service queries. The third type of SAP packet is service responses.

SAP Service Response Types

There are two types of service response packets: General Service responses (discussed earlier in this chapter) and Nearest Service responses. Both response types use the same format, as shown in Figure 9.7.

SAP Response packet

format

Packet Type (2 bytes)

Server Type (2 bytes)

Server Name (48 bytes)

If a server name is less than 48 bytes in length, it will be padded with 0's following the server name to maintain the 48-byte field length.

Network Address (4 bytes)

Node Address (6 bytes)

Socket (2 bytes)

Intermediate Networks (2 bytes)

Note: SAP responses can contain information for up to seven servers by repeating the server type through intermediate networks fields in a single SAP response.

General Service responses are currently used only for the Service Information broadcasts. Each of these SAP responses can contain information about up to seven servers.

The Nearest Service Response packets are sent in reply to Nearest Service queries and can contain information about only one server—the server with the least number of intermediate networks that matches the server type in the SAP Service Query packet. For example, if a server contains bindery entries for three known servers, FS1, FS2, and FS3, that are located one, two, and three hops away, respectively, the server will report information only about the closest one, FS1.

SAP Service Response Packet Format

Both General and Nearest Service responses use the same packet structure. The packets are differentiated within the response type field.

RESPONSE TYPE

The response type field contains either 0x0002, for SAP General Service responses, or 0x0004, for Nearest Service responses.

SERVER TYPE

The server type field identifies the type of service available. The server type numbers for responses are the same as the server types defined for queries.

SERVER NAME

The server name field contains the object name of the server. This name can be up to 48 bytes long and must be unique within each server type. For example, you can have a print server (type 0x0047) and file server (type 0x0004) that have the name SALES1, but you cannot have two file servers named SALES1. NetWare server names are assigned when the operating system is configured or installed; print server names are defined within PCONSOLE.

NETWORK ADDRESS

The network address is a 4-byte number that identifies the network address of the server listed.

NODE ADDRESS

The node address number identifies the node address of the server. Net-Ware 3.x-based services will advertise 0x00-00-00-00-00-01 as the service node address.

SOCKET

The socket field identifies the socket number on which the server will receive all service requests. For example, a server type 0x0004 will receive NCP requests on socket 0x0451.

INTERMEDIATE NETWORKS

The intermediate networks field identifies the number of routers between a server and the client (the hop count). NetWare 3.x-based servers will advertise NCP services with the value of 1 in the intermediate networks field when broadcasting on the local network. This is due to the internal IPX network upon which NCP services reside. The network extending from the LAN adapter is one hop away from the internal IPX LAN. (This concept is covered in more detail toward the end of this chapter.)

Monitoring Excessive SAP Traffic

As NetWare LANs expand to include additional servers, SAP traffic also increases. Since each server must transmit a Server information broadcast every 60 seconds, a network with many servers will experience a large amount of SAP traffic.

Using the SAP filter developed by Novell (FILTER.NLM), you can restrict which services are advertised across routers throughout the internet. This technique reduces the overall SAP traffic. This filter may also restrict the servers a client can access, thus providing additional network security. Careful planning is necessary before installing the SAP filter to ensure that users can still access all required servers.

How can you determine the current number of SAPs on your network? Using the LANalyzer, you can create an application that tracks the number of packets using the value 0x0452 in the socket fields of an IPX header.

Novell's internal network was experiencing workstation timeouts because the network was constantly flooded with SAP traffic. This prompted Novell to create the FILTER.NLM, which provides for SAP filtering. Originally developed to reduce the SAP traffic on Novell's own network, this filter NLM was released to the public in early 1992.

A single SAP packet can have one of the following socket designation combinations, depending upon the type of SAP packet:

▸ Source socket 0x0452 and destination socket 0x0452 are used for Service information broadcasts.

▸ Dynamically assigned source socket (in the range of 0x4001–0x7FFF) and destination socket 0x0452 are used for Nearest Service Query broadcasts.

▸ Source sockets of 0x0452 and client-assigned destination sockets are used for Nearest Service responses.

You need to look at both source and destination sockets to ensure that you catch all SAP packets. Figure 9.8 shows a LANalyzer application that was created to monitor all SAP traffic on the network. The first channel, SAP-SR, filters on the value 0x0452 in the source socket field. The second channel, SAP-DEST, filters on the value 0x0452 in the destination socket field.

FIGURE 9.8

Filtering on both source and destination sockets ensures that you capture all SAP packets.

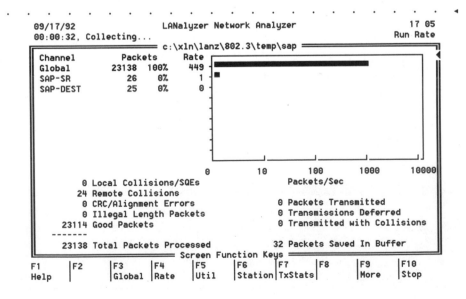

In Figure 9.8, the peak number of SAP packets per second is less than 1% of the total number of packets on the network. Excessive SAP traffic is not yet a concern on this network. Monitoring SAP traffic on a growing network will help determine when SAP filtering becomes necessary.

Next you will use SAP information to determine the types of services that are currently available on a network.

Identifying Servers and Availability

Using the LANalyzer for NetWare, you can capture SAP information broadcast packets (General Service responses) on a NetWare LAN to identify all services available on the network. If a workstation is unable to connect to a server, you may wish to verify the server's availability first. In Figure 9.9, you are viewing a SAP information broadcast from the server, TRAIN1.

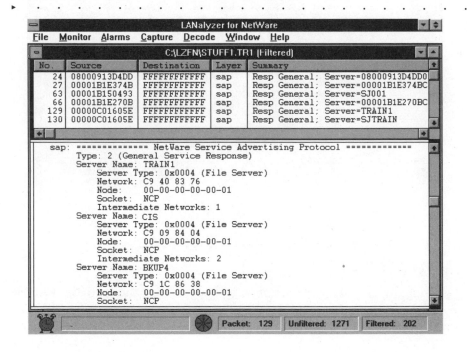

F I G U R E 9.9

SAP information broadcasts identify servers available on the network.

The intermediate networks field indicates the number of hops to the service. As shown in Figure 9.10, if the value in this field is 16, the service is not available; it is considered unreachable.

Unreachable services may be an indication of network problems. If a router goes down, you may see a sudden increase in unreachable services. Later in this chapter, you will learn about the "server shutdown" packets that also contain the "unreachable" designation in the intermediate networks field.

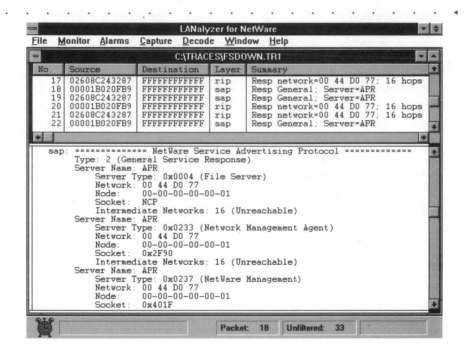

Image text:

LANalyzer for NetWare

File Monitor Alarms Capture Decode Window Help

C:\TRACES\FSDOWN.TR1

No.	Source	Destination	Layer	Summary
17	02608C243287	FFFFFFFFFFFF	rip	Resp network=00 44 D0 77; 16 hops
18	00001B020FB9	FFFFFFFFFFFF	sap	Resp General; Server=APR
19	02608C243287	FFFFFFFFFFFF	sap	Resp General; Server=APR
20	00001B020FB9	FFFFFFFFFFFF	rip	Resp network=00 44 D0 77; 16 hops
21	02608C243287	FFFFFFFFFFFF	rip	Resp network=00 44 D0 77; 16 hops
22	00001B020FB9	FFFFFFFFFFFF	sap	Resp General; Server=APR

```
sap: ============ NetWare Service Advertising Protocol ============
        Type: 2 (General Service Response)
        Server Name: APR
            Server Type: 0x0004 (File Server)
            Network: 00 44 D0 77
            Node:    00-00-00-00-00-01
            Socket:  NCP
            Intermediate Networks: 16 (Unreachable)
        Server Name: APR
            Server Type: 0x0233 (Network Management Agent)
            Network: 00 44 D0 77
            Node:    00-00-00-00-00-01
            Socket:  0x2F90
            Intermediate Networks: 16 (Unreachable)
        Server Name: APR
            Server Type: 0x0237 (NetWare Management)
            Network: 00 44 D0 77
            Node:    00-00-00-00-00-01
            Socket:  0x401F
```

Packet: 18   Unfiltered: 33

Actively Gathering Service Information

Using the LANalyzer, you can actively determine the services available on the network. The LANalyzer v3.11A contains a predefined application, SERVERVU, for finding the network services. By broadcasting a Nearest

Service Request packet, as shown in Figure 9.11, you can receive information of the nearest servers on the network. All servers on the local network will respond. This application is configured to capture routing information packets as well. The routing packets contain information about other networks that can be explored.

```
09/17/92                    LANalyzer Network Analyzer                19 09
00:00:32, Collecting...                                              Run Station
=================== c:\xln\lanz\802.3\netware\802.3\servervu ===================
Stations seen: 7
                         Packet Rate    Total Packets    Avg. Size     Errors
No.  Station Address     Rcv   Xmt      Rcv     Xmt      Rcv   Xmt     Rcv   Xmt
1    exos651575          1     0        140     0        114   -
2    SALES1              0     0        0       7        -     114
3    ADMIN-02            0     0        0       7        -     114
4    MKTG-45             0     0        0       7        -     114
5    SALES2              0     0        0       7        -     114
6    BKUP-FS1            0     0        0       7        -     114
7    OPS-01              0     0        0       7        -     114
8
9
10
11
12
13
14
15
16
========================= Screen Function Keys ========================
F1      F2      F3       F4     F5      F6       F7      F8      F9      F10
Help            Global   Rate   Util    Station  TxStats         More    Stop
```

F I G U R E 9.11

Results of the SERVERVU application

"Server Shutdown" Packets

The SAP Protocol also allows servers to announce that they are going down. A properly downed server will broadcast a "server shutdown" packet to notify all routers and servers on the network that it will no longer be available. This information is propagated throughout the network, and the server and router binderies will be updated to reflect the server's absence.

As shown in Figure 9.12, a "server shutdown" packet is simply a response packet indicating that the server is now considered unreachable, 16 hops away. A server will also broadcast RIP packets announcing that services cannot be reached through it in a similar way (see Chapter 10).

F I G U R E 9.12

Servers transmit a "server
shutdown" packet when
they are brought down.

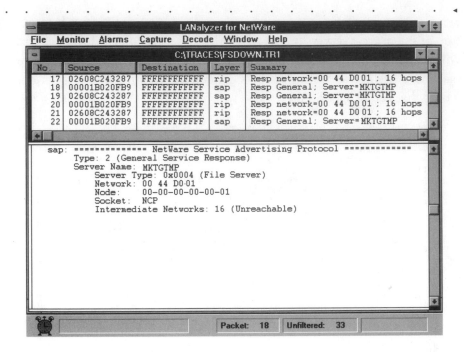

SAP Intermediate Networks Field

As you work more in depth with analyzers, you may notice a strange feature of NetWare 3.x that is viewed in SAP packets sent from the servers. As shown in Figure 9.13, a LANalyzer for NetWare has been placed on network C9-99-01-64.

Earlier, this chapter discussed the internal IPX network and indicated that NetWare 3.x file servers advertise NCP services as one network away due to the internal IPX network address (the virtual LAN within the v3.x server). Interestingly, with NetWare v3.x, there seems to be a Novell "implementation" issue that causes all NLM-based servers to advertise themselves as farther away than the NCP server itself.

Viewing local SAP packets

Server Name: SF-01
Type: 0x0004 (File Server)
Socket: 0x451 NCP
Hops: 1

Server Name: PS01
Server Type: 0x0047 (Advertising Print Server)
Socket: 0x8060 (Print Server)
Hops: 2

LANalyzer for
NetWare

Network: C9-99-01-64

NW 3.x Server

For example, in Figure 9.14, a NetWare 3.x server broadcasts a SAP that states

▸ The file server (NCP) is one hop away.

▸ The print server is two hops away.

Although the network and node addresses reflect that both the file server
and print server are on the same network, the print server is actually considered one network farther away—remote to the file server itself. Figure
9.15 illustrates the logical interpretation of this SAP anomaly.

This "implementation" issue should be fixed in future versions of Net-
Ware to indicate that NLM-based services are the same distance from the
local network as NCP services.

As discussed in this chapter, the Service Advertising Protocol is used by
NetWare servers and routers to exchange information about available servers on the internetwork and their distance from the local network. With
the LANalyzer, you have examined these packets and differentiated between SAP information broadcasts and Nearest Service Query and Response
packets. You have also actively gathered a listing of services available on the
network by using a SAP broadcast.

On NetWare LANs, it is necessary to understand which routes are available to access these services once you have identified them. The next chapter examines the Routing Information Protocol (RIP), which provides you with this information.

▶ . . . . ◀

F I G U R E   9.14

An NLM-based service will advertise itself as two hops away on the local LAN.

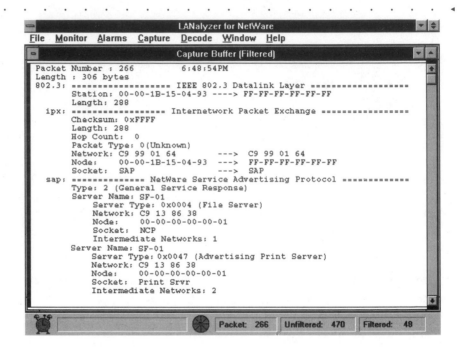

```
                                  LANalyzer for NetWare
 File   Monitor   Alarms   Capture   Decode   Window   Help

                            Capture Buffer (Filtered)

 Packet Number : 266            6:48:54PM
 Length : 306 bytes
 802.3: ==================== IEEE 802.3 Datalink Layer ====================
        Station: 00-00-1B-15-04-93 ----> FF-FF-FF-FF-FF-FF
        Length: 288
   ipx: ================== Internetwork Packet Exchange ==================
        Checksum: 0xFFFF
        Length: 288
        Hop Count:  0
        Packet Type: 0(Unknown)
        Network: C9 99 01 64      --->  C9 99 01 64
        Node:    00-00-1B-15-04-93 --->  FF-FF-FF-FF-FF-FF
        Socket:  SAP              --->   SAP
   sap: ============== NetWare Service Advertising Protocol ==============
        Type: 2 (General Service Response)
        Server Name: SF-01
            Server Type: 0x0004 (File Server)
            Network: C9 13 86 38
            Node:    00-00-00-00-00-01
            Socket:  NCP
            Intermediate Networks: 1
        Server Name: SF-01
            Server Type: 0x0047 (Advertising Print Server)
            Network: C9 13 86 38
            Node:    00-00-00-00-00-01
            Socket:  Print Srvr
            Intermediate Networks: 2

                              Packet: 266   Unfiltered: 470   Filtered: 48
```

▶ . . . . ◀

F I G U R E   9.15

Logical interpretation of SAP service hop determinations

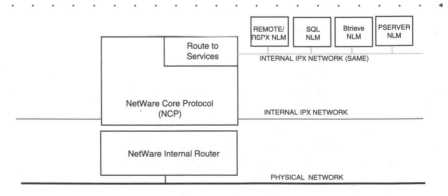

Routing
Information
Protocol

The previous chapters have discussed how packets are addressed before being transmitted. There are two distinct address types used on NetWare LANs: the hardware address and the software address.

The *hardware address* is specified in the Ethernet header source and destination fields. This address corresponds to the address on the local network interface card. Providing this address alone, however, can get packets routed only through the local LAN, not through the internet. Nor can this information alone allow you to cross from one network type to another (between ARCnet and Ethernet, for example).

You therefore need to assign software addresses as well. *Software addresses* are independent of the media upon which they rely. They are the same regardless of whether a packet is traveling across an Ethernet, a Token Ring, or an ARCnet LAN. In NetWare, the software address is called the *internetwork address*. The internetwork address includes a 4-byte network address (assigned during installation of the operating system) and a 6-byte node address. The node address portion is "borrowed" from the node's physical hardware address. In the case of physical addresses that are shorter than 6 bytes (such as ARCnet), the address is padded with preceding 0's.

The IPX header defined in Chapter 6 contains the internetwork address and indicates the final destination network of the packet. This information is used for routing purposes. It is also necessary for routers to provide information about the networks to which they are directly attached or to which they may route packets. This way, when a client transmits a packet across the network, it can address the packet to the closest router, which, in turn, forwards the packet on to the next router, and so on, until the packet reaches the final destination network.

Routing information is passed between servers and routers by Novell's Routing Information Protocol (RIP). This routing information is contained in routing information tables located at each router and server on the network.

This chapter explains the functionality of NetWare's RIP, examines the packet structure used, and provides several analysis techniques for viewing and streamlining routing networks. Finally, the chapter defines the steps required to test routing efficiencies on a NetWare LAN.

Routing Information Protocol Functionality

As shown in Figure 10.1, RIP packets utilize the IPX Protocol for transport and designate the value 0x0453 in the IPX socket field.

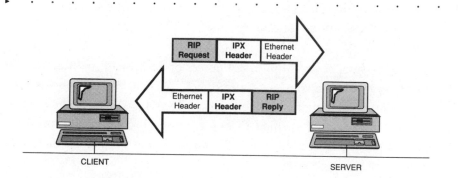

FIGURE 10.1

RIP uses IPX for transport.

IPX routers will transmit their routing information on the network in five specific circumstances:

▸ **When a router initializes:** When you bring up a new router, it broadcasts a RIP packet to inform other network routers that it is available to forward packets between networks.

▸ **When a router requires initial routing information:** Besides presenting information of routes it is making available, routers request information of all other routers on the network so they can configure their routing information tables.

▸ **Periodically, to maintain current routing tables:** Every 60 seconds, NetWare IPX routers transmit a RIP broadcast packet to ensure that all routers maintain current routing information tables.

▶ **To notify routers of a change in routing configurations:** When a router has changed any information in its routing information tables, it broadcasts the new information to guarantee that all routers have correct information in their tables.

▶ **To notify other routers that they are going down:** If a router is being properly "downed," it broadcasts routing information indicating that all routes through it are unreachable so other routers can find alternate routes.

If a router shuts down from loss of power or because of malfunctions, it may not be able to transmit a "going down" packet. Because of this possibility, all routers maintain a timeout mechanism. If an entry in the routing information table is not verified through routing broadcasts within three minutes, it is purged from the table. It is assumed that the route is no longer available.

When IPX routers transmit their routing information, they must follow specific rules. Their broadcasts must be local broadcasts only, and they must use the Best Information Algorithm (BIA). To understand the RIP packets that traverse the local system, it is necessary to first examine why these packets are local only and what the algorithm provides you.

Local Broadcasts and the Best Information Algorithm

RIP broadcasts are restricted to the local network only and allow routers to propagate the routing information onto other networks. Each router maintains a table of known routes and broadcasts this information on each locally attached segment. Other routers will receive this information, update their routing information tables, and transmit an up-to-date routing information packet.

For example, in Figure 10.2, router A is a NetWare v3.11 server (SALES1). There are two network interface cards in this server, with IPX

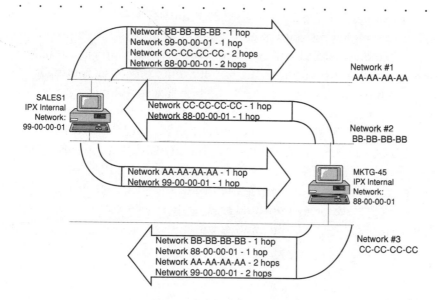

bound to both. One network is assigned the network address AA-AA-AA-AA, the other BB-BB-BB-BB. The router will advertise any remote networks to which it provides routing services.

Since the server is a NetWare v3.11 operating system, it will also have an IPX internal network address that will be broadcast. This is important because clients must be able to route to the internal network for services, just as they would route to LAN A on a NetWare 2.x server.

RIP packets are not allowed to cross routers. Instead, each router will accept the information, update its tables, and transmit current information to its locally attached networks.

The Best Information Algorithm states that

- ▸ Routers may not transmit information back onto the network upon which it was received.

- ▸ Routers may not transmit information about the network upon which they are transmitting.

For example, in Figure 10.2, SALES1 and MKTG-45 connect networks 1, 2, and 3, providing routing services. SALES1 is physically attached to networks 1 and 2. SALES1 will transmit routing information about network 1 onto network 2. According to the BIA, it cannot broadcast routing information about network 2 onto network 2. This is acceptable since nodes on network 2 do not need to route packets when communicating with local network nodes. MKTG-45 receives the RIP packet from SALES1, updates its tables, and transmits a RIP packet onto network 3, announcing that it is a router to networks 1 and 2. In accordance with the BIA, MKTG-45 does not announce this information back onto the local network 2. If it did, nodes on the local segment would assume there were two routes to network 1, one through SALES1 and another through MKTG-45.

Routing Information Packet Format

Now that NetWare's routing functionality has been defined, let's examine the Routing Information Protocol packet formats.

There are two types of RIP packets that use the same packet formats: the request packets and the response packets. As shown in Figure 10.3, RIP packets have the value 0x0453 in the IPX socket field.

PACKET TYPE

The type field designates whether the packet is a request for routing information or a reply containing routing information. The two type field values are

Request   0x0001

Response   0x0002

Request packets are transmitted by workstations that want to locate a route to a network. Responses are transmitted by routers and indicate the networks to which they can route. As shown in Figure 10.3, RIP Response

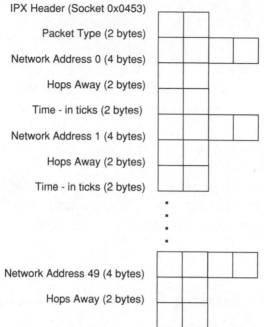

IPX Header (Socket 0x0453)

Packet Type (2 bytes)

Network Address 0 (4 bytes)

Hops Away (2 bytes)

Time - in ticks (2 bytes)

Network Address 1 (4 bytes)

Hops Away (2 bytes)

Time - in ticks (2 bytes)

Network Address 49 (4 bytes)

Hops Away (2 bytes)

F I G U R E 10.3

RIP packet format

packets can contain information on up to 50 networks (network 0 through network 49).

NETWORK ADDRESS

If the packet is a RIP request, the network address field will contain the network that is being sought. The value 0xFF-FF-FF-FF indicates that the RIP request is for all known networks.

HOPS AWAY

The hops away field is valid only on response-type packets and contains the number of routers that a packet must cross to reach a network. For example, in Figure 10.2, SALES1 would transmit RIP Response packets onto network 2, indicating that there is one hop between clients on network 2 and network 1.

On RIP requests, the hop field will contain the value 0xFFFF. (The decimal equivalent is 65535.)

TIME—IN TICKS

The time field is valid only for reply packets and indicates the time required to reach the remote network. One tick is equivalent to $\frac{1}{18}$ of a second.

On request packets, this field is padded with 0xFFFF. (The decimal equivalent is 65535.)

When routers are functioning properly, they broadcast RIP information every 60 seconds. If a router is being brought down, however, it will notify all other routers that it cannot provide services anymore.

Router "Going Down" Packets

In order to provide this information, routers broadcast a "going down" RIP packet on all attached networks, as shown in Figure 10.4. This function

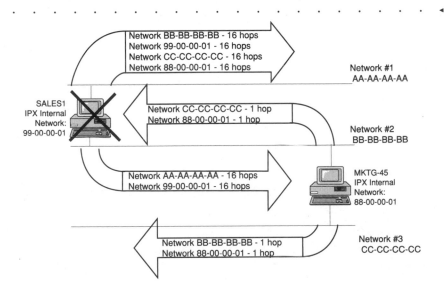

FIGURE 10.4

Routers transmit a "going down" packet to all attached networks.

is performed by all internal and external NetWare routers (v2.x and v3.x).

These packets contain the same routing information that is normally transmitted on the networks, but the hop count is now 16. Sixteen hops is considered unreachable. Upon receiving this new information, routers will update their routing tables and remove any routes that are no longer available. Figure 10.4 shows a "going down" packet from SALES1 indicating that networks AA-AA-AA-AA and 99-00-00-01 are no longer reachable through that router. As shown in Figure 10.5, router "going down" packets indicate that attached networks are 16 hops away.

This information is useful when troubleshooting network communications that occur over a router. For example, if a particular route seems sluggish, you can track whether it is "losing" its routing tables and intermittently transmitting a "going down" packet to local networks, as shown in Figure 10.6.

The RIP is also used during a workstation's initial network connection to find the route to the server responding most quickly.

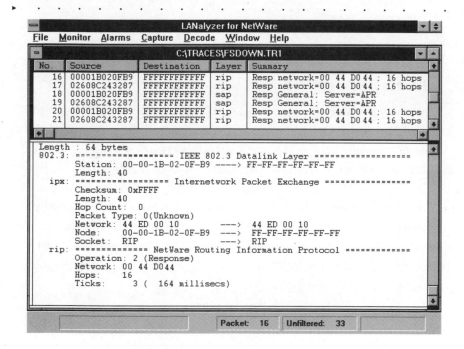

FIGURE 10.5

Router "going down" packets indicate attached networks are 16 hops away.

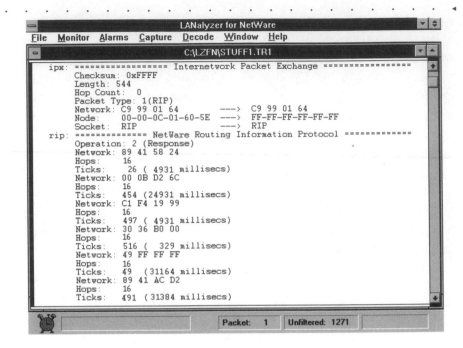

Using RIP During Connection Establishment

When a workstation launches the shell program (NETX.COM), it broadcasts a SAP packet to locate the server able to respond the most quickly. The SAP packet contains the responding server's network address. The workstation must then find a route to that server. It does this by using a RIP Request broadcast. As shown in Figure 10.7, a workstation transmits a RIP Request broadcast onto the local network. In this packet, the workstation indicates the network number it wishes to locate (as learned from the SAP reply, defined above). The router that provides routing services to the desired network will respond. In Figure 10.7, the client is requesting a route to network 00-00-11-62.

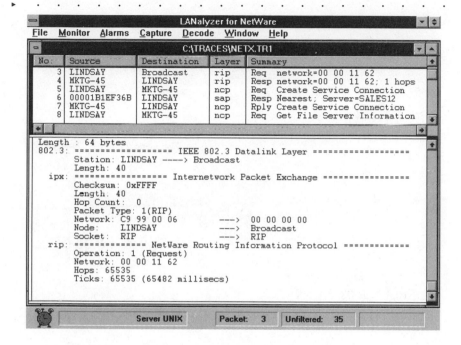

Testing Routing Efficiencies

Using the LANalyzer, you can test network routes and determine their efficiencies. The LANalyzer contains a predefined application, ROUTVIEW, that transmits an IPX diagnostic packet (see Chapter 11) to workstations and servers on the other side of a router. The responses are time stamped upon receipt. You can use this information to determine the round-trip delay through network routers.

Figure 10.8 shows an internetwork of five LANs connected by routers. The LANalyzer is placed on network AA-AA-AA-AA. In this example, you will test the round-trip delay between network AA-AA-AA-AA and network EE-EE-EE-EE, crossing four routers.

To determine available routes from the local network, you can first filter on all RIP broadcasts on the network; this will provide a listing of all known networks, routers to use when accessing the remote LAN, and the distance

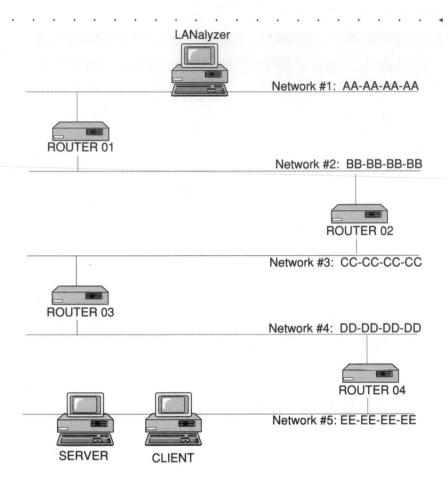

F I G U R E 10.8

Five networks connected by routers

from the local network (in hops). As shown in Figure 10.9, the router advertising services to network EE-EE-EE-EE is called ROUTER01.

Using the LANalyzer's predefined ROUTVIEW application, you can transmit diagnostic packets across the network to the remote LAN. As the active stations on the network respond, their packets are saved in the trace buffer.

You must edit the ROUTVIEW application in order to capture and time-stamp the packet you are transmitting across the network. This will give

NOTE
Chapter 11 focuses on creating and using these dianostic packets.

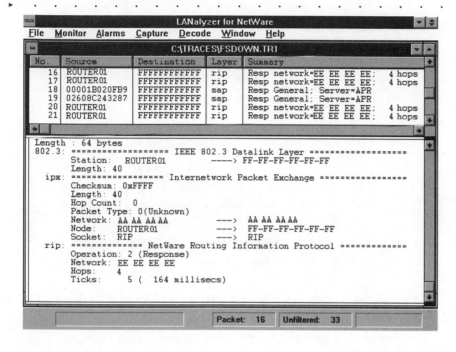

you a reference point when determining round-trip delay time for communicating across the four routers.

The LANalyzer ROUTVIEW application should be configured to capture the following packets:

Channel router	All RIP packets
Channel nodes	Responses to test packets
Channel test	Test packets transmitted

After the application is run, the trace display provides a listing of all responding nodes and their response times. As shown in the LANalyzer trace display in Figure 10.10, the fastest round-trip time to a server on the network is 130.075 ms (milliseconds).

The time stamp is shown in *relative format*. This format indicates the time of packet receipt based on the first packet in the buffer. When the first

▶ . . . . ◀

Time stamps provide the round-trip delay time.

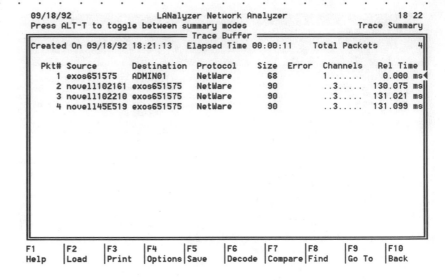

```
09/18/92              LANalyzer Network Analyzer                    18 22
Press ALT-T to toggle between summary modes                   Trace Summary
                        ══════════ Trace Buffer ══════════
║Created On 09/18/92 18:21:13   Elapsed Time 00:00:11   Total Packets      4║
║                                                                           ║
║  Pkt# Source      Destination Protocol   Size  Error  Channels   Rel Time ║
║    1 exos651575   ADMIN01     NetWare     68           1.......    0.000 ms◀
║    2 novel1102161 exos651575  NetWare     90           ..3.....  130.075 ms║
║    3 novel1102210 exos651575  NetWare     90           ..3.....  131.021 ms║
║    4 novel145E519 exos651575  NetWare     90           ..3.....  131.099 ms║
║                                                                           ║
║                                                                           ║
║                                                                           ║
║                                                                           ║
║                                                                           ║
║                                                                           ║
║                                                                           ║
║                                                                           ║
║                                                                           ║
║                                                                           ║

F1     F2     F3     F4      F5     F6     F7      F8    F9     F10
Help   Load   Print  Options Save   Decode Compare Find  Go To  Back
```

packet is received, it is time-stamped as 0.00 ms. Another is received, and it is time-stamped based on the first packet's arrival time of 0.00 ms. You can tell that the second packet (the response) arrived approximately 130 ms after the test packet was sent.

If the response time is considered inadequate, there may be a problem with either the node tested or one of the routers connecting to the remote network. First, test several more nodes located on network EE-EE-EE-EE. If all nodes respond at approximately the same rate, you can rule out the possibility that the delay is isolated to the first node you tested on the network. You can now assume that the delay is caused by a router. To test this theory, you can perform the same test on network DD-DD-DD-DD and measure the average round-trip response time. You can perform this test on all the networks connecting network AA-AA-AA-AA to network EE-EE-EE-EE in order to determine which router may be causing the slow response through the network.

As shown in Figure 10.11, it is evident that the router between networks BB-BB-BB-BB and CC-CC-CC-CC seems to be introducing an unacceptable delay into the network communications. This router may be faulty or insufficient for the routing load it is required to handle.

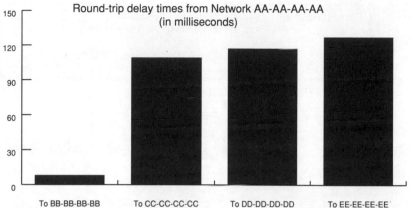
Round-trip delay times from Network AA-AA-AA-AA
(in milliseconds)

To test a single device's response across the network, you can address the diagnostic packet to the station's node address in the IPX header. This tests round-trip response time from a single network node, as shown in Figure 10.12.

This chapter has examined NetWare's Routing Information Protocol functionality and packet structures. You know that by filtering on packets that contain the value 0x0453 in the IPX socket fields, you can view RIP packets and determine available and unavailable routes. These packets will also define the distance between the current network and remote networks on the internetwork. RIP packets are also useful when testing the efficiency of a certain route.

Chapter 11 examines how IPX Diagnostic packets can be sent across routers to test routing delays. It also examines the many uses for the Diagnostic Responder and shows how to transmit these packets using the LANalyzer.

FIGURE 10.12

Testing the response time
of a single remote
network node

Ethernet Header: To 00-00-1B-23-90-12 (Router 01)
                     From 08-00-20-65-15-75 (LANalyzer)

IPX Header: To Network 88-00-00-01, Node 00-00-00-00-00-01
                     From Network AA-AA-AA-AA, Node 08-00-20-65-15-75

LANalyzer
Node Address: 08-00-20-65-15-75

Network #1: AA-AA-AA-AA

Node Address: 00-00-1B-23-90-12

ROUTER 01

Network #2: BB-BB-BB-BB

ROUTER 02

Network #2: BB-BB-BB-BB

IPX Internal Network Address: 88-00-00-01
Node address: 00-00-00-00-00-01

CHAPTER II

NetWare
Diagnostic
Packets

Up to this point, you have examined how many of the NetWare protocols work, including IPX, SPX, NCP, SAP, and RIP. There is, however, one NetWare protocol that is rarely explained, although it is most useful in analyzing NetWare LANs. This protocol is the Diagnostic Responder.

This chapter examines Novell's Diagnostic Responder services and packet structures. It also reviews several ways in which you can use the Diagnostic Responder for network analysis.

On a NetWare LAN, it is helpful to be able to "ping" another network system, or transmit a single packet that requires a direct response. It is also helpful to receive workstation configuration information with the response. You can use the Diagnostic Responder for

- Connectivity testing

- Configuration information gathering

Connectivity Testing

When workstations load IPX.COM or IPXODI.COM, they automatically load the Diagnostic Responder. It is possible, however, to load IPX without the Diagnostic Responder. Figure 11.1 indicates the load options for IPX.

NetWare v2.x and 3.x servers will always have the Diagnostic Responder capability enabled.

FIGURE 11.1

Loading options for IPX

NetWare IPX/SPX Protocol v1.20 (911120)
(C) Copyright 1990, 1991 Novell, Inc. All Rights Reserved.

Available command line options:
    IPXODI   -Installs IPX, SPX and Diagnostic Responder
    IPXODI D -Installs IPX and SPX
    IPXODI A -Installs IPX
    IPXODI U -Removes resident IPXODI from memory
    IPXODI ? -Displays this help screen

All servers and clients that have the Responder loaded must transmit a response upon receipt of a diagnostic packet that is addressed to their node address or 0xFF-FF-FF-FF-FF-FF (broadcast). This response from the server or client indicates that it can receive and transmit packets successfully. As shown in Figure 11.2, the response also contains configuration information about the server or client.

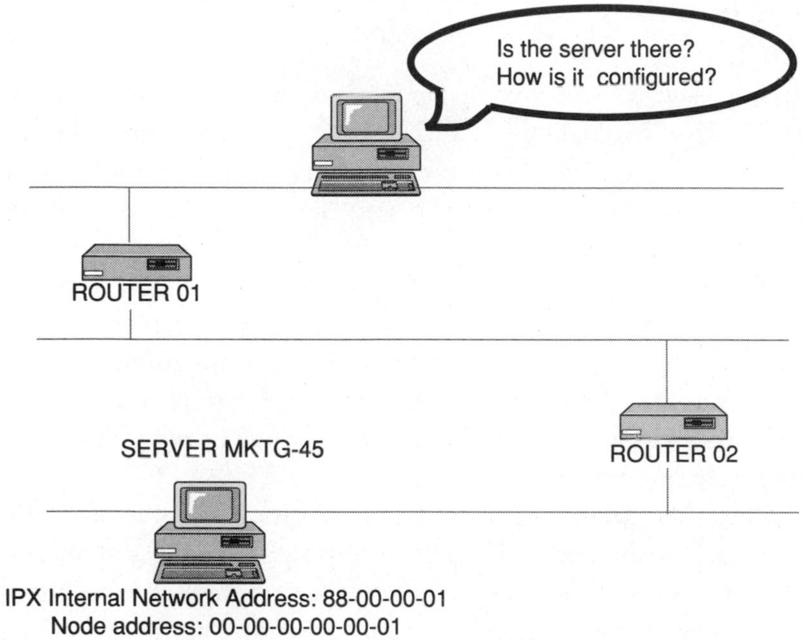

FIGURE 11.2

The Diagnostic Responder can be used to test connectivity, and it also provides configuration information.

Configuration Information Gathering

When a server or client replies, it transmits a Configuration Response packet that indicates the components that are present at the server or client. The Configuration Response packet will also include the number of instances for each component.

Servers and clients may report that they have components such as

- ▶ IPX/SPX
- ▶ Router driver
- ▶ File server/router
- ▶ LAN driver
- ▶ Shell

The Diagnostic Responder component list still mistakenly calls a NetWare router a "bridge." Throughout this chapter the correct terminology, "router," is used; however, you may still see the term "bridge" on many of the screens shown herein. Also in this chapter, the term "LAN driver" replaces the term "shell driver." The correct term is "LAN driver" since it relates to the driver used for the network interface card (NE2000.COM, NE1000.COM, and so on).

In order to obtain configuration information from a server or a client, an application or protocol analyzer can transmit a Configuration Request packet to the desired server or client. As shown in Figure 11.3, a single Configuration Response packet may contain a list of one or more components that are part of the responding system.

In Chapter 10, the Diagnostic Responder was used to test the round-trip delay time across routers. Although the LANalyzer includes applications that have predefined Diagnostic Request packet transmit channels, it may be desirable to create a customized Diagnostic Request packet to meet your specific needs.

Diagnostic Request Packet Structure

A Diagnostic Request packet is defined by the value 0x0456 in the IPX header destination socket field, as shown in Figure 11.4. The diagnostic request information follows the IPX header.

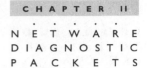

FIGURE 11.3

Responding nodes supply
configuration information.

```
─                          LANalyzer for NetWare                    ▼ ◆
File   Monitor   Alarms   Capture   Decode   Window   Help
─                              C:\LZFN\DIAG.TR1                      ▼ ▲
No.   Source          Destination    Layer   Summary
  1   APRICOTFT       FS-TRAIN        diag    Number of Exclusion Addresses=0
  2   FS-TRAIN        APRICOTFT       diag    SPX Diag Socket=0x4002; 3 Componen
  3   APRICOTFT       FS-BLDG4        diag    Number of Exclusion Addresses=0
  4   FS-BLDG4        APRICOTFT       diag    SPX Diag Socket=0x4002; 3 Componen
  5   APRICOTFT       FS-TRAIN        diag    Number of Exclusion Addresses=0
  6   FS-TRAIN        APRICOTFT       diag    SPX Diag Socket=0x4002; 3 Componen

diag:  ================ IPX Diagnostic Support Protocol ================
       Major Version: 1
       Minor Version: 0
       SPX Diagnostic Socket: 0x4002
       Number of Components: 3
       Component ID: 0 (IPX / SPX)
       Component ID: 1 (Bridge Driver)
       Component ID: 6 (File Server / Bridge)
       Number of Local Networks: 2
          Local Network Type: 1 (Non-dedicated File Server (virtual board))
             Network Address1: 44 ED FF F0
             Node     Address1: 00-00-00-00-00-01
          Local Network Type: 0 (LAN Board)
             Network Address2: 44 ED 00 10
             Node     Address2: FS-TRAIN

                        Packet:  2    Unfiltered:  14
```

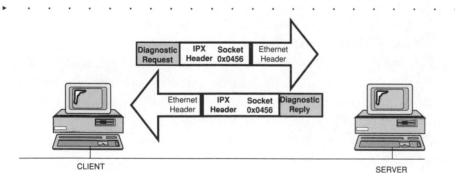

FIGURE 11.4

Diagnostic packets use the
socket number 0x0456.

The diagnostic request information may be quite simple, requesting all information from each station being addressed. It may also, however, become quite complex, allowing you to broadcast a Diagnostic Request packet on the network and then, within the Diagnostic Request packet, specify stations that should *not* respond. The structure of the Diagnostic Request packet is shown in Figure 11.5.

▶ . . . . ◀

F I G U R E II.5

Diagnostic Request packet

structure

IPX Header (Socket 0x0456)

Exclusion Address Count (1 byte)

Exclusion Address 0 (6 bytes)

Exclusion Address 79 (6 bytes)

EXCLUSION ADDRESS COUNT

The exclusion address count field defines the number of stations that will be requested not to respond. These are *exclusion addresses*. A 0 in this field indicates that all stations should respond. The maximum value for this field is 80 (exclusion address 0 through 79).

EXCLUSION ADDRESS

If, in the IPX header, the packet is addressed to broadcast, all stations will respond to the packet. If you do not wish to receive a response from a server or client, you must put its node address in the exclusion address field. You can exclude up to 80 stations from responding.

Figure 11.6 shows a Diagnostic Request packet that has two stations listed in the exclusion address field.

When nodes respond, they transmit a Diagnostic Response packet. Nodes must respond within 0.5 seconds of receipt of the Diagnostic Request packet. If you are testing a large network, these responses add to the overall network utilization and may cause some sluggishness during the response phase.

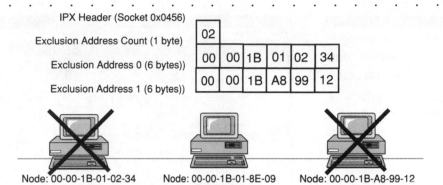

Diagnostic Response Packet Structure

If a node receives a packet addressed to it specifically or addressed to broadcast that contains the value 0x0456 in the destination socket field, the node understands it is a diagnostic packet. By looking within the diagnostic packet, the station can determine whether or not it should respond. If the station's node address is not listed in the exclusion address field, it will respond with a Diagnostic Response packet.

The Diagnostic Response packet information follows the IPX header and is transmitted from the diagnostic configuration socket number 0x0456, as shown in Figure 11.7.

The packet will vary in length, depending upon the number of components reported from the responding node. Figure 11.8 shows the Diagnostic Response packet structure.

MAJOR/MINOR VERSION

The major and minor fields indicate the version of the Diagnostic Responder that is installed in the responding station. Currently, you may commonly find version 1.0 (major version 1, minor version 0) or version 1.1 from responding stations.

FIGURE 11.7

A Diagnostic Response packet is transmitted from socket number 0x0456, decoded as "Configure" by the LANalyzer for NetWare.

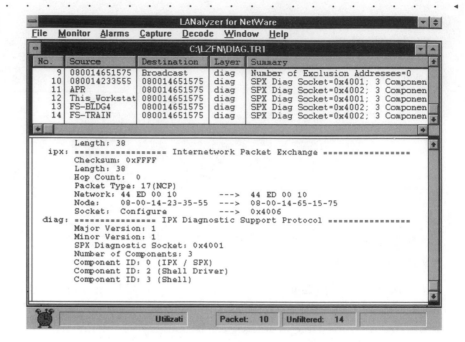

FIGURE 11.8

Diagnostic Response packet structure

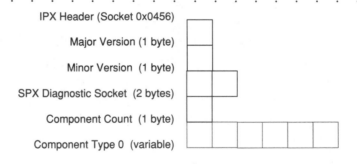

IPX Header (Socket 0x0456)

Major Version (1 byte)

Minor Version (1 byte)

SPX Diagnostic Socket (2 bytes)

Component Count (1 byte)

Component Type 0 (variable)

SPX DIAGNOSTIC SOCKET NUMBER

The SPX diagnostic socket number field identifies the socket number to which all SPX diagnostic responses can be addressed. The SPX Diagnostic Responder is available for third-party development.

COMPONENT COUNT

The component count field defines the number of components that are found within this response packet.

COMPONENT TYPE

The component type field contains information about one of the components, or active processes, at the responding node. The component structure can be either simple or extended.

Simple Component Structures

A simple component structure contains a single, 1-byte field that is called the component ID field. Simple structures are used to identify the following component types:

Simple component type 0:   IPX/SPX

Simple component type 1:   Router drivers

Simple component type 2:   LAN drivers

Simple component type 3:   Shells

Simple component type 4:   VAPs

Figure 11.7, shown earlier, shows a Diagnostic Response packet that is reporting three simple components: IPX/SPX, the LAN driver (shell driver), and the shell. The packet contains only 38 bytes of data—30 bytes for the IPX header and 8 bytes for the diagnostic response information.

Extended Components

The extended component structure reports specific information about such components as routers, file servers/routers, and nondedicated IPX/SPX. A response using an extended component structure is shown in Figure 11.9.

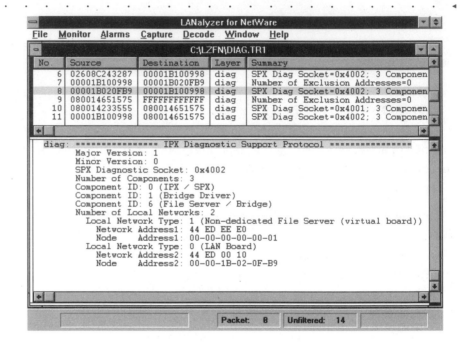

Extended Component ID   The first field, component ID, defines the component type number. Extended component type numbers include

Extended component type 5:   Router

Extended component type 6:   File server/router

Extended component type 7:   Nondedicated IPX/SPX

Number of Local Networks   The number of local networks field denotes the number of local networks that this component may communicate with. For example, a file server/router component will communicate with at least one network for a dedicated NetWare 2.x server (with a single network interface card). The file server/router component will communicate with at least two networks if it is a NetWare 3.x system; one network is the internal IPX network, and the second is the network interface card. The network type, network address, and node address will be listed for each of the networks that the component communicates with.

Local Network Type   The local network type field contains a number that indicates the type of network the component communicates with. The network types include

Network type 0:   LAN board

Network type 1:   Nondedicated file server (virtual board)

Network type 2:   Redirected remote line

NetWare 3.x will always have a nondedicated file server (virtual board) extended component listed. This is the internal IPX network defined upon installation of the server.

Network Address   The network address field contains the 4-byte network address assigned to the network listed in the local network type field.

Node Address Field   The node address field contains the 6-byte node address that accompanies the network address listed above. Redirected remote lines have a node address of 0x00-00-00-00-00-00. NetWare v3.x IPX internal networks have a node address of 0x00-00-00-00-00-01.

Figure 11.9, shown earlier, depicts a Diagnostic Response packet from a NetWare v3.11 server. Based on the response, you can determine that the server has the IPX internal network address of 44-ED-EE-E0 and the network address of 44-ED-00-10.

NOTE
NetWare 3.x servers place their internal IPX network address and node address of 0x00-00-00-00-00-01 in IPX headers when they communicate. To find the actual network address and node address of the LANs to which the server is connected, view the network address field and node address field of the first extended component with network type 0 (LAN board).

COMPONENT TYPE DESCRIPTIONS

The following provides a brief description of component types that can be found in Diagnostic Response packets.

▶ **Type 0: IPX/SPX:** The actual IPX/SPX process or module in a dedicated NetWare file server, dedicated NetWare router, or NetWare client.

▶ **Type 1: Router drivers:** The LAN board driver process in a file server or router, whereas "LAN driver" refers to the client LAN board driver.

▶ **Type 2: LAN Drivers:** The client LAN board driver, such as NE2000.COM, NE1000.COM, etc.

▶ **Type 3: Shells:** The DOS shell/emulation module in the workstation (NETX.COM).

▶ **Type 4: VAPs:** The DOS shell/emulation module loaded on a NetWare v2.x server or an external router for VAP support.

▶ **Type 5: Router:** The routing component in an external NetWare router.

▶ **Type 6: File Server/Router:** The routing component in a NetWare file server (internal router).

▶ **Type 7: Nondedicated IPX/SPX:** The IPX/SPX process on a NetWare 2.x nondedicated file server, an external nondedicated router, or a NetWare v3.x internal virtual LAN (IPX internal network).

Creating Diagnostic Tests

As mentioned earlier in this chapter, you can use the Diagnostic Responder to test connectivity or gather configuration information about a server or client.

When creating a diagnostic test, you must first determine which network and nodes you wish to send the Diagnostic Request packet to and whom the responses should be sent to. This information will be placed in the IPX header of the Diagnostic Request packet.

The remote or local network address should be placed in the destination network address field. The value 0x00-00-00-00 can be used to indicate the local network. The node address of the destination client or server should be placed in the destination node address field. The value 0xFF-FF-FF-FF-FF-FF indicates that all nodes on the designated network should respond. Your network address should be placed in the source network address field. If you wish the responses to be transmitted to another network, however, you can place that network address in the source network address field instead. When you use the LANalyzer, the source node field can contain a fictitious node address. To capture the responses addressed to that node, the LANalyzer can be configured to filter for all Diagnostic Response packets sent to that node address.

Figure 11.10 shows a Diagnostic Request packet being transmitted to all nodes on network BB-BB-BB-BB.

After the IPX header, information regarding the intended recipients can be indicated. If you wish all workstations (as indicated by broadcast addressing in the IPX header) to reply, the value in the exclusion count field should be 0x00. If, however, you do not wish certain stations to reply, you can indicate an exclusion address count and then list the node addresses that should not respond. For example, perhaps you want only workstations, not servers, to respond.

In Figure 11.11, a Diagnostic Request packet is being sent to all nodes on network BB-BB-BB-BB again. Following the IPX header, however, it is specified that workstation 0x00-00-1B-03-98-3D should not respond. All other nodes on the network should respond.

As shown in Chapter 10, you can use the Diagnostic Responder to test round-trip delay times across routers. You can also use it to test client and server connectivity. By simply addressing the IPX header to the desired client or server, you can test whether it is responding. Figure 11.12 shows

FIGURE 11.10

*The IPX header contains
the destination and source
information for diagnostic
packets.*

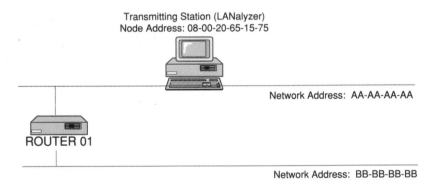

Checksum (2 bytes)	FF	FF			
Length (2 bytes)	00	1F			
Transport Control (1 byte)	00				
Packet Type (1 byte)	04				
Destination Node Address (6 bytes)	FF	FF	FF	FF	FF	FF
Destination Network Address (4 bytes)	BB	BB	BB	BB	
Destination Socket (2 bytes)	04	56			
Source Node Address (6 bytes)	08	00	20	65	15	75
Source Network Address (4 bytes)	AA	AA	AA	AA	
Source Socket (2 bytes)	40	23			
Exclusion Address Count (1 byte)	00				

Transmitting Station (LANalyzer)
Node Address: 08-00-20-65-15-75

Network Address: AA-AA-AA-AA

ROUTER 01

Network Address: BB-BB-BB-BB

a connectivity test transmitted directly to server SALES1, as shown in the destination network and destination node fields of the IPX header.

Since all servers have the Diagnostic Responder enabled, they should respond to the request. However, since the Diagnostic Responder is IPX based, there is no guarantee that the requests arrived on the remote network. In that case, you may wish to send a request to all nodes to ensure that you can access the remote network. If other stations reply successfully

Listing a node address in the exclusion address field indicates that a node should not respond to the Diagnostic Request packet.

Checksum (2 bytes)	FF	FF			
Length (2 bytes)	00	25			
Transport Control (1 byte)	00				
Packet Type (1 byte)	04				
Destination Node Address (6 bytes)	FF	FF	FF	FF	FF	FF
Destination Network Address (4 bytes)	BB	BB	BB	BB	
Destination Socket (2 bytes)	04	56			
Source Node Address (6 bytes)	08	00	20	65	15	75
Source Network Address (4 bytes)	AA	AA	AA	AA	
Source Socket (2 bytes)	40	23			
Exclusion Address Count (1 byte)	01				
Exclusion Address (6 bytes)	00	00	1B	03	98	3D

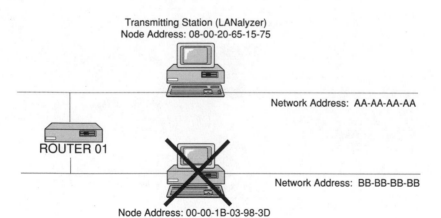

Transmitting Station (LANalyzer)
Node Address: 08-00-20-65-15-75

Network Address: AA-AA-AA-AA

ROUTER 01

Network Address: BB-BB-BB-BB

Node Address: 00-00-1B-03-98-3D

but the server does not, you can determine that it is either not connected or not running on the network.

The Diagnostic Responder can be a tremendously helpful tool for testing the network response and connectivity. Since the responses provide configuration information about servers and clients, it can also be used for

FIGURE 11.12

Testing the connectivity of
server SALES1

Field						
Checksum (2 bytes)	FF	FF				
Length (2 bytes)	00	1F				
Transport Control (1 byte)	00					
Packet Type (1 byte)	04					
Destination Node Address (6 bytes)	00	00	00	00	00	01
Destination Network Address (4 bytes)	C9	00	00	01		
Destination Socket (2 bytes)	04	56				
Source Node Address (6 bytes)	08	00	20	65	15	75
Source Network Address (4 bytes)	AA	AA	AA	AA		
Source Socket (2 bytes)	40	23				
Exclusion Address Count (1 byte)	00					

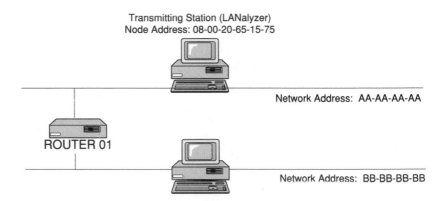

Transmitting Station (LANalyzer)
Node Address: 08-00-20-65-15-75

Network Address: AA-AA-AA-AA

ROUTER 01

Network Address: BB-BB-BB-BB

Server SALES1
IPX Internal Network Address: 99-00-00-01
Node Address: 00-00-00-00-00-01

information gathering. The Diagnostic Responder is also used by Novell's NetWare Management System and third parties to "discover" network devices.

There are two LANalyzer applications that are designed to transmit Diagnostic Request packets and filter for responses. These applications are NODEVIEW and ROUTVIEW.

You can use NODEVIEW to check the connectivity of NetWare nodes, and you can use ROUTVIEW to check nodes and servers on the other side of a router.

This chapter has defined several uses for the Diagnostic Responder, including connectivity testing and configuration information gathering. By looking at the Diagnostic Responder Request packet format, you have seen how to transmit to an entire network, a group of selected nodes, or specific, individual stations.

The next chapter covers some miscellaneous packets that are found on NetWare LANs. These include the NetWare Watchdog packets, Serialization packets, and message packets.

Miscellaneous
Netware
Protocols

Thus far, this book has examined the most commonly used NetWare protocols, IPX, SPX, NCP, and so on. However, there are special needs on a NetWare LAN that are handled using some unique packets that do not fit into the previously defined protocols. These unique packets include

▶ Watchdog packets

▶ Serialization packets

▶ Message packets

This chapter examines the packet structure and functionality of each of these services.

Up to this point you have seen how workstations communicate with servers. However, it is necessary to maintain an active network connection in order to communicate. This connectivity is held in check by NetWare's Watchdog protocol.

Watchdog Protocol

The Watchdog protocol provides constant validation of active workstation connections and notifies the NetWare operating system when a connection may be terminated as a result of lengthy periods without communicating.

When a workstation is logged in but is not being used, the Watchdog continuously questions the workstation to ensure that the connection is still valid. Workstations are queried according to their connection number, given during the login process. If a workstation does not transmit any packets to a server within 4 minutes 56.6 seconds (a settable parameter), a Watchdog packet will be transmitted to the station, as shown in Figure 12.1.

WATCHDOG FRAME FORMAT
As shown in Figure 12.2, there are only two fields contained in a Watchdog packet after the IPX header: connection number and signature character.

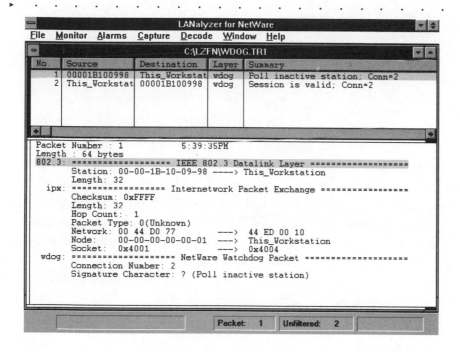

FIGURE 12.1

Watchdog queries include a station's connection number.

IPX Header

Connection Number (1 byte)

Signature Character (1 byte)

FIGURE 12.2

Watchdog packet structure

The connection number field indicates the connection number given to the station during the login process. The signature character field contains the value 0x3F (ASCII character ?), which is used to poll an inactive station.

If no response is received from the workstation, the server transmits ten additional Watchdog Query packets at 59.3-second intervals. If the workstation still does not respond, the server terminates the workstation's connection. It is possible to modify the Watchdog timings and retry count.

The Watchdog parameters are set at the NetWare v3.x file server prompt, using the following syntax:

NUMBER OF WATCHDOG PACKETS=n

DELAY BETWEEN WATCHDOG PACKETS=n

DELAY BEFORE FIRST WATCHDOG PACKET=n

The number of Watchdog packets sent defaults to 10 but can be set for 5 to 100 packets. The delay between Watchdog packets defaults to 59.3 seconds but can be set from 9.9 seconds up to 10 minutes 26.2 seconds. The delay before transmitting the first Watchdog packet defaults to 4 minutes 56.6 seconds but can be set from 15.7 seconds up to 20 minutes 52.3 seconds.

When an active workstation responds to the server, it sends a Watchdog Response packet indicating that the workstation connection is still in use. Figure 12.3 depicts a Watchdog Response packet.

FIGURE 12.3

Watchdog Response packet

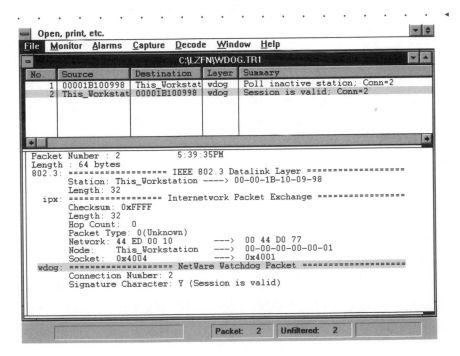

In the signature character field, the value 0x59 (ASCII Y) indicates that the connection is still valid although it hasn't transmitted data for the amount of time indicated in the Delay Before First Watchdog Packet parameter.

The Watchdog feature ensures that workstation connections are tested for validity if they have not transmitted recently. Definable parameters allow NetWare v3.x networks to determine how the Watchdog feature performs. If connections are a precious resource, the Watchdog feature can be tuned to be more aggressive and wait shorter periods of time before terminating a station's connection.

Serialization Packets

NetWare is sold in "per server" versions. Each version of NetWare can be loaded on only one file server. To ensure that a single version of NetWare is not being loaded on multiple servers, the operating system broadcasts copy-protection packets, called Serialization packets, to determine if there are multiple copies of the same operating system on the network.

Serialization packets are 36 bytes in length (including the IPX header), as shown in Figure 12.4.

These Serialization packets are transmitted approximately every 66 seconds. Figure 12.5 shows the Serialization packet structure.

Serialization packets are transmitted to another file server's internal IPX address. Serialization packets contain only one field, the serialization data field. This information is used to notify other servers of the operating system serialization number. These packets are always addressed to the serialization socket number 0x0457.

If multiple servers use the same operating system, the servers will broadcast "Copyright violation" messages to all users.

FIGURE 12.4

Serialization packets use IPX for transport.

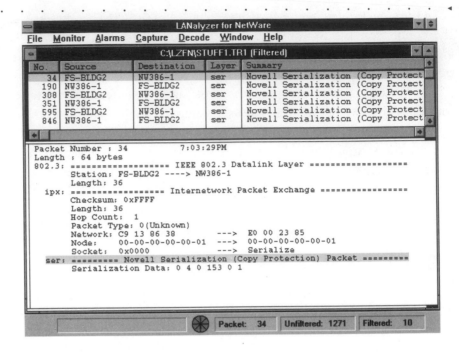

```
                          LANalyzer for NetWare                      ▼ ▲
 File   Monitor   Alarms   Capture   Decode   Window   Help
 ▭                     C:\LZFN\STUFF1.TR1 [Filtered]                ▼ ▲
 No.   Source        Destination   Layer   Summary
    34 FS-BLDG2      NW386-1        ser     Novell Serialization (Copy Protect
   190 NW386-1       FS-BLDG2       ser     Novell Serialization (Copy Protect
   308 FS-BLDG2      NW386-1        ser     Novell Serialization (Copy Protect
   351 NW386-1       FS-BLDG2       ser     Novell Serialization (Copy Protect
   595 FS-BLDG2      NW386-1        ser     Novell Serialization (Copy Protect
   846 NW386-1       FS-BLDG2       ser     Novell Serialization (Copy Protect
 ◀

 Packet Number : 34              7:03:29PM
 Length : 64 bytes
 802.3: ==================== IEEE 802.3 Datalink Layer ====================
         Station: FS-BLDG2 ----> NW386-1
         Length: 36
   ipx: ================== Internetwork Packet Exchange ==================
         Checksum: 0xFFFF
         Length: 36
         Hop Count: 1
         Packet Type: 0(Unknown)
         Network: C9 13 86 38        --->   E0 00 23 85
         Node:    00-00-00-00-00-01  --->   00-00-00-00-00-01
         Socket:  0x0000             --->   Serialize
   ser: ========= Novell Serialization (Copy Protection) Packet =========
         Serialization Data: 0 4 0 153 0 1



          ✦  Packet:  34    Unfiltered: 1271   Filtered:  10
```

FIGURE 12.5

Serialization packet structure

IPX Header (Destination Socket 0x0457)

Serialization Data (6 bytes)

Sending Messages

NetWare allows users to send messages from stations and the console to specific stations, groups, users, or the console. To the user, NetWare's messaging system appears to be a peer-to-peer operation, bypassing the NetWare server. It is not.

NetWare reserves a message buffer for each attached workstation. The console, however, displays the message received immediately. The buffer stores messages and notifies the recipient that a message is pending. Users receive a banner on their screen that displays the message sent to them.

The following lists the steps taken to transmit a message from a user named Jane to a user named Fred:

1 · Send the message addressed to a user, group, or connection number: SEND "Backup at 7:00 P.M." to Fred [Enter].

2 · Get Jane's login information and then scan the bindery for the login name "Fred."

3 · Get Fred's connection number and transmit the message to his message buffer.

4 · The server notifies Fred that he has a message waiting and, if Fred has not run CASTOFF, he requests the message from the server.

The packets shown in Figures 12.6 through 12.9 are seen when executing the steps listed above.

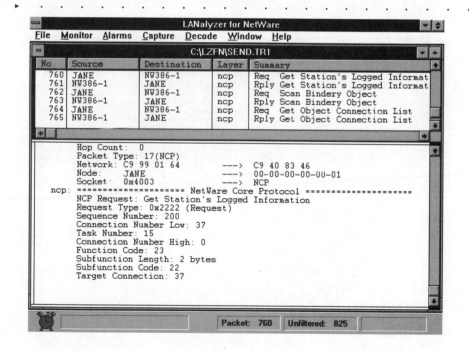

FIGURE 12.7

*Request Fred's connection
number.*

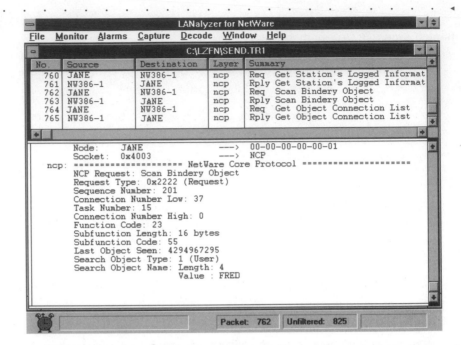

FIGURE 12.8

*Transmit the message to
the server.*

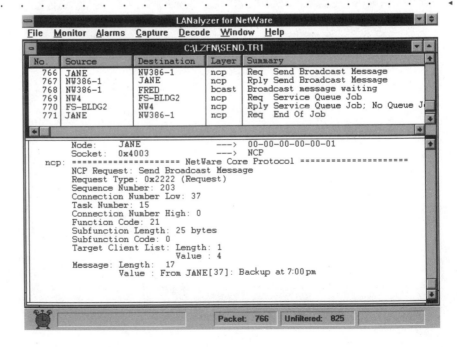

▶ . . . . ◀

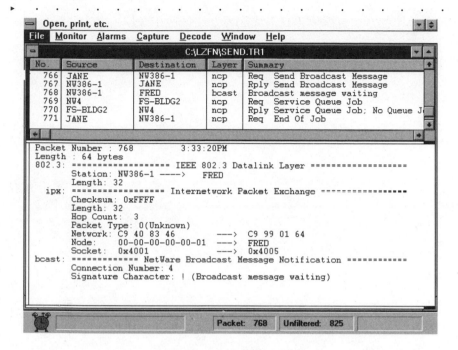

FIGURE 12.9

The server notifies Fred's station of a message waiting.

The packets covered in this chapter are unique. The Watchdog and Serialization packets do not fit into the standard SAP, RIP, or NCP structure and format. NetWare's messaging is also unique in that it doesn't use the true NCP structure when notifying users that a message is waiting.

Part III of this book defines various performance benchmarking, testing, and optimization techniques that can be used on NetWare Ethernet LANs.

Performance Benchmarking, Testing, and Optimization

Part III focuses on the methods available to benchmark network performance and create a baseline against which to compare current performance. You will perform tests on the network to determine if your cabling system is overloaded or if a component is unable to keep up with the load on the network and look at methods for characterizing server performance based on the types of requests a server is handling, and explore options available for optimizing the network.

In Chapter 13 you will look at factors that should be documented for the network, such as utilization, packets per second, errors per second, and the purpose of maintaining an accurate baseline.

In Chapter 14 you will work with several methods of stress-testing a network, learn to differentiate between "dumb" and "intelligent" loads, and determine which would be most appropriate for testing a cabling system or an individual network component.

Chapter 15 looks at specific NCP requests and replies to determine if the upper-layer protocol, NetWare, is performing properly. You will look at the initial attachment process and the login process, learn the three netware server connection priorities, and explore methods of using protocol analyzers to test security on the network.

Chapter 16 examines the types of requests a server is required to handle most often and those that may overload a server.

CHAPTER 13

Creating a Network Baseline

This chapter defines the purpose of creating and tracking network performance over time. Although your network seems to be performing properly, you have noticed some slight degradation in performance over the last several months. In order to document the increasing network load or decreasing network performance, you need some sort of benchmark information to compare the current status against. This is the primary purpose of creating and maintaining network baseline reports.

A baseline is simply a "snapshot" of network health. As your network grows in complexity and size, you can refer back to your baseline report to chart its growth and performance.

What Is Included in a Baseline Report?

Baseline reports can include various specialized bits of information about a network, such as router statistics, LAN driver statistics, and so on. There are, however, several key characteristics of network performance that should be included in all baseline reports.

These key characteristics include

- ▶ Utilization
- ▶ Error rates
- ▶ Packets per second
- ▶ Kilobytes per second
- ▶ Most active servers
- ▶ Request Being Processed packets

Within practical limits, this could be done for mission-critical servers and clients on the network as well.

UTILIZATION TRENDS

Utilization increase is a common symptom of a network that has grown over time. As new workstations and applications are added to the network, more users and more data are dependent upon the cabling system for transport. By documenting this change, you can prepare for further growth and justify the expense required to enhance the network.

When charting utilization statistics, it is desirable to create a utilization trend graph. A trend graph plots information over a certain time period, such as a week or month. A statistics graph that provides only 20 minutes of utilization information would be misleading for later comparisons. Perhaps the utilization was being charted at a time when the network was busier than normal, such as during the morning hours when everyone is logging into the network. Figure 13.1 shows a utilization trend graph as it appears on the LANalyzer for NetWare screen.

Analyzers generally allow you to export network statistics in various formats. You can then import the information into a spreadsheet program to provide further analysis. When exporting statistics for use in a spreadsheet,

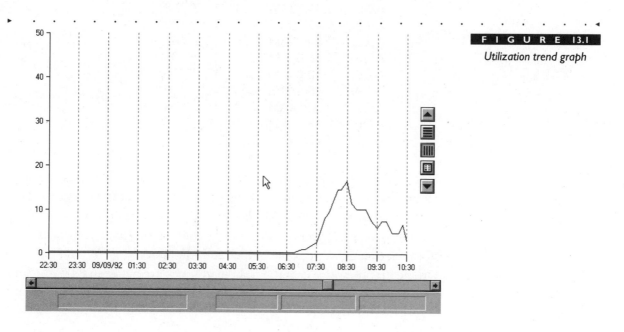

FIGURE 13.1

Utilization trend graph

be certain to select the proper delimiter value for the spreadsheet program you are using. A delimiter such as a comma or tab will separate the fields of the information for proper interpretation by a spreadsheet program. Figure 13.2 shows a file that has been exported using comma separation.

F I G U R E 13.2

File exported with

comma-separated fields

```
"Date","Time","Pkts/Sec","Avg. Errors","Util","Kb/Sec"
"7/9/92","3:15:03AM","687","1","13","161"
"7/9/92","3:30:03AM","444","1","7","93"
"7/9/92","3:45:03AM","808","1","14","167"
"7/9/92","4:00:03AM","515","1","9","108"
"7/9/92","4:15:03AM","787","1","15","183"
"7/9/92","4:30:03AM","723","1","14","172"
"7/9/92","4:45:03AM","616","1","11","136"
"7/9/92","5:00:04AM","546","1","10","123"
"7/9/92","5:15:03AM","607","1","10","125"
"7/9/92","5:30:03AM","427","1","7","89"
"7/9/92","5:45:04AM","387","1","7","84"
"7/9/92","6:00:04AM","381","1","7","83"
"7/9/92","6:15:03AM","401","1","7","85"
"7/9/92","6:30:03AM","401","1","7","85"
"7/9/92","6:45:03AM","437","1","7","88"
"7/9/92","7:00:03AM","395","1","7","85"
"7/9/92","7:15:03AM","420","1","7","85"
"7/9/92","7:30:04AM","361","1","6","75"
"7/9/92","7:45:04AM","349","1","6","76"
"7/9/92","8:00:04AM","329","1","6","74"
"7/9/92","8:15:04AM","363","1","6","80"
"7/9/92","8:30:04AM","342","1","6","74"
```

Notice that the fields are separated by commas. The titles are also separated by commas. Figure 13.3 shows how the data can be plotted. This example uses a bar graph to display the utilization trend information. By viewing Figure 13.3, you can see several characteristics of your network's performance, such as peak load times and idle times.

On the graph, notice that the peak load times are between 8:00 A.M. and 9:00A.M., 5:00 P.M., and 12:00 A.M. These are the times when people are

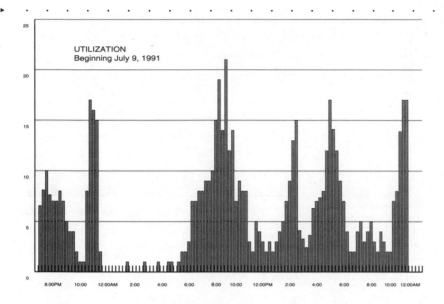

FIGURE 13.3

A comma-separated file can be imported by many spreadsheet programs.

logging into the network, logging out of the network, and when backup is being performed, respectively.

Based on the information presented, you may decide to set your utilization alarm threshold at 25%, since you do not normally exceed 21% utilization at the peak time of the day.

ERROR RATES

Error rate trend information should also be included in the baseline report. This ensures that you are aware of your typical error rates over time. As the network grows, the error rates may also increase. As discussed in Chapter 5, increased errors may be a symptom of network growth, cabling bottlenecks or miswiring, or possibly a component failure.

Figure 13.4 shows a trend graph for error rates. This trend information has been exported and plotted on a line graph. The typical number of errors on this network ranges from 0 to 4 errors in every 15-minute period.

Based on this graph and the preceding utilization graph, you can see that your errors are closely related to network utilization. As the network grows, both utilization and errors will most likely increase. If, however, errors

FIGURE 13.4

Error rate trend information

plotted on a line graph

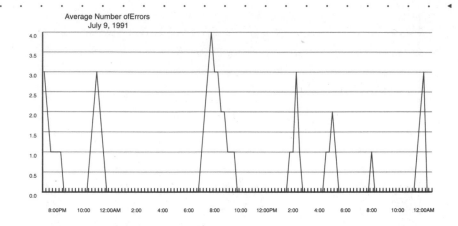

increase and utilization does not, it indicates a possible component problem, such as a faulty network interface card or transceiver.

PACKETS PER SECOND

Tracking the number of packets per second on the network will give you a general idea of the amount of traffic on the wire. This is not the same as utilization since utilization is based on the number of kilobytes on the wire per second. Packets can range in size and do not directly correspond with utilization. Utilization may increase as the result of an increase in either the number of packets on the wire or the size of packets.

On a NetWare LAN, the number of packets per second defines the number of requests, replies, and information packets that are typically serviced by the network. If the number of packets increases but the utilization does not, you can assume that the number of small packets has increased, thereby not causing an increase in bandwidth utilization.

Figure 13.5 shows a trend graph for packets per second in an area graph. You can easily see the peak times for requests, replies, and information packets on the network.

As you add NetWare servers to your network, you may see the number of packets per second steadily rise. This may be a result of the number of SAP and RIP broadcasts that are propagated throughout the network. The

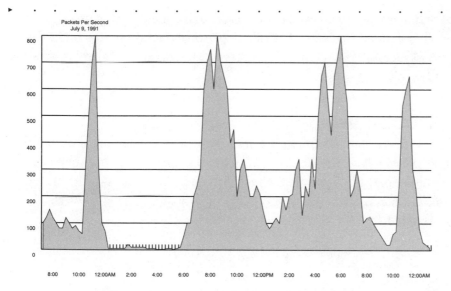

Packets Per Second
July 9, 1991

FIGURE 13.5

Packets-per-second trend graph

excessive number of SAP packets seen on large NetWare LANs prompted the creation of Novell's RESTRICT.NLM product, which selectively limits SAP packets passed by NetWare routers.

KILOBYTES PER SECOND

By tracking kilobytes per second, you can determine the actual through-put of your network—the number of kilobytes transmitted per second.

The utilization statistics are based upon kilobytes per second and determine a percentage of bandwidth in use compared to the maximum possible (10 Mbps).

MOST ACTIVE SERVERS

Be aware of the most active servers on the network. Maintaining a list of the top three servers will help you distribute the load among them as you add applications and users.

To measure server activity, track the number of packets per second from the server over several days or a week. If you place too many users on a single server, the server may begin transmitting Request Being Processed

NOTE
In Chapter 16, you will graph server performance statistics.

packets. By keeping an eye on the servers that are most often used, you may be able to avoid server overload. If performance decreases but Request Being Processed packets are not observed, the server's LAN card may be the bottleneck.

NOTE
In Chapter 16, you will look more closely at the cause of Request Being Processed packets.

REQUEST BEING PROCESSED PACKETS

If a server cannot reply to a client because it is busy performing other tasks, it will transmit a Request Being Processed packet. This indicates that the server may be overloaded. A few of these packets may not signal a problem, but a constantly increasing number is a sign that the server is being overloaded.

When Should a Baseline Be Created?

Baseline information should be gathered on a healthy network during a time when conditions are normal. In order to create a baseline that is indicative of normal network activity, the baseline information should be gathered when the network is performing under normal conditions. You can recompile baseline information after adding a new server, workstation, router, or application, if desired. As mentioned earlier in this chapter, the purpose of a baseline is to provide a "snapshot" of normal network activity. You can contrast future network reports against the baseline for comparative purposes. This historical data viewed in total shows the "evolution" of your network and may indicate future trends.

An additional use of baselining is the prediction of network performance based on planned changes. For example, if a client GUI (graphical user interface) were being considered for all stations on the network, a "typical" station using the new GUI could be tested. Its usage could be multiplied by the anticipated total number of stations in the implementation planned and added to the baseline to define estimated performance.

$$\text{Baseline} + (\text{new traffic} \times \text{number of stations}) = \text{estimated future}$$
$$\text{baseline}$$

Comparing Current Network Performance against the Baseline

In order to track network growth and health, you can gather statistics months later than the baseline was created and compare the information against the baseline.

For example, in Figure 13.6, you can see a graph of the current network utilization in comparison to a network baseline created in January 1992. The network administrator wanted to know how the network had been affected by the addition of several workstations and a database server.

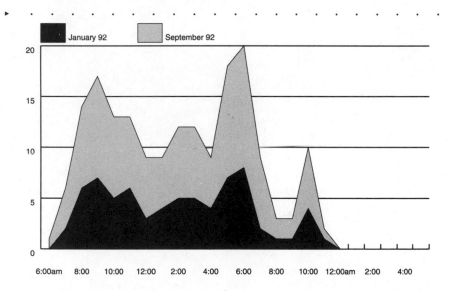

FIGURE 13.6

Comparing utilization information in September 1992 against the baseline of daily activity created in January

By appending September's utilization information to January's baseline information, a comparative chart of utilization growth has been created. The utilization chart is for a 24-hour period beginning at 6:00 A.M. Although the idle times have not changed significantly—from midnight to 5:30 A.M., the network goes unused—overall utilization during the work hours has increased quite a bit.

This chapter has examined some key elements that should be included in a baseline report, such as utilization, error rate, and packets per second. You have also viewed a comma-separated trend file and the charts that were created from the data. Finally, you compared current network activity against the baseline to verify that bandwidth utilization has increased over an eight-month period.

In the next chapter, you will stress-test the network cabling system and an individual component.

CHAPTER 14

Stress-Testing Techniques

The previous chapters have discussed how Ethernet LANs should work and some of the warning signs of an overloaded network component or cabling system. In this chapter, you will take a proactive step in testing components and the cabling system. By performing load tests on the network, you can test a single component, groups of components, or the media.

There are two types of loads that can be generated onto the network:

- Dumb loads

- Intelligent loads

Before you begin generating load tests on the network, a word of warning: Be very selective of when you perform load tests, since they will most likely degrade network performance. The tests are designed to find the point at which a component or network cabling system becomes the bottleneck for communications. You should perform these tests during the evenings or on a weekend, when the network is less actively used.

Dumb Loads

Dumb loads are designed to test the cabling system bandwidth and determine how much additional load the media can sustain without performance degradation.

When you are generating traffic that is not addressed to any particular device and that contains no meaningful information, it is called a dumb load. You can use these loads to test the network cabling system. In Chapter 3, you used a dumb load (GENLOAD test) to test access to the network cabling system. As shown in Figure 14.1, the GENLOAD application can be configured to transmit packets to an invalid node address of 0x00-00-00-00-00-00. No station will respond to this address; therefore, you are not testing a component.

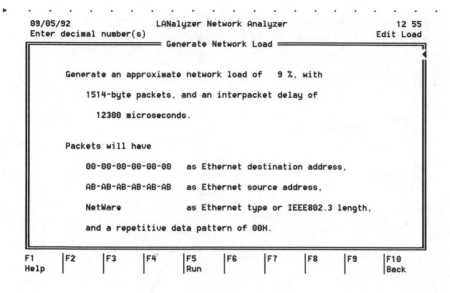

FIGURE 14.1

*The GENLOAD application
is designed to generate a
dumb load.*

Using the GENLOAD application, you can generate varying amounts of load onto the network and view your transmission statistics to evaluate network access. In Figure 14.2, the results of running a GENLOAD test have been plotted. During the test, the percentage of transmissions that were successfully transmitted on the first attempt has been noted. As the load increases on the network, successful first attempts decrease.

It is clear from the graph that the access to the medium begins to decline when there is a network load of approximately 35%–40%. From 40% to 50%, the decline in performance is quite noticeable. The following table lists the statistics for Figure 14.2:

NETWORK LOAD	SUCCESSFUL TRANSMISSIONS
10%	100%
20%	98%
30%	97%
40%	90%
50%	58%

NETWORK LOAD	SUCCESSFUL TRANSMISSIONS
60%	46%
70%	44%

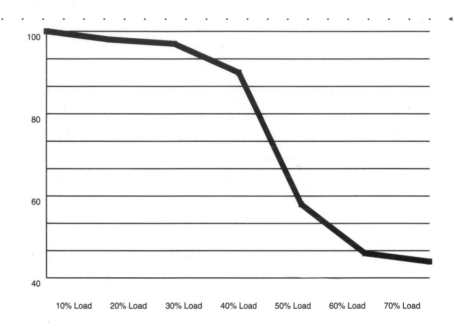

FIGURE 14.2

Results of testing the network access under various loads

Many people stress-test their networks based on user response. This method requires you to generate a reasonable load onto the network for a full work day and wait for any network users to complain about network performance. If the load is unnacceptable, the symptoms encountered may include workstation timeouts and/or slow file transfers. If, however, no users complain, you know that there is some margin for growth on the network.

Now that you know your margin for growth, you can determine if network sluggishness is due to a bottleneck in the cabling system. If, at a later date, users begin to complain of slow file transfers, check the utilization. If you are within your acceptable bandwidth utilization amount, there may be some other problem causing the slowness, such as an overloaded server or router.

Although not a very scientific method for stress-testing the network cabling system, testing acceptable bandwidth utilization based on user response gives a realistic measure of how much performance degradation users will permit.

Intelligent Loads

Intelligent loads are used to test a particular device on a network, such as a router, server, or network interface card. When generating an intelligent load, the packets are addressed to a particular device, often with some reply requested, as shown in Figure 14.3.

One example of using an intelligent load test is when testing the response from a server's network interface card. By transmitting various loads consisting of SAP requests to a NetWare server, you can test the server card's ability to buffer packets and respond.

For example, an intelligent load test can be performed on a NetWare v3.x server that has a 16-bit card installed. By transmitting gradually increasing

NOTE
NetWare v3.x servers will adjust parameters, such as packet receive buffers, in response to load demands. This type of "regulation" should be considered when drawing conclusions from your tests.

An intelligent load
may be used to test
individual components.

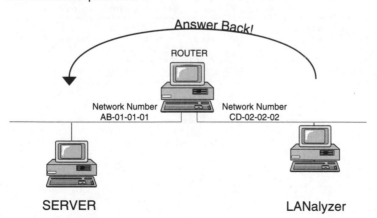

FIGURE 14.3
Intelligent loads are transmitted to a particular device on the network.

loads of SAP packets, you can determine at what point the card is unable to keep up. If, however, you substitute a 32-bit card in the server, you should see a dramatic increase in performance. This increase in performance is not due to any changes in the server except the 32-bit network interface card. You can use this type of load test to justify the purchase of a faster card for the server or a router.

Stress Tests

There are two LANalyzer applications designed specifically for stress testing. The first one, GENLOAD, has been covered in this chapter and in Chapter 3.

The second test, VARLOAD, generates a random load between 1% and 7%. As shown in Figure 14.4, there are three transmit channels defined in

FIGURE 14.4

The VARLOAD application
has three predefined
channels to transmit 64-,
633-, and 1082-byte
packets.

```
09/09/92                LANalyzer Network Analyzer                    21 51
Enter a name                                                    Edit Transmit
╔═══════════════════════ c:\xln\lanz\802.3\general\varload ═══════════════════╗
║TRANSMIT                                                                      ◀
║Channel                      Delay              Preamble    Coll.
║Name       Active  Count    (100us)  CRC  Collide  Bytes    Backoff
║64byte     No        1         0     Good   No   8 (normal) Normal
║633byte    No        1         0     Good   No   8 (normal) Normal
║1082byte   No        1         0     Good   No   8 (normal) Normal
║           No        1         0     Good   No   8 (normal) Normal
║           No        1         0     Good   No   8 (normal) Normal
║           No        1         0     Good   No   8 (normal) Normal
║──────────────────────────────────────────────────────────────────────
║MULTIPACKET TRANSMISSION
║Txall      Yes      Inf       200    Good   No   8 (normal) Normal
║
║Transmit serially with the following relative frequencies:
║           64byte      30        633byte    20       1082byte   50
║                        0                    0                   0
║
║Transmit after _     00:00:00 hours or    _
╚══════════════════════════════════════════════════════════════════════════════╝
F1    |F2     |F3   |F4      |F5   |F6     |F7      |F8   |F9     |F10
Help  |Revert |Save |Options |Mode |Packet |Receive |Xmit |Alarms |Back
```

VARLOAD:

- ▸ 64-byte packets
- ▸ 633-byte packets
- ▸ 1082-byte packets

Each transmit channel is defined as a dumb load by default, transmitting to destination address 0x-00-00-00-00-00-00. To make the application transmit an intelligent load, edit the transmit channel and provide a destination address, as shown in Figure 14.5.

In this example, you are transmitting packets to a file server. Since the packet is addressed to the server, it will attempt to process the packet.

As Figure 14.6 shows, once VARLOAD is running, the Global screen shows the packet size distribution on the network and the current load.

Bridges and routers are good candidates for testing. Use multiple tests with various size packets to determine if bridging/routing efficiency is affected by packet size. Many internetworking devices have built-in error monitoring that may supply useful information for test results. If two

```
09/09/92              LANalyzer Network Analyzer            21 52
Enter decimal number(s)                                   Edit Packet
============ c:\xln\lanz\802.3\general\varload ============
64byte                      Protocol Type  DATA
Packet Length (Generated: 60    Transmitted: as generated)

Ethernet
     Destination Address              novel11EF22C
     Source Address                   exos651575
     Type                             NetWare

Data Length  46                   Data Offset 0    EBCDIC display
0000  E3 88 89 A2 40 89 A2 40   91 A4 A2 A3 00 00 00 00   This is just....
0010  81 40 A3 85 A2 A3 40 97   81 83 92 85 A3 00 00 00   a test packet...
0020  00 00 00 00 00 00 00 00   00 00 00 00 00 00         ..............




F1    |F2    |F3    |F4    |F5    |F6     |F7   |F8    |F9    |F10
Help  |Copy  |Paste |Type  |ASCII |Zoom In|Fill |      |      |Back
```

FIGURE 14.5

Using VARLOAD to transmit to a particular device

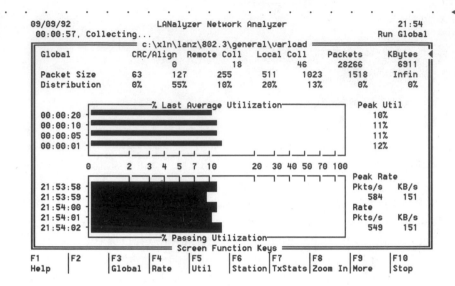

LANalyzers are available, monitor the generated load on the far side of the internetworking device to ensure accurate packet bridged/routed rates and observe any bridge- or router-induced errors.

Whenever possible, try to add intelligence to your load test by emulating the type of traffic that will most likely occur on your network. For example, if you wish to simulate graphics users, transmit large packet sizes.

This chapter has examined two types of loads that can be transmitted onto the network: dumb loads and intelligent loads. You have learned that you can use dumb loads to test the nework cabling system and that intelligent loads are best suited to testing a particular device on the network.

The next chapter analyzes NetWare NCP communications, such as attachment and login.

Testing NCP Communications

Chapter 7 covered the NetWare Core Protocol. This chapter views various communications between clients and servers using NCP requests and replies. By placing a LANalyzer on a network segment and filtering on the client-server communications, you can gain a clearer understanding of how clients attach to the desired server, log in, and gain access to network services in the NetWare environment.

This chapter covers four specific topics:

- Connection procedure

- Login procedure

- NetWare security

- Directory access/rights

The Connection Procedure

When a client executes the NETX.COM (or other shell file), it generates a Get Nearest Server SAP broadcast on the local network. Either a server on the local network or a NetWare router can reply to this request. The replies will provide the name and network address of the nearest server. In Figure 15.1 you can see the NETX sequence.

The NETX sequence follows seven steps:

1 · Find the nearest server (primary) and the route to it.

2 · Create the connection and negotiate the buffer size.

3 · Query the primary server's bindery for the network address to the preferred server.

4 · Locate the route to the preferred server.

5 · Create a connection to the preferred server and negotiate the buffer size.

6 · Destroy the connection to the primary server.

7 · Issue the logout command to the preferred server.

No.	Source	Destination	Layer	Size	Summary
1	LINDSAY	Broadcast	sap	0064	Query Nearest File Server
2	FS2	LINDSAY	sap	0114	Resp Nearest;Server=FS2
3	LINDSAY	Broadcast	rip	0064	Req network=00 00 11 62
4	FS2	LINDSAY	rip	0064	Resp network=00 00 11 62; 1 hops
5	LINDSAY	FS2	ncp	0064	Req Create Service Connection
6	FS2	LINDSAY	ncp	0064	Rply Create Service Connection
7	LINDSAY	FS2	ncp	0064	Req Get File Server Information
8	FS2	LINDSAY	ncp	0184	Rply Get File Server Information
9	00001B110014	LINDSAY	sap	0114	Resp Nearest; Server=SANFRAN1
10	LINDSAY	FS2	ncp	0064	Req Negotiate Buffer Size
11	FS2	LINDSAY	ncp	0064	Rply Negotiate Buffer Size
12	LINDSAY	FS2	ncp	0084	Req Read Property Value
13	FS2	LINDSAY	ncp	0186	Rply Read Property Value
14	LINDSAY	Broadcast	rip	0064	Req network=C9 40 83 46
15	00001B15089F	LINDSAY	sap	0114	Resp Nearest; Server=TOM-P-SERVER
16	00001B331232	LINDSAY	sap	0114	Resp Nearest; Server=PETESERVER
17	00001B03F363	LINDSAY	sap	0114	Resp Nearest; Server=ADMINISTRAT
18	00001B1EF36B	LINDSAY	sap	0114	Resp Nearest; Server=FS1
19	00001B1E1047	LINDSAY	sap	0114	Resp Nearest; Server=PURCHASING
20	00001B3321C3	LINDSAY	sap	0114	Resp Nearest; Server=SW-FS02
21	00001B1E5CCD	LINDSAY	sap	0114	Resp Nearest; Server=SW-FS01
22	00001B32EE91	LINDSAY	sap	0114	Resp Nearest; Server=SW-FS04
23	00001B1E5CD8	LINDSAY	sap	0114	Resp Nearest; Server=SW-FS05
24	00001B036448	LINDSAY	sap	0114	Resp Nearest; Server=SW-FS06
25	00001B036448	LINDSAY	rip	0064	Resp network=C9 40 83 46; 1 hops
26	LINDSAY	SALES1	ncp	0064	Req Create Service Connection
27	SALES1	LINDSAY	ncp	0064	Rply Create Service Connection
28	LINDSAY	SALES1	ncp	0064	Req Get File Server Information
29	SALES1	LINDSAY	ncp	0184	Rply Get File Server Information
30	LINDSAY	SALES1	ncp	0064	Req Negotiate Buffer Size
31	SALES1	LINDSAY	ncp	0064	Rply Negotiate Buffer Size
32	LINDSAY	SALES1	ncp	0064	Req Destroy Service Connection
33	SALES1	LINDSAY	ncp	0064	Rply Destroy Service Connection
34	LINDSAY	SALES1	ncp	0064	Req Logout
35	SALES1	LINDSAY	ncp	0064	Rply Logout
36	LINDSAY	SALES1	ncp	0064	Req Get File Server Date and Tim
37	SALES1	LINDSAY	ncp	0064	Rply Get File Server Date and Tim

FIGURE 15.1

The NETX sequence

STEP 1: FIND THE NEAREST SERVER (PRIMARY) AND THE ROUTE TO IT

In packet number 1, the client, LINDSAY, is requesting the nearest server. Packet number 2 shows that FS2 responded the most quickly. Even though other servers will reply to the Get Nearest Server request (packets 9 and 15–24), the client will ignore these responses. Packet number 3 depicts that the client is requesting the route to the server FS2.

STEP 2: CREATE THE CONNECTION AND NEGOTIATE THE BUFFER SIZE

In packets 5, 7, and 10, the client is creating the connection, obtaining information about the server, and negotiating the buffer size.

STEP 3: QUERY THE PRIMARY SERVER'S BINDERY FOR THE NETWORK ADDRESS TO THE PREFERRED SERVER

If the Preferred Server option is placed in the client's NET.CFG file or at the command line ("NETX PS=[server name]"), the client will query the server that responded first to the Get Nearest Server SAP for the network address of the preferred server. This query (packet 12) is made through the use of a Get Property Value NCP. However, if the client did not request a specific server, it will retain a connection to the original server that answered the Get Nearest Server query.

By viewing packet number 12, as shown in Figure 15.2, you can see that the client is requesting the network address of server SALES1.

FIGURE 15.2

The client requests the network address of its preferred server.

```
Packet Number : 12              11:56:11PM
Length : 84 bytes
802.3: =================== IEEE 802.3 Datalink Layer ===================
        Station: LINDSAY ---> 00-AA-00-0C-75-9F        Length: 66
    ipx: =================== Internetwork Packet Exchange==================
        Checksum: 0xFFFF                  Length: 65
        Hop Count: 0                      Packet Type: 17(NCP)
        Network: C9 99 00 06       ->  00 00 11 62
        Node:    LINDSAY           ->  00-00-00-00-00-01
        Socket:  0x4003            ->  NCP
    ncp: ===================== NetWare Core Protocol=====================
        NCP Request: Read Property Value
        Request Type: 0x2222 (Request)
        Sequence Number: 3
        Connection Number Low: 1
        Task Number: 0
        Connection Number High: 0
        Function Code: 23
        Subfunction Length: 26 bytes
        Subfunction Code: 61
        Object Type: 4 (File Server)
        Object Name: Length: 6
                    Value : SALES1
        Segment Number: 1
        Property Name: Length: 11
                    Value : NET_ADDRESS
```

STEP 4: LOCATE THE ROUTE TO THE PREFERRED SERVER

In packet number 14 of Figure 15.1, the client is requesting the route to the network upon which the preferred server is located, C9-40-83-46.

STEP 5: CREATE A CONNECTION TO THE PREFERRED SERVER AND NEGOTIATE THE BUFFER SIZE

Next, the client creates the connection to the preferred server, obtains server information, and negotiates the buffer size. The client and server will agree to use the lowest buffer size negotiated. This occurred in packets 26 to 31 of Figure 15.1.

STEP 6: DESTROY THE CONNECTION TO THE PRIMARY SERVER

Since the original server is no longer required, the client destroys the connection (packets 32 and 33).

STEP 7: ISSUE THE LOGOUT COMMAND TO THE PREFERRED SERVER

To ensure that any past connections are clear for the client, it issues a Logout command to the server (packets 34 and 35).

NETWARE SERVER CONNECTION PRIORITIES

When you are connecting to a NetWare LAN, there are three server connection priorities available:

- ▶ Primary server
- ▶ Preferred server
- ▶ Default server

The *primary server* is the one you attached to during the NETX sequence. Even if you included a Preferred Server= command in your NET.CFG file, you can still attach initially to another server.

The *preferred server* is the one that you explicitly logged into by typing **LOGIN [SERVER NAME]/[USER NAME]** or that you placed in your NET.CFG file by using the PS= option.

The *default server* is the server implied by the client's default drive.

Now that you have established a connection with either the primary or the preferred server, you can begin the login process.

The Login Process

Users are often surprised at the number of packets required to complete the login process. There are, however, several files that are downloaded to the workstation during the login process. These files can include

LOGIN.EXE (login executable file)

NET$LOG.DAT (system login script)

LOGIN.DAT (user login script)

CAPTURE.EXE (port redirection executable file)

PRINTCON.DAT (print job configuration file)

NET$PRN.DAT (printer device defintion file)

Figure 15.3 shows some of the NCP calls used during the login process. Remember, the NETX sequence has already occurred and the user has a connection to the server (see Figure 15.1).

The number of packets required for the login process is dependent upon commands within the login scripts. Each executable command within a login script may require another file to be downloaded to the client's station. For example, if you place two capture statements within the login script, the CAPTURE.EXE file will be downloaded twice, once for each statement.

No.	Source	Destination	Layer	Size	Summary
1	LINDSAY	FS2	ncp	0064	Req Open File LOGIN
2	FS2	LINDSAY	ncp	0064	Rply Open File; Failure
3	LINDSAY	FS2	ncp	0064	Req Get Directory Path
4	FS2	LINDSAY	ncp	0066	Rply Get Directory Path SYS:LOGIN
5	LINDSAY	FS2	ncp	0064	Req File Search Initialize /LOGIN
6	FS2	LINDSAY	ncp	0064	Rply File Search Initialize
7	LINDSAY	FS2	ncp	0074	Req File Search Continue LOGIN.COM
8	FS2	LINDSAY	ncp	0064	Rply File Search Continue; Failure
9	LINDSAY	FS2	ncp	0064	Req File Search Initialize /LOGIN
10	FS2	LINDSAY	ncp	0064	Rply File Search Initialize
11	LINDSAY	FS2	ncp	0074	Req File Search Continue LOGIN.EXE
12	FS2	LINDSAY	ncp	0088	Rply File Search Continue LOGIN.E
13	LINDSAY	FS2	ncp	0076	Req Open File /LOGIN/LOGIN.EXE
14	FS2	LINDSAY	ncp	0092	Rply Open File LOGIN.EXE
15	LINDSAY	FS2	ncp	0068	Req Read LOGIN.EXE; 30 bytes
16	FS2	LINDSAY	ncp	0088	Rply Read; 30 bytes
17	LINDSAY	FS2	ncp	0068	Req Read LOGIN.EXE; 512 bytes
18	FS2	LINDSAY	ncp	0570	Rply Read; 512 bytes
19	LINDSAY	FS2	ncp	0068	Req Read LOGIN.EXE; 1024 bytes

(Download LOGIN.EXE to the client)

No.	Source	Destination	Layer	Size	Summary
253	LINDSAY	FS2	ncp	0068	Req Read LOGIN.EXE; 30 bytes
254	FS2	LINDSAY	ncp	0088	Rply Read; 30bytes
255	LINDSAY	FS2	ncp	0064	Req Close File LOGIN.EXE
256	FS2	LINDSAY	ncp	0064	Rply Close File
257	LINDSAY	FS2	ncp	0064	Req Get Bindery Access Level
258	FS2	LINDSAY	ncp	0064	Rply Get Bindery Access Level
259	LINDSAY	FS2	ncp	0084	Req Read Property Value
260	FS2	LINDSAY	ncp	0186	Rply Read Property Value
261	LINDSAY	Broadcast	rip	0064	Req network=C9 40 83 46
262	SALES1	LINDSAY	rip	0064	Resp network=C9 40 83 46; 1 hops
263	LINDSAY	SALES1	ncp	0064	Req Create Service Connection
264	SALES1	LINDSAY	ncp	0064	Rply CreateService Connection
265	LINDSAY	SALES1	ncp	0064	Req Get FileServer Information
266	SALES1	LINDSAY	ncp	0184	Rply Get FileServer Information
267	LINDSAY	SALES1	ncp	0064	Req Negotiate Buffer Size
268	SALES1	LINDSAY	ncp	0064	Rply Negotiate Buffer Size
269	LINDSAY	FS2	ncp	0064	Req End Of Job
270	FS2	LINDSAY	ncp	0064	Rply End Of Job
271	LINDSAY	SALES1	ncp	0064	Req End Of Job
272	SALES1	LINDSAY	ncp	0064	Rply End Of Job
273	LINDSAY	FS2	ncp	0064	Req Logout
274	FS2	LINDSAY	ncp	0064	Rply Logout
275	LINDSAY	SALES1	ncp	0064	Req Logout
276	SALES1	LINDSAY	ncp	0064	Rply Logout
277	LINDSAY	FS2	ncp	0064	Req Destroy Service Connection
278	FS2	LINDSAY	ncp	0064	Rply Destroy Service Connection
279	LINDSAY	SALES1	ncp	0070	Req Get Bindery Object ID
280	SALES1	LINDSAY	ncp	0110	Rply Get Bindery Object ID
281	LINDSAY	SALES1	ncp	0064	Req Get Log Key
282	SALES1	LINDSAY	ncp	0064	Rply Get Log Key
283	LINDSAY	SALES1	ncp	0070	Req Get Bindery Object ID
284	SALES1	LINDSAY	ncp	0110	Rply Get Bindery Object ID
285	LINDSAY	SALES1	ncp	0078	Req Keyed Login
286	SALES1	LINDSAY	ncp	0064	Rply Keyed Login; Failure

FIGURE 15.3

NCP calls during the login process

FIGURE 15.3

NCP calls during the login

process (continued)

287	LINDSAY	SALES1	ncp	0064	Req	Get Log Key
288	SALES1	LINDSAY	ncp	0064	Rply	Get Log Key
289	LINDSAY	SALES1	ncp	0070	Req	Get Bindery Object ID
290	SALES1	LINDSAY	ncp	0110	Rply	Get Bindery Object ID
291	LINDSAY	SALES1	ncp	0078	Req	Keyed Login
292	SALES1	LINDSAY	ncp	0064	Rply	Keyed Login
293	LINDSAY	SALES1	ncp	0066	Req	Alloc Permanent Directory Ha
294	SALES1	LINDSAY	ncp	0064	Rply	Alloc Permanent Directory Ha
295	LINDSAY	SALES1	ncp	0064	Req	Deallocate Directory Handle
296	SALES1	LINDSAY	ncp	0064	Rply	Deallocate Directory Handle
297	LINDSAY	SALES1	ncp	0066	Req	Set Directory Handle LOGIN
298	SALES1	LINDSAY	ncp	0064	Rply	Set Directory Handle
299	LINDSAY	SALES1	ncp	0064	Req	Get File Server Date and Tim
300	SALES1	LINDSAY	ncp	0064	Rply	Get File Server Date and Tim
301	LINDSAY	SALES1	ncp	0064	Req	Get Bindery Access Level
302	SALES1	LINDSAY	ncp	0064	Rply	Get Bindery Access Level
303	LINDSAY	SALES1	ncp	0064	Req	Get Station's Logged Informa
304	SALES1	LINDSAY	ncp	0118	Rply	Get Station's Logged Informa
305	LINDSAY	SALES1	ncp	0064	Req	Get Internet Address
306	SALES1	LINDSAY	ncp	0068	Rply	Get Internet Address
307	LINDSAY	SALES1	ncp	0086	Req	Read Property Value
308	SALES1	LINDSAY	ncp	0186	Rply	Read Property Value
309	LINDSAY	SALES1	ncp	0082	Req	Search for File SYS:PUBLIC/N
310	SALES1	LINDSAY	ncp	0088	Rply	Search for File NET$LOG.DAT
311	LINDSAY	SALES1	ncp	0082	Req	Open File SYS:PUBLIC/NET$LOG
312	SALES1	LINDSAY	ncp	0092	Rply	Open File NET$LOG.DAT
313	LINDSAY	SALES1	ncp	0068	Req	Read NET$LOG.DAT; 512 bytes

The following lists the general sequence for logging in to a NetWare server:

1 • Locate and download the LOGIN.EXE file from the server you attached to (primary server).

2 • Find out your privileges in the LOGIN directory.

3 • Locate the server you wish to log in to (preferred server).

4 • Create the service connection and obtain information about the server.

5 • Negotiate the buffer size.

6 • End the job with both the servers and log out from each.

7 • Destroy your connection with the primary server.

8 • Submit your password.

9 · Allocate a directory handle for LOGIN.

10 · Get additional information regarding bindery access and client/server information.

STEP 1: LOCATE AND DOWNLOAD THE LOGIN.EXE FILE FROM THE SERVER YOU ATTACHED TO (PRIMARY SERVER)

In Figure 15.3, note in packet 2 an Open File; Failure response from the server. These are common in NetWare when you are opening a file; this response indicates that either the file is not in the directory where you are located or you haven't typed the entire file name. The system must attempt to execute the file name you typed by first placing a .COM extension at the end. If that fails, it then places an .EXE extension at the end of the file name. Finally, it attempts to open the file with .BAT as the extension.

In packet 13, the client has found the LOGIN.EXE file and is requesting to open it. Packets 15 through 254 were used to download the file LOGIN.EXE to the client.

STEP 2: FIND OUT YOUR PRIVILEGES IN THE LOGIN DIRECTORY

In packet number 257, Get Bindery Access Level is the NCP call to get your privileges in the LOGIN directory. By default, you are given "anyone read, anyone write" privileges to the LOGIN directory. After you log in, you are granted "logged read, logged write" privileges to the LOGIN directory.

STEP 3: LOCATE THE SERVER YOU WISH TO LOG IN TO (PREFERRED SERVER)

If the server you are attached to (the primary server) is not the one you have requested in your login argument, you query the server bindery for the network address of the server you want to log in to (your preferred server) (packets 259 and 260).

NOTE
Even though you do not specify "preferred server" when loading the shell, the server you explicitly log in to becomes your preferred server.

STEP 4: CREATE THE SERVICE CONNECTION AND OBTAIN INFORMATION ABOUT THE SERVER

In packet 263, you can see that the Create Service Connection (NCP type 1111) is issued to the preferred server.

STEP 5: NEGOTIATE THE BUFFER SIZE

Next, the station and the server negotiate buffer sizes. Once they each report their maximum buffer sizes, their communications will occur using the lowest buffer size negotiated during this phase (packets 267 and 268). If they are not using Novell's Large Internet Packet (LIP) protocol and there is a router between the client and the server, they will default to 576-byte packets.

STEP 6: END THE JOB WITH BOTH THE SERVERS AND LOG OUT FROM EACH

The client then ends the job with both servers and sends a Logout NCP request to each (packets 269–276). This ensures that any connections that had been previously held open for the client are terminated.

STEP 7: DESTROY YOUR CONNECTION WITH THE PRIMARY SERVER

Now that the client has connected to the preferred server, it sends a Destroy Service Connection NCP (NCP request type 5555) to the primary server (packets 277 and 278). The client no longer has any connection or association with that server until it explicitly requests it or reloads NETX.

STEP 8: SUBMIT YOUR PASSWORD

Packets 285 through 292 consist of an exchange of a *log key*—the specific encryption sequence—from the server and the encrypted password from the client.

STEP 9: ALLOCATE A DIRECTORY HANDLE FOR LOGIN

In packet 297, the client requests that a directory handle be set for the login directory. The client is now prepared to use a directory handle for the LOGIN directory of its preferred server.

STEP 10: GET ADDITIONAL INFORMATION REGARDING BINDERY ACCESS AND CLIENT/SERVER INFORMATION

In packets 299 through 308, the client is requesting information regarding rights, internet address, and logged information. The rights granted at this time are "logged read, logged write"; these are the privileges required to access the system login script. The Internet Address includes the network number and workstation node address. The station's logged information is a synopsis of station information such as login name, login time, and user ID (\MAIL\[USER ID]).

Once the client has completed the steps listed above, it can then begin to read the system login script (NET$LOG.DAT), user login script (\MAIL\[USER ID]\LOGIN.DAT), CAPTURE.EXE file, print job configuration file (PRINTCON.DAT), and printer device definitions (NET$PRN.DAT).

Now let's examine NetWare's security process and how you can use the LANalyzer to detect intruders on the network.

NetWare Security

NetWare's security cannot be broken into by using a protocol analyzer. Passwords are encrypted with a one-way encryption scheme. The encryption scheme is dynamic, constantly changing the key, so a password is never encrypted the same way twice. In fact, if you provide the wrong password when logging in, the server will give a second login key for your second attempt at the password.

As shown during the login procedure, the client requests the log key from the server. It then applies the key to the password before sending it to the server. Figure 15.4 shows a client requesting the encryption key (packet 275), receiving the encryption key (packet 276), and transmitting the encrypted password to the server (packet 279).

If the password is incorrect, the server replies with a Keyed Login; Failure response, as shown in Figure 15.4.

F I G U R E   15.4

Keyed Login; Failure indicates that the password is incorrect.

271	LINDSAY	SALES1	ncp	0064	Req Logout
272	SALES1	LINDSAY	ncp	0064	Rply Logout
273	LINDSAY	SALES1	ncp	0070	Req Get Bindery Object ID
274	SALES1	LINDSAY	ncp	0110	Rply Get Bindery Object ID
275	LINDSAY	SALES1	ncp	0064	Req Get Log Key
276	SALES1	LINDSAY	ncp	0064	Rply Get Log Key
277	LINDSAY	SALES1	ncp	0070	Req Get Bindery Object ID
278	SALES1	LINDSAY	ncp	0110	Rply Get Bindery Object ID
279	LINDSAY	SALES1	ncp	0078	Req Keyed Login
280	SALES1	LINDSAY	ncp	0064	Rply Keyed Login; Failure
281	LINDSAY	SALES1	ncp	0064	Req Get Log Key
282	SALES1	LINDSAY	ncp	0064	Rply Get Log Key
283	LINDSAY	SALES1	ncp	0070	Req Get Bindery Object ID
284	SALES1	LINDSAY	ncp	0110	Rply Get Bindery Object ID
285	LINDSAY	SALES1	ncp	0078	Req Keyed Login
286	LINDSAY	SALES1	ncp	0078	Req Keyed Login
287	SALES1	LINDSAY	ncp	0064	Rply Rqst Being Processed; Conn=1
288	LINDSAY	SALES1	ncp	0078	Req Keyed Login
289	SALES1	LINDSAY	ncp	0064	Rply Rqst Being Processed; Conn=1
290	SALES1	LINDSAY	ncp	0064	Rply Keyed Login; Failure

When a user attempts to log in, the client process (shell) makes two attempts to supply a password to the server before informing the user of a failure. When the first attempt to supply an encrypted password fails (packet 280), the client asks for a second log key (packet 281) and resubmits the password with the new key (packet 285). If this second attempt also fails, the message "Access to server denied" is displayed and the user must reissue the LOGIN.EXE command.

Now let's look at how to tell if the user name was incorrectly entered at the workstation.

INCORRECT USER NAME
If the client types the wrong user name, the server notifies the client that the object is not in the bindery, as shown in Figure 15.5.

```
Packet Number : 285          5:26:17PM
Length : 66 bytes
802.3: =================== IEEE 802.3 Datalink Layer ===================
         Station: LINDSAY ——> SALES1
         Length: 48
  ipx: =================== Internetwork Packet Exchange =================
         Checksum: 0xFFFF
         Length: 48
         Hop Count:  0
         Packet Type: 17(NCP)
         Network: C9 99 00 06        ->  C9 40 83 46
         Node:    LINDSAY            ->  00-00-00-00-00-01
         Socket:  0x4003            ->  NCP
  ncp: =================== NetWare Core Protocol =====================
         NCP Request: Get Bindery Object ID
         Request Type: 0x2222 (Request)
         Sequence Number: 5
         Connection Number Low: 11
         Task Number: 1
         Connection Number High: 0
         Function Code: 23
         Subfunction Length: 9 bytes
         Subfunction Code: 53
         Object Type: 1 (User)
         Object Name: Length: 5
                      Value : LAURA


Packet Number : 286          5:26:17PM
Length : 64 bytes
802.3: =================== IEEE 802.3 Datalink Layer ===================
         Station: SALES1 ——> LINDSAY
         Length: 38
  ipx: =================== Internetwork Packet Exchange =================
         Checksum: 0xFFFF
         Length: 38
         Hop Count:  0
         Packet Type: 17(NCP)
         Network: C9 40 83 46        ->  C9 99 00 06
         Node:    00-00-00-00-00-01  ->  LINDSAY
         Socket:  NCP               ->  0x4003
  ncp: =================== NetWare Core Protocol =====================
         NCP Reply: Get Bindery Object ID
         Reply Type: 0x3333 (Reply)
         Sequence Number: 5
         Connection Number Low: 11
         Task Number: 1
         Connection Number High: 0
         Completion Code: 252 (No Such Object)
         Connection Status: 0x00
```

FIGURE 15.5

The response No Such Object indicates that the user name does not exist in the bindery.

The user will still be prompted to enter the password, however. This has always been considered a security feature since it masks whether the user name was wrong or the password was wrong.

As shown in this section, if a user complains that he cannot access the NetWare server, you can simply view the packets transmitted during the login process to determine if they are submitting the wrong password or user name.

Watching for Unauthorized Network Users

Some protocol analyzers can alert you to unauthorized users even before they execute LOGIN.EXE. As shown in Figure 15.1, when a client issues NETX.COM, it begins transmitting SAP and RIP packets on the wire. Analyzers such as the LANalyzer have a "new station" alarm that can be triggered each time a new node address is discovered.

In Figure 15.6, you are viewing a LANalyzer log file listing the users that have been discovered and the detection dates and times. If desired, you can have an audible alarm or an alarm banner (visual alarm) notify you of a new user, as well.

This has become a fairly common procedure for network security enhancements. The administrator can set up the application to run in the evening and log all new station access information to a single file. If a new station is detected at midnight, when no one should be accessing the network, the log file provides the node address of the user, as shown in Figure 15.6.

Although NetWare's time restrictions are generally sufficient for keeping users off the network during certain off-business hours, you can use the LANalyzer to track attempts by unknown stations, such as portables, to gain access to the network at any time.

Next, you will see how the server replies to stations attempting to read or write files without the appropriate directory or file privileges.

```
Log : 09/10/92 19:26:16 New station with address exosC16258detected
Log : 09/10/92 19:26:16 New station with address novell134230Fdetected
Log : 09/10/92 19:26:16 New station with address novell1E8667detected
Log : 09/10/92 19:26:16 New station with address cisco021602detected
Log : 09/10/92 19:26:16 New station with address novell133E9BDdetected
Log : 09/10/92 19:26:16 New station with address exosC14126detected
Log : 09/10/92 19:26:16 New station with address exos556013detected
Log : 09/10/92 19:26:16 New station with address novell102A4A2detected
Log : 09/10/92 19:26:17 New station with address novell1E8474detected
Log : 09/10/92 19:26:17 New station with address novell131D74Bdetected
Log : 09/10/92 19:26:17 New station with address novell1E5188detected
Log : 09/10/92 19:26:17 New station with address novell1E5A6Cdetected
Log : 09/10/92 19:26:17 New station with address novell15199Cdetected
Log : 09/10/92 19:26:17 New station with address novell1315391detected
Log : 09/10/92 19:26:17 New station with address novell103E112detected
Log : 09/10/92 19:26:17 New station with address novell190ED5detected
Log : 09/10/92 19:26:17 New station with address novell1032464detected
Log : 09/10/92 19:26:17 New station with address novell1326EE6detected
Log : 09/10/92 19:26:17 New station with address hp13F8E4detected
Log : 09/10/92 19:26:17 New station with address novell130C4D3detected
Log : 09/10/92 19:26:18 New station with address novell1E1BD9detected
Log : 09/10/92 19:26:18 New station with address novell13458DFdetected
Log : 09/10/92 19:26:18 New station with address novell1E8456detected
Log : 09/10/92 19:26:19 New station with address novell1E375Ddetected
Log : 09/10/92 19:26:19 New station with address novell131B695detected
Log : 09/10/92 19:26:20 New station with address novell131AA8Fdetected
Log : 09/10/92 19:26:21 New station with address novell1E248Ddetected
Log : 09/10/92 19:26:21 New station with address novell1350774detected
Log : 09/10/92 19:26:21 New station with address novell1E866Adetected
Log : 09/10/92 19:26:23 New station with address novell1351DC3detected
Log : 09/10/92 19:26:25 New station with address novell102F04Edetected
Log : 09/10/92 19:26:25 New station with address intel0C759Fdetected
Log : 09/10/92 19:26:25 New station with address novell1315410detected
Log : 09/10/92 19:26:26 New station with address novell1E8631detected
Log : 09/10/92 19:26:27 New station with address intel0C76F4detected
Log : 09/10/92 19:26:27 New station with address novell1E85E6detected
Log : 09/10/92 19:26:29 New station with address novell1315092detected
Log : 09/10/92 19:26:29 New station with address novell1E1047detected
Log : 09/10/92 19:26:29 New station with address novell1EF36Bdetected
Log : 09/10/92 19:26:29 New station with address novell1E5987detected
Log : 09/10/92 19:26:29 New station with address novell130FF9Bdetected
Log : 09/10/92 19:26:29 New station with address novell131A234detected
Log : 09/10/92 19:26:29 New station with address00-00-0E-1A-CE-46 detected
Log : 09/10/92 19:26:29 New station with address novell1318E7Edetected
Log : 09/10/92 19:26:29 New station with address intel044E1Cdetected
Log : 09/10/92 19:26:29 New station with address novell135040Ddetected
Log : 09/10/92 19:26:29 New station with address novell141C057detected
Log : 09/10/92 19:26:30 New station with address novell1E1AA5detected
Log : 09/10/92 19:26:31 New station with address exosF10530detected
Log : 09/10/92 19:26:32 New station with address novell1E119Edetected
Log : 09/10/92 19:26:34 New station with address novell130386Adetected
Log : 09/10/92 19:26:34 New station with address novell103CEC1detected
Log : 09/10/92 19:26:34 New station with address exosC40940detected
Log : 09/10/92 19:26:34 New station with address exosC38746detected
Log : 09/10/92 19:26:34 New station with address exos565529detected
Log : 09/10/92 19:26:35 New station with address novell19101Adetected
```

FIGURE 15.6

LANalyzer alarm log file

Viewing Access Rights/Privileges

When a client attempts to write a file to the server, the client must first determine what rights it has to the directory in which it is located. This information is supplied through the Get Bindery Access Level NCP call. The client wishing to write to the directory will request its bindery privilege information, and the server will supply it.

In Figure 15.7, the station is attempting to write a file, TEMP.BAT, to the PUBLIC directory. Packet 5 is the NCP request, Create File. Packet 6 is the NCP reply.

In packet number 6, you can see the server returning the NCP Create File reply with a completion code of 132 (no create privileges). This is why the user cannot save his file to the PUBLIC directory.

In Figure 15.8, you are viewing a user's attempt to delete a file from the PUBLIC directory.

Packet 11 is the user's request to delete the file SYSCON.EXE. In packet 12, the server replies, stating that the request is denied because the file is flagged Read Only. Using the LANalyzer, you can set up an application that filters on requests to delete files (function code 68) if you are concerned about the integrity and safety of data.

This chapter has examined the NETX sequence for attaching to a primary server and differentiated among the three server connection priorities (primary, preferred, and default). You have viewed the login procedure as well as an attempt to create and delete a file without proper access privileges.

The next chapter focuses on characterizing NetWare server performance.

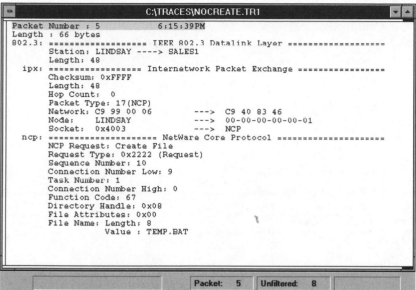

*The user attempts to write
to the PUBLIC directory.*

```
─  ▭                    C:\TRACES\NOCREATE.TR1                    ▼ ▲
Packet Number : 5              6:15:39PM
Length : 66 bytes
802.3: ================== IEEE 802.3 Datalink Layer ==================
       Station: LINDSAY ----> SALES1
       Length: 48
  ipx: ================== Internetwork Packet Exchange ================
       Checksum: 0xFFFF
       Length: 48
       Hop Count:  0
       Packet Type: 17(NCP)
       Network: C9 99 00 06      --->  C9 40 83 46
       Node:    LINDSAY          --->  00-00-00-00-00-01
       Socket:  0x4003           --->  NCP
  ncp: ================== NetWare Core Protocol ===================
       NCP Request: Create File
       Request Type: 0x2222 (Request)
       Sequence Number: 10
       Connection Number Low: 9
       Task Number: 1
       Connection Number High: 0
       Function Code: 67
       Directory Handle: 0x08
       File Attributes: 0x00
       File Name: Length: 8
                  Value : TEMP.BAT




                              Packet:  5    Unfiltered:  8
```

```
─  ▭                    C:\TRACES\NOCREATE.TR1                    ▼ ▲
Packet Number : 6              6:15:39PM
Length : 64 bytes
802.3: ================== IEEE 802.3 Datalink Layer ==================
       Station: SALES1 ----> LINDSAY
       Length: 38
  ipx: ================== Internetwork Packet Exchange ================
       Checksum: 0xFFFF
       Length: 38
       Hop Count:  0
       Packet Type: 17(NCP)
       Network: C9 40 83 46      --->  C9 99 00 06
       Node:    00-00-00-00-00-01 --->  LINDSAY
       Socket:  NCP              --->  0x4003
  ncp: ================== NetWare Core Protocol ===================
       NCP Reply: Create File
       Reply Type: 0x3333 (Reply)
       Sequence Number: 10
       Connection Number Low: 9
       Task Number: 1
       Connection Number High: 0
       Completion Code: 132 (No Create Privileges)
       Connection Status: 0x00






                              Packet:  6    Unfiltered:  8
```

FIGURE 15.8

*The user without rights
attempts to delete a file.*

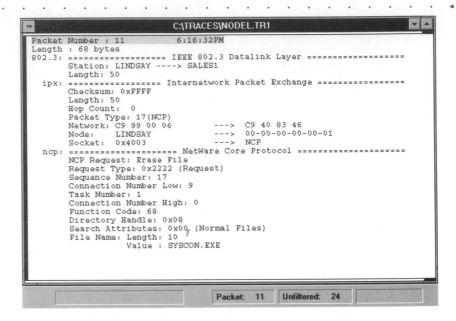

```
┌─────────────────────────────────── C:\TRACES\NODEL.TR1 ──────────────────────────┐
│                                                                                   │
│ Packet Number : 11              6:16:32PM                                         │
│ Length : 68 bytes                                                                 │
│ 802.3: =================== IEEE 802.3 Datalink Layer ===================          │
│         Station: LINDSAY ----> SALES1                                             │
│         Length: 50                                                                │
│   ipx: =================== Internetwork Packet Exchange ===================       │
│         Checksum: 0xFFFF                                                           │
│         Length: 50                                                                │
│         Hop Count:  0                                                              │
│         Packet Type: 17(NCP)                                                       │
│         Network: C9 99 00 06          --->  C9 40 83 46                            │
│         Node:    LINDSAY              --->  00-00-00-00-00-01                      │
│         Socket:  0x4003               --->  NCP                                   │
│   ncp: =================== NetWare Core Protocol ===================               │
│         NCP Request: Erase File                                                   │
│         Request Type: 0x2222 (Request)                                            │
│         Sequence Number: 17                                                        │
│         Connection Number Low: 9                                                   │
│         Task Number: 1                                                             │
│         Connection Number High: 0                                                  │
│         Function Code: 68                                                          │
│         Directory Handle: 0x08                                                     │
│         Search Attributes: 0x00 (Normal Files)                                    │
│         File Name: Length: 10                                                      │
│                    Value : SYSCON.EXE                                             │
│                                                                                   │
│                                        Packet:  11   Unfiltered:  24              │
└───────────────────────────────────────────────────────────────────────────────────┘
```

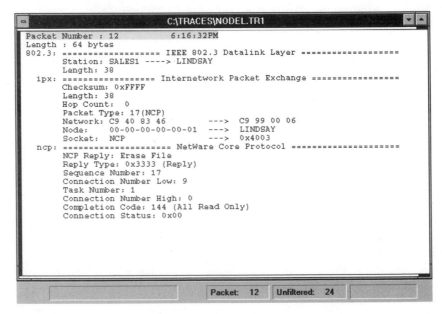

```
┌─────────────────────────────────── C:\TRACES\NODEL.TR1 ──────────────────────────┐
│                                                                                   │
│ Packet Number : 12              6:16:32PM                                         │
│ Length : 64 bytes                                                                 │
│ 802.3: =================== IEEE 802.3 Datalink Layer ===================          │
│         Station: SALES1 ----> LINDSAY                                             │
│         Length: 38                                                                │
│   ipx: =================== Internetwork Packet Exchange ===================       │
│         Checksum: 0xFFFF                                                           │
│         Length: 38                                                                │
│         Hop Count:  0                                                              │
│         Packet Type: 17(NCP)                                                       │
│         Network: C9 40 83 46          --->  C9 99 00 06                            │
│         Node:    00-00-00-00-00-01    --->  LINDSAY                               │
│         Socket:  NCP                   --->  0x4003                               │
│   ncp: =================== NetWare Core Protocol ===================               │
│         NCP Reply: Erase File                                                      │
│         Reply Type: 0x3333 (Reply)                                                │
│         Sequence Number: 17                                                        │
│         Connection Number Low: 9                                                   │
│         Task Number: 1                                                             │
│         Connection Number High: 0                                                  │
│         Completion Code: 144 (All Read Only)                                      │
│         Connection Status: 0x00                                                   │
│                                                                                   │
│                                        Packet:  12   Unfiltered:  24              │
└───────────────────────────────────────────────────────────────────────────────────┘
```

CHAPTER 16

Characterizing
Server Performance

Previous chapters have discussed the nature of NCP-based communications. Clients send a request to the server, and the server replies. However, what if a client sends a request to a server and the server is too busy handling other requests? The server cannot process the client's request. This chapter focuses on NetWare server performance. First, you will examine a NetWare server that is not overloaded. You will characterize the types of requests the server typically handles. Next, you will analyze network traffic involving a server that is overloaded. Finally, you will determine the cause of the server overload and learn about the steps available to relieve burdened NetWare servers.

Setting Up a Server Workload Test

In order to characterize the server's workload, you must follow these steps:

1 · Determine the server to examine.

2 · Create an application to filter on NCP traffic.

3 · Plot the data.

STEP 1: DETERMINE THE SERVER TO EXAMINE

Unless you specify a single server within the application you create, you will be characterizing all servers' performance information. To characterize traffic from a single NetWare v3.x server, filter on the server's internal IPX address in the IPX header. Figure 16.1 shows a packet that has been received from a NetWare v3.x server. Note that the address in the IPX header differs from the address in the Ethernet header. Remember, if a packet has crossed a router, the Ethernet source address will be the physical address of the router, not the server. Therefore, the server's address must go in the IPX header's source address (or destination address) field, not the Ethernet header's source address (or destination address) field.

```
┌─────────────────────────────────────────────────────────────────┐
│ ▭                    LANalyzer for NetWare                    ▼│◆│
│ File  Monitor  Alarms  Capture  Decode  Window  Help             │
│ ┌───────────────────────────────────────────────────────────┐▼│▲│
│ │ ▭                     Capture Buffer                      ▼│▲│ │
│ │ Packet Number : 2           6:05:18PM                         │ │
│ │ Length : 64 bytes                                             │ │
│ │ 802.3: =================== IEEE 802.3 Datalink Layer ======== │ │
│ │        Station: 00-00-1B-15-04-93 ----> 08-00-09-13-D4-DD     │ │
│ │        Length: 38                          Router to Workstation │ │
│ │   ipx: ================ Internetwork Packet Exchange ======== │ │
│ │        Checksum: 0xFFFF                                        │ │
│ │        Length: 38                                             │ │
│ │        Hop Count: 4                        Server to Workstation │ │
│ │        Packet Type: 17(NCP)                                   │ │
│ │        Network: C9 13 86 38      --->  C9 99 01 64            │ │
│ │        Node:    00-00-00-00-00-01 --->  08-00-09-13-D4-DD    │ │
│ │        Socket:  NCP              --->  0x4000                 │ │
│ │   ncp: ================ NetWare Core Protocol =============== │ │
│ │        NCP Reply: Service Queue Job                           │ │
│ │        Reply Type: 0x3333 (Reply)                             │ │
│ │        Sequence Number: 87                                    │ │
│ │        Connection Number Low: 1                               │ │
│ │        Task Number: 1                                         │ │
│ │        Connection Number High: 0                              │ │
│ │        Completion Code: 213 (No Queue Job)                    │ │
│ │        Connection Status: 0x00                                │ │
│ │                                                               │ │
│ └───────────────────────────────────────────────────────────┘ │
│              │  Packet:  2  │  Unfiltered:  5  │                 │
└─────────────────────────────────────────────────────────────────┘
```

F I G U R E 16.1

The IPX header specifies the server being examined; the Ethernet header specifies the router that forwarded the packet onto the local network.

If you do not know the internal IPX address of the server, log in to the network and type **SLIST**. You will receive a listing of all server names, internal IPX addresses (or LAN card A addresses for NetWare 2.x servers), and node addresses, as shown in Figure 16.2.

Known NetWare File Servers	Network	Node Address Status
FS1	[A87666][	1]
FS2	[A190FF9A][	1]
FS3	[A88AA88A][	1]
FS4	[CC007000][	1]
MKTG-45	[C9408346][	1]
MKTG-SE	[C0000016][	1]
SALES1	[C9138638][	1]
SALES2	[C0CB4117][	1]
SALES3	[1020001][	1]

Total of 9 file servers found.

F I G U R E 16.2

The SLIST command lists all known servers on the network, as well as their network and node addresses.

You can identify NetWare 3.x servers by the node address 0x00-00-00-00-00-01. Once you have determined the server whose local traffic you would like to characterize, place your analyzer on that server's network, as shown in Figure 16.3. This ensures that you are viewing all traffic to and from that server; routers and bridges are not filtering out traffic. If a server is acting as a router between multiple networks, you may wish to examine the server's activity on each of the attached networks. If you examine only one of the networks to which the server is attached, you are not creating a complete report of the server's activity; you are only gathering server activity information for the local network.

In the example, you can place your LANalyzer on either segment of the same network as the server SALES1, the server you are going to characterize local traffic for.

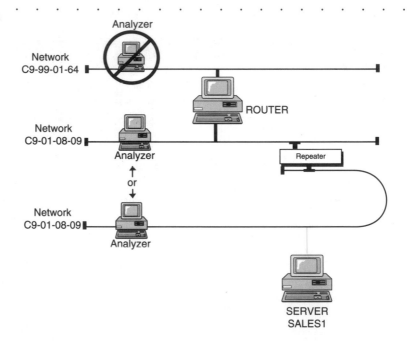

FIGURE 16.3

Place your analyzer on the server's network.

STEP 2: CREATE AN APPLICATION TO FILTER ON NCP TRAFFIC

Set up an application that filters on specific NCP function codes. The application should also capture broadcast packets (addressed to FF-FF-FF-FF-FF-FF in the Ethernet header), routed packets (greater than 0 in transport control field), and Request Being Processed packets (NCP type 9999). The application must filter on these Request Being Processed packets in order to locate servers that are potentially overloaded. Later in this chapter, you will examine the implications of these Request Being Processed packets.

You must also determine the collection time and sampling period for your application. For how long do you want to collect data, and at what frequency? For example, perhaps you want to characterize server traffic at 2:00 P.M. You may wish to collect data for 15 minutes, sampling every 20 seconds.

In Figure 16.4, the LANalyzer's predefined application, PERFORM, is being used to characterize the performance of the server SALES1. The PERFORM application is filtering on delay (Request Being Processed packets), broadcasts, logins, file reads/writes, messages, queues, bridge (routed packets), and all NetWare traffic in general.

STEP 3: PLOT THE DATA

To obtain a clear view of server performance, you can plot the data using a spreadsheet program. In Figure 16.5, the data has been exported in CSV (comma-separated value) format. Next, the data was imported into the spreadsheet and a line graph format was selected to graph the data.

By viewing this graph, you can see that most requests made from server SALES1 are file requests. In this application, the server SALES1 is not transmitting any Request Being Processed packets. You can determine, therefore, that the server is keeping up with client requests. If users are complaining of slow responses from the network, you can determine that the server is not at fault. Once this has been determined, you can look at other sources

The LANalyzer PERFORM
application characterizes
server performance.

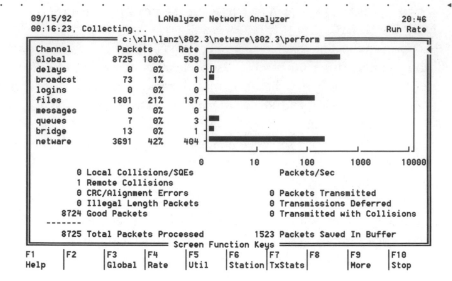

The data is plotted in a line
graph format.

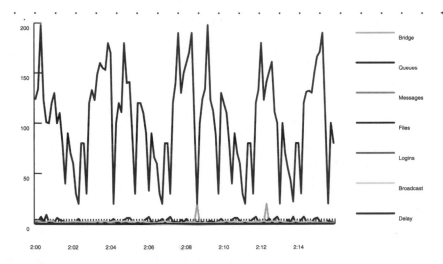

for the network delay, such as an overloaded cabling system. The next step would be to test the utilization on the server's segment and the client's segment, as defined in Chapter 3.

Next, you will locate an overloaded server, characterize the traffic, and determine the possible cause for the overload condition.

Locating an Overloaded Server

To locate a server that is not keeping up with client requests, you must look for Request Being Processed packets on the network.

NetWare servers include a flow control mechanism that enables them to report an overload condition to client shells. When a client sends requests to a server, the client shell expects a response within the IPX timeout period.

When a workstation does not receive a response within the timeout period, it assumes the server has not received the original request. It reexecutes the request. This retransmission function is useful if packets are lost or network access is interrupted. This may be the result of an overloaded cabling segment—the server may not be able to access the media to reply. This reexecution process, however, does not indicate an overloaded server. To help control workstation requests to an overloaded server, Novell has created the unique NCP type 9999, Request Being Processed, to indicate an overloaded server.

When a client transmits a request to an overloaded server, the server replies with a Request Being Processed packet, as shown in Figure 16.6.

These Request Being Processed packets are a clear indication that the server cannot keep up with all the work it is currently handling. However, it is not necessarily the fault of the workstation that received the Request Being Processed packet. It may be due to other processes the server is handling. Later in this chapter, you will determine the cause of a server

NOTE
The terms "IPX timeout value" and "IPX retry count" are misleading; it is actually the client shell that will timeout and reexecute the request, not IPX. To maintain consistency with the NET.CFG configuration options, however, this chapter uses the terms that contain 'IPX.'

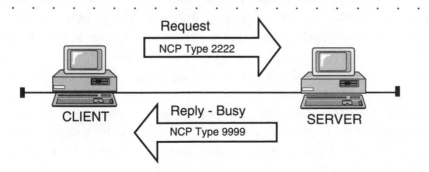

A client requests services, but the server replies that it is busy.

overload condition. First, let's continue to examine the communications between a client and an overloaded server.

Upon receipt of a Request Being Processed packet, the workstation resets its IPX timeout timer and continues to wait for a reply. If the client does not receive any reply within the timeout value, it reexecutes the request. The server can either execute the request and transmit a reply or, if it is busy, transmit another Request Being Processed packet.

A client can reexecute a request up to 20 times without receiving any reply (including a Request Being Processed packet) before giving up. This amount is configurable, however, in the NET.CFG file. For example, you can add the line "IPX RETRY = 50" to make the client more persistent on a busy or problem network segment. When the retry count is reached, the user receives a network error message indicating that the station experienced an "Error Receiving from Server [server name]," indicating that the server did not reply within the timeout value. Remember, however, that you are looking for Request Being Processed packet responses to indicate an overloaded server.

To locate a server that is overloaded, you must create an application that filters on the Request Being Processed NCP type 9999, as shown in Figure 16.7.

When viewing the trace, the NetWare v3.x server that is sending the Request Being Processed packet places its internal IPX address in the IPX header source address field, as shown in Figure 16.8.

Many analyzers provide a name table that allows substitution of the server's name for the internal IPX address. If, however, the server name is not shown within the IPX header, you can use the SLIST command to determine the server name, as discussed earlier in this chapter. In Figure 16.8, a server with the internal IPX network address of C9-40-83-46 has been identified as an overloaded server. By reviewing Figure 16.2, you will discover that it is the MKTG-45 server that is indicating an overload condition.

How many Request Being Processed packets are too many? A few overload packets throughout the day may not cause noticable delay to the users. When users begin to complain of slow response from the server, however, and the server is indicating an overload condition, the number of Request

```
09/15/92                    LANalyzer Network Analyzer                    22:03
Enter hexadecimal number(s)                                           Edit Pattern
╔══════════════ c:\xln\lanz\802.3\netware\802.3\perform ══════════════╗
║↑Station XX XX XX XX XX XX <---- XX XX XX XX XX XX                     ◄
║Type    XXXX
║
║Data:
║Offset    Label              Value
║0000      Checksum           XXXX
║0002      Length             XXXXX
║0004      Transport Ctl      XXX
║0005      Packet Type        XXX
║0006      Dest Network       XX XX XX XX
║000A      Dest Node          XX XX XX XX XX XX
║0010      Dest Socket        XXXX
║0012      Src  Network       XX XX XX XX
║0016      Src  Node          XX XX XX XX XX XX
║001C      Src  Socket        XXXX
║001E      Req Type           9999
║0024      Function Code      XXX
║0025      Function Len       XXXXX
║0027      SubFunction Code   XXX
╚══════════════════════════════════════════════════════════════════════╝

F1    |F2    |F3    |F4    |F5     |F6    |F7    |F8    |F9    |F10
Help  |Copy  |Paste |      |EBCDIC |      |Clear |      |      |Back
```

A filter is set up to look for Request Being Processed packets.

```
┌──────────────────────── LANalyzer for NetWare ────────────────────────┐▼♦
│ File  Monitor  Alarms  Capture  Decode  Window  Help                   │
│┌──────────────────────────── C:\TRACE ─────────────────────────────┐▼♦│
││ Packet Number : 288          5:27:38PM                              │  │
││ Length : 64 bytes                                                   │  │
││ 802.3: ================= IEEE 802.3 Datalink Layer ================= │  │
││        Station: 00-00-1B-03-64-48 ----> 00-00-1B-1E-F2-2C           │  │
││        Length: 38                                                   │  │
││   ipx: ================= Internetwork Packet Exchange ============== │  │
││        Checksum: 0xFFFF                                             │  │
││        Length: 38                                                   │  │
││        Hop Count:  0                        ── Internal IPX Address │  │
││        Packet Type: 17(NCP)                                         │  │
││        Network: C9 40 83 46      ---> C9 99 00 06                   │  │
││        Node:    00-00-00-00-00-01  --->  00-00-1B-1E-F2-2C          │  │
││        Socket:  NCP                --->  0x4003                     │  │
││   ncp: ================= NetWare Core Protocol =================== │  │
││        NCP Message: Request Being Processed                         │  │
││        Reply Type: 0x9999 (Request Being Processed)                 │  │
││        Connection Number Low: 11                                    │  │
││        Task Number: 1                                               │  │
││        Connection Number High: 0                                    │  │
││                                                                     │  │
│└─────────────────────────────────────────────────────────────────────┘  │
│              ┌───────────────┬─────────────┬──────────────┐            │
│              │ Packet:  288  │ Unfiltered: 299 │            │
└────────────────────────────────────────────────────────────────────────┘
```

A Request Being Processed packet contains the server's internal IPX address.

Being Processed packets has most likely become excessive for your network. Next, you will determine the cause of the overload condition.

Determining the Cause of Server Overload

When an overloaded server has been located, you can determine the cause of the overload and take corrective action to improve performance. These are the steps for characterizing an overloaded server's traffic:

1 · Run the server characterization application.

2 · Plot the results.

3 · Look for relationships between traffic and Request Being Processed packets.

STEP 1: RUN THE SERVER CHARACTERIZATION APPLICATION

The characterization application (defined earlier in this chapter) must filter on the overloaded server's address (the internal IPX address for NetWare 3.x servers). The analyzer should also be placed on the segment that the server is on, as shown in Figure 16.9. It should be noted that NetWare servers may have multiple network segments attached; only delay packets sent from the server onto the network local to the analyzer will be seen.

FIGURE 16.9

Filter on SALES1's traffic on the local segment

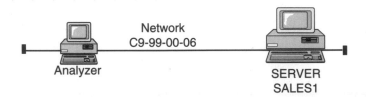

Analyzer

Network
C9-99-00-06

SERVER
SALES1

Internal IPX Network Address: 0xC9-40-83-46
Internal Node Address: 0x00-00-00-00-00-01

Next, define an appropriate length for the test and sampling rate. In this example, you will run the characterization application for 15 minutes, sampling every 20 seconds.

STEP 2: PLOT THE RESULTS

After running the application, plot the results using a spreadsheet program. Figure 16.10 shows the results plotted using a line graph.

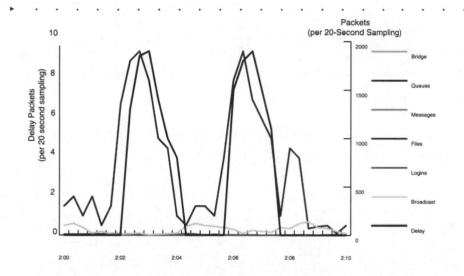

F I G U R E 16.10

The results are plotted

using a line graph.

STEP 3: LOOK FOR RELATIONSHIPS BETWEEN TRAFFIC AND REQUEST BEING PROCESSED PACKETS

The final step in determining the cause of the overload condition requires interpretation of the plotted results. Since Request Being Processed packets are sent when servers are busy, look for a correlation between the Request Being Processed packets and a specific type of activity, such as printing requests or file activity. For example, Figure 16.11 shows only the broadcast packets and the Request Being Processed packets being plotted. You can see there is no relationship between the increase in broadcasts and the Request Being Processed packets. Therefore, you can state that the broadcasts are not causing the server overload.

F I G U R E 16.11

*Broadcast requests
compared with Request
Being Processed packets*

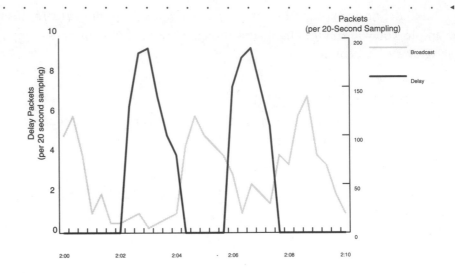

Next, you will compare file activity to Request Being Processed packets. Figure 16.12 shows the graphed results.

F I G U R E 16.12

*File activity compared with
Request Being Processed
packets*

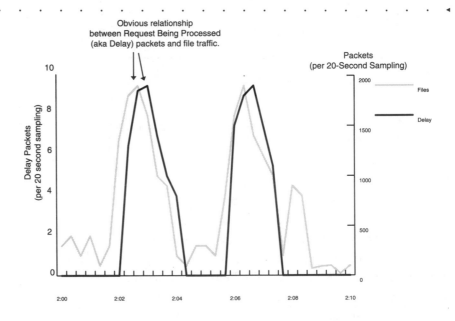

As you can see, the file requests show a direct relationship to the Request Being Processed packets. This indicates that they are causing the server overload condition.

Now let's examine the possible solutions to various server overload conditions.

Balancing Server Loads

Based on the results of the server workload test, you can take several steps to remedy performance problems.

OVERLOAD DUE TO BROADCAST ACTIVITY

If the server is being overloaded due to an extreme number of broadcast requests, track down the source of the requests. For example, if a server begins to report an overload condition at the same time a high number of broadcasts occurs, view the trace to determine who is sending the broadcasts onto the network. Perhaps a workstation has a corrupt shell causing it to send repeated Get Nearest Server packets onto the LAN. The server will respond to each of these packets, eventually causing an overload situation. Replace the faulty shell.

OVERLOAD DUE TO FILE ACTIVITY

If the server is reporting an overload associated with extremely high file activity, check the server to determine if it has enough memory. Most file requests should be serviced from cache on a NetWare server. Check the Monitor screen to see the number of requests being serviced from cache. Chances are that an overload due to file activity indicates a need to increase the server memory.

OVERLOAD DUE TO ROUTED ACTIVITY

If a server cannot handle requests because it is busy routing packets, consider moving the routing responsibility from the server to an external router or another server. It is also possible to redistribute applications or user accounts to minimize the need to route traffic.

OVERLOAD DUE TO PRINT ACTIVITY

If the server is reporting an overload due to excessive print activity, consider moving the queues to another server, or find out which users are most actively sending queue requests. Determine if they can submit jobs to queues on another server.

Another option involves reviewing the queue system and determining if too many users are spooling to a single queue on the network. Redistribute queues across the network, if desired.

You can use this same type of approach to troubleshoot overload due to other NCP request types as well.

In this chapter you have characterized performance on a server that is not overloaded by creating an application filtering on certain NCP function and subfunction codes. This application helped you locate an overloaded server. After plotting the results, you determined the cause of the overload on the network.

Part IV of this book focuses on the features and benefits provided by protocol analyzers.

Protocol Analyzers — Overview and Features

Part IV focuses on the key benefits that protocol analysis can offer through various product features. Review these features to determine which would suit your analysis needs.

Chapter 17 examines the benefits that protocol analysis provides at the physical, data link, and network layers, and reviews analysis options for the upper-layer protocols.

Chapter 18 defines the four primary statistics needed to create a solid baseline and shows you how to differentiate between short-term, real-time statistics and long-term trend statistics.

Chapter 19 shows how to determine the most active stations communicating with a server and those using the most bandwidth on the network and how to locate stations that are transmitting errors onto the LAN.

Chapter 20 examines alarm thresholds and alarm actions that can be used to alert you to unusual or error conditions on the network.

Chapter 21 discusses capture filters (pre-filters) and display filters (post-filters) and takes a look at filtering with Boolean operands.

Chapter 22 discusses creating a network load, packet addressing, various packets that can be copied and transmitted back onto the network, and how to re-create network events.

Chapter 23 defines several protocols you can decode by using an analyzer and examines three methods for viewing decoded data.

CHAPTER 17

Overview of Protocol Analyzers

In Parts I, II, and III of this book, you used several techniques for analyzing, troubleshooting, and optimizing NetWare Ethernet LANs. By this time, you should be familiar with many of the features offered by protocol analyzers. This chapter defines the various benefits of protocol analyzers. It also examines the configuration options, such as hardware and software, or software only.

Protocol analyzers offer a tremendous amount of information about network performance, and you can use them to analyze networks from the physical-layer through the upper-layer protocols. This chapter begins by examining protocol analyzer features for physical-layer analysis.

Physical Layer Analysis

Many analyzers have the capability to test the cabling system on the network. Although a TDR (time domain reflectometer) has been the standard industry tool for testing cabling, many analyzers now include this feature as well. Figure 17.1 shows the LANalyzer's cable check being run on a network.

FIGURE 17.1

LANalyzer cable check

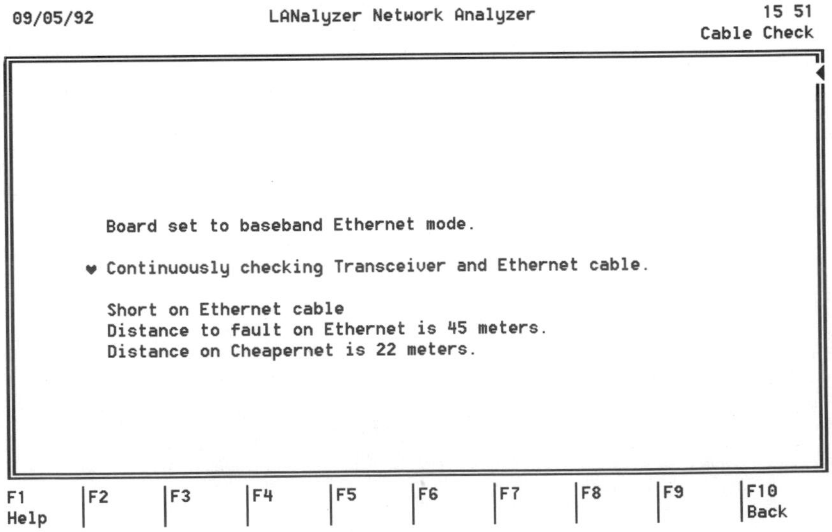

```
09/05/92              LANalyzer Network Analyzer              15 51
                                                         Cable Check



         Board set to baseband Ethernet mode.

       ♥ Continuously checking Transceiver and Ethernet cable.

         Short on Ethernet cable
         Distance to fault on Ethernet is 45 meters.
         Distance on Cheapernet is 22 meters.




   F1    |F2    |F3    |F4    |F5    |F6    |F7    |F8    |F9    |F10
   Help  |      |      |      |      |      |      |      |      |Back
```

The LANalyzer utilizes the rudimentary TDR functionality built into the Ethernet chipset to determine opens (cable breaks) or shorts (contact between conductor and ground). By sending a signal down the cabling system, timing the return signal (if any), and determining if the return signal was in phase or out of phase, the LANalyzer can determine if the cable is experiencing a short or an open condition. You can use analyzers that provide this type of functionality to troubleshoot network backbones and segments, as well as drop cables.

Data Link Layer Analysis

Chapters 4 and 5 of this book were dedicated to data link layer analysis. In these chapters, you viewed several methods for determining frame errors. Analyzers provide a method for looking beyond the workstation error messages to the traffic on the wire.

Analyzers can report an assortment of Ethernet errors, such as

- Local collisions

- Late collisions

- Remote collisions

- Short packets

- Long packets

- CRC/alignment errors

- Jabber

NOTE
Many analyzer vendors use the term "fragments" to define collisions.

Of course, you must understand the implications of each error to determine the cause for the network errors.

Many analyzers do not report all the errors listed above. When purchasing an analyzer, determine what errors it will report and how it defines each error.

As shown in Figure 17.2, you can use an analyzer to determine the source of errors as well. This provides a streamlined method for catching hardware or software errors on the network.

F I G U R E   17.2

You can use the analyzer to determine the source of errors.

```
09/05/92                    LANalyzer Network Analyzer                  21 24
Press ALT-T to toggle between summary modes                     Trace Summary
                          === b:\crc ===
Created On 09/05/92 20:15:32   Elapsed Time 00:00:19    Total Packets     2600

  Pkt# Source        Destination  Protocol    Size  Error  Channels IntPkt Time
   344 novel11EF22C  BLDG4        NetWare       74   CRC    12......   0.403 ms◄
   345 novel11EF22C  BLDG4        NetWare       74   CRC    12......   0.403 ms◄
   346 novel1187450  MKTG         NetWare       64          1.......   0.475 ms
   347 MKTG          novel11EF22C NetWare      184          1.......   0.770 ms
   348 MKTG          novel11EF22C NetWare      184          1.......   0.770 ms
   349 exos8e4501    SALES        NetWare       64          1.......   0.561 ms
   350 BLDG4         novel11EF22C NetWare       64          1.......   0.671 ms
   351 3com90d0b5    SALES        NetWare       64          1.......   0.412 ms
   352 SALES         novel11EF22C NetWare      184          1.......   0.756 ms
   353 novel1897612  ADMIN1       NetWare       64          1.......   0.559 ms
   354 novel1897612  ADMIN1       NetWare       64          1.......   0.559 ms
   355 novel11EF22C  SALES        NetWare       64   CRC    12......   0.392 ms
   356 SALES         novel11EF22C NetWare       64          1.......   0.545 ms
   357 novel11EF22C  BLDG4        NetWare      568   CRC    12......   1.002 ms
   358 BLDG4         novel11EF22C NetWare      390          1.......   1.343 ms
   359 novel1674590  BLDG4        NetWare       64          1 ......   0.521 ms
   360 BLDG4         novel11EF22C NetWare      184          1.......   0.733 ms

F1     F2     F3     F4      F5     F6     F7      F8    F9     F10
Help   Load   Print  Options Buffer Decode Compare Find  Go To  Back
```

Network Layer Analysis

The network layer provides routing information for the internetwork. In a NetWare environment, the IPX header provides routing information and is used to send a packet throughout a large NetWare internet. At this layer, analyzers can be used to determine the distance between clients and servers. This information helps determine if a network cabling system needs reconfiguration or if applications or clients should be moved to other networks because of routing inefficiencies.

In Figure 17.3, you are viewing a LANalyzer application called HOP-COUNT that registers all traffic based upon the number of hops seen in the transport control field of the IPX header.

Generally, most troubleshooting analysis happens at the network layer and below. These are the errors that an administrator can usually handle,

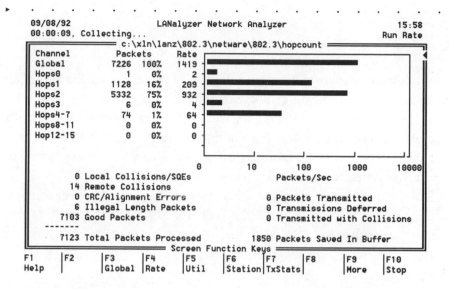

```
09/08/92                  LANalyzer Network Analyzer           15:58
00:00:09, Collecting...                                     Run Rate
┌═══════════ c:\xln\lanz\802.3\netware\802.3\hopcount ═══════════┐
│ Channel     Packets   Rate                                     ◄│
│ Global       7226     100%   1419                               │
│ Hops0           1       0%      2                               │
│ Hops1        1128      16%    209                               │
│ Hops2        5332      75%    932                               │
│ Hops3           6       0%      4                               │
│ Hops4-7        74       1%     64                               │
│ Hops8-11        0       0%      0                               │
│ Hop12-15        0       0%      0                               │
│                                                                 │
│                          0    10      100    1000     10000     │
│          0 Local Collisions/SQEs       Packets/Sec              │
│         14 Remote Collisions                                    │
│          0 CRC/Alignment Errors         0 Packets Transmitted   │
│          6 Illegal Length Packets       0 Transmissions Deferred│
│       7103 Good Packets                 0 Transmitted with Collisions │
│       -------                                                   │
│       7123 Total Packets Processed   1850 Packets Saved In Buffer │
└════════════════════ Screen Function Keys ════════════════════┘
F1    |F2   |F3     |F4   |F5    |F6      |F7      |F8  |F9    |F10
Help  |     |Global |Rate |Util  |Station |TxStats |    |More  |Stop
```

such as swapping out a bad network interface card, reloading a LAN driver, and distributing resources or clients to another network or segment.

However, when a problem does occur above the network layer, analyzers can be used to interpret the communications occurring on the wire. For example, if an application does not load properly from the server, you may wish to use a protocol analyzer to see the downloading process on the wire.

Upper-Layer Protocol Analysis

Upper-layer protocol analysis deals with the transport-, session-, presentation-, and application-layer protocols. In the NetWare environment, these include

▸ SPX

▸ Packet burst

▸ NCP

▸ RIP

▸ SAP

Analysis at this level requires a solid understanding of the protocol's method of communicating. For example, if you wanted to determine whether a network was utilizing the packet burst protocol when it should, you would need a general understanding of how packet burst connections are created, as shown in Figure 17.4. This, in turn, would help you understand why connections may be getting refused by the servers.

Another example involves the analysis of an SPX session between a client and the server. In order to understand why the SPX session is aborting, you can use an analyzer to "listen" to the connection-oriented services on the wire.

F I G U R E 17.4

Analyzers can be used to determine why a packet burst connection is being refused at the server.

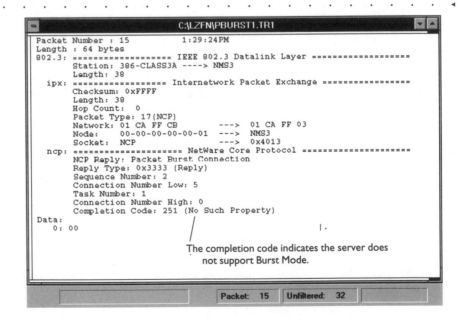

```
C:\LZFN\PBURST1.TR1
Packet Number : 15              1:29:24PM
Length : 64 bytes
802.3: ==================== IEEE 802.3 Datalink Layer ====================
       Station: 386-CLASS3A ----> NMS3
       Length: 38
  ipx: ================== Internetwork Packet Exchange ==================
       Checksum: 0xFFFF
       Length: 38
       Hop Count:  0
       Packet Type: 17(NCP)
       Network: 01 CA FF CB        --->  01 CA FF 03
       Node:    00-00-00-00-00-01  --->  NMS3
       Socket:  NCP                --->  0x4013
  ncp: ==================== NetWare Core Protocol ====================
       NCP Reply: Packet Burst Connection
       Reply Type: 0x3333 (Reply)
       Sequence Number: 2
       Connection Number Low: 5
       Task Number: 1
       Connection Number High: 0
       Completion Code: 251 (No Such Property)
Data:
  0: 00                                              |.

                          Packet:  15   Unfiltered:  32
```

The completion code indicates the server does not support Burst Mode.

You can also use analyzers to measure performance of an upper-layer protocol, such as NCP. After installing new NetWare shells, if you wished to determine whether they were enhancing performance, you could create an application that filters on the station using the new shell. Comparing current performance against the previous shell's performance can help determine if the new shell is more efficient than its predecessor.

You can also examine applications with analyzers. When the workstation loads an application from the server, analyzers can capture the traffic between the server and workstation to see the application download to the client system, as well as any supplemental files the application relies on. For example, if a WordPerfect user continuously complains of having the wrong working environment (such as an unusual color scheme or units instead of points for measurement), you can view the download sequence to determine what .SET file is being loaded with the application, as shown in Figure 17.5.

```
┌──────────────────────── C:\TRACES\WPEXE.TR1 ──────────────────────┐
│ No. │ Source  │ Destination │ Layer │ Summary                         │
│ 539 │ LINDSAY │ SALES1      │ ncp   │ Req  Set Directory Handle /HOME/LC│
│ 540 │ SALES1  │ LINDSAY     │ ncp   │ Rply Set Directory Handle         │
│ 541 │ LINDSAY │ SALES1      │ ncp   │ Req  Get Directory Path           │
│ 542 │ SALES1  │ LINDSAY     │ ncp   │ Rply Get Directory Path VOL1:HOME/│
│ 543 │ LINDSAY │ SALES1      │ ncp   │ Req  Set Directory Handle /HOME/LC│
│ 544 │ SALES1  │ LINDSAY     │ ncp   │ Rply Set Directory Handle         │
│ 545 │ LINDSAY │ SALES1      │ ncp   │ Req  Open File /HOME/LCHAPPEL/APPS.│
│ 546 │ SALES1  │ LINDSAY     │ ncp   │ Rply Open File WP.FIL             │
│ 547 │ LINDSAY │ SALES1      │ ncp   │ Req  Get Current Size of File WP.F│
│ 548 │ SALES1  │ LINDSAY     │ ncp   │ Rply Get Current Size of File     │
│ 549 │ LINDSAY │ SALES1      │ ncp   │ Req  Get Directory Path           │
│ 550 │ SALES1  │ LINDSAY     │ ncp   │ Rply Get Directory Path VOL1:HOME/│
│ 551 │ LINDSAY │ SALES1      │ ncp   │ Req  Set Directory Handle /HOME/LC│
│ 552 │ SALES1  │ LINDSAY     │ ncp   │ Rply Set Directory Handle         │
│ 553 │ LINDSAY │ SALES1      │ ncp   │ Req  Get Directory Path           │
│ 554 │ SALES1  │ LINDSAY     │ ncp   │ Rply Get Directory Path VOL1:HOME/│
│ 555 │ LINDSAY │ SALES1      │ ncp   │ Req  Set Directory Handle /HOME/LC│
│ 556 │ SALES1  │ LINDSAY     │ ncp   │ Rply Set Directory Handle         │
│ 557 │ LINDSAY │ SALES1      │ ncp   │ Req  Read WP.FIL; 1024 bytes      │
│ 558 │ SALES1  │ LINDSAY     │ ncp   │ Rply Read; 1024 bytes             │
│ 559 │ LINDSAY │ SALES1      │ ncp   │ Req  Read WP.FIL; 1024 bytes      │
│ 560 │ SALES1  │ LINDSAY     │ ncp   │ Rply Read; 1024 bytes             │
│ 561 │ LINDSAY │ SALES1      │ ncp   │ Req  Get Directory Path           │
│ 562 │ SALES1  │ LINDSAY     │ ncp   │ Rply Get Directory Path VOL1:HOME/│
│ 563 │ LINDSAY │ SALES1      │ ncp   │ Req  Set Directory Handle /HOME/LC│
└──────────────────────────────────────────────────────────────────┘
          Packet:  546    Unfiltered:  939
```

FIGURE 17.5

The analyzer interprets downloading of an application and any supplemental files.

Preceding chapters have given other examples of how you can use analyzers to troubleshoot and optimize the network. These include

- ▸ Creating a baseline
- ▸ Stress-testing the cabling system
- ▸ Stress-testing a component
- ▸ Route testing
- ▸ Utilization gauging
- ▸ Growth planning

Besides reviewing the features and capabilities of analyzers, you need to be aware that analyzers are available in two standard configurations: hardware/software, or software only.

Hardware/Software Analyzer Kits

NOTE
The analyzer features defined within this book are based on the capability of Novell's LANalyzer and LANalyzer for NetWare products. Check with your analyzer vendor to determine product capabilities.

Hardware/software solutions are generally more expensive due to the cost of the interface board (and sometimes the PC) that accompanies the software.

The specialized cards that are included with the system can provide additional functionality such as

- ▸ On-board buffering
- ▸ On-board processor
- ▸ Greater transmit capabilities

The specialized cards often include an on-board buffer for packet capture. This type of buffering is generally faster than saving packets to a disk or system memory, and it allows the analyzer to keep up with higher traffic network systems.

The on-board processor that is included on these cards frees the PC from handling all the processing required for capturing packets and maintaining statistics information. On a higher traffic network system, these on-board processors provide a more powerful analyzer system.

The specialized hardware systems also provide greater transmit capabilities. For example, the LANalyzer allows users to simultaneously transmit and receive packets. The ability to capture and decode improperly framed data and transmit errors onto the network is also a capability enabled by hardware/software solutions.

One drawback of hardware/software solutions is cost. Hardware/software solutions are generally more expensive than software-only solutions because of the specialized hardware prices. Hardware/software systems range in price, generally starting at around $10,000.

Another drawback of hardware/software solutions is the lack of portability of these systems. In order to analyze a network with a hardware/software system, you must take to the site either a portable system with the hardware installed or the specialized card and software in hopes of finding a system to use on site.

Software-Only Solutions

Software-only solutions are becoming more popular because of their cost and portability.

Software-only solutions do not require expensive specialized boards and are therefore generally less expensive. Software-only solutions range in price, starting at around $900. For smaller networks and cost-conscious users, the software-only option allows access to a protocol analyzer without the high price tag.

The software-only solutions offer greater portability as well. To analyze a network, it is possible with a software-only solution to take just a set of disks to a customer site. However, it may still be more convenient to carry a portable unit with the software preinstalled.

These systems rely upon the processing power of the PC they are installed in and are dependent upon the LAN driver that accompanies the software. As an example, the LANalyzer for NetWare includes the latest drivers from Novell (drivers for NetWare 4.0). These drivers can operate in "promiscuous" mode, allowing all errors seen on the wire to be filtered up to the LANalyzer for NetWare application for statistics gathering.

This chapter has covered the general features of analyzers, from the ability to analyze physical-layer protocols to the ability to analyze upper-layer protocols. Whether you are considering purchasing a hardware/software or software-only solution, there is a variety of options analyzers offer to the network administrator or support technician.

The next chapter focuses on statistics-gathering options for short-term or trend information.

CHAPTER 18

Network
Statistics

In this book you have viewed a variety of statistics regarding network performance. For example, you have viewed utilization trend information that indicates typical network utilization. You have also looked at error trends on the network. This chapter examines how statistics information is gathered and the types of data that can be saved in statistics files.

Statistics are created from the packets viewed on the wire by the analyzer, as shown in Figure 18.1.

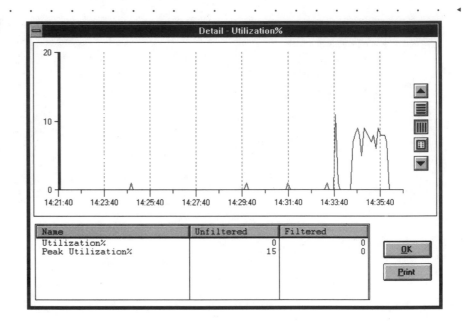

Incrementing Statistics Counters

When a packet is viewed, the analyzer can make a determination upon the type of packet—error packet, broadcast, and so on—and increment the appropriate statistics counter. You can configure the analyzer to track the types of packets you are most interested in. For example, if a NetWare broadcast packet is seen by the analyzer, the following counters may be affected:

- ▶ NetWare packets

- ▶ Good packets (packets that comply with Ethernet standards)

- ▶ Broadcast packets (all)

- ▶ SAP broadcast packets

- ▶ Packets between 64 and 127 bytes

- ▶ Packets per second

- ▶ Kilobytes per second

- ▶ Current bandwidth utilization

Statistics information can be presented in many different ways, including bar graphs, line graphs, gauges, and digital counters. In Figure 18.2, you are viewing the LANalyzer's Global Statistics screen. This screen displays information on *all* network activity.

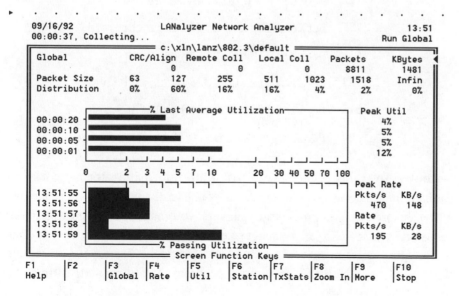

FIGURE 18.2

LANalyzer's Global

Statistics screen

On the Global Statistics screen, you are presented with statistics information such as

▶ Packet size distribution

▶ Total number of packets

▶ Total number of kilobytes

▶ Average utilization over sampling periods

▶ Utilization for the current sampling period

▶ Average kilobytes per second

▶ Peak kilobytes per second

The packet size distribution is listed across the top of the screen. The size columns are interpreted as follows:

HEADING	INTERPRETATION
63	Between 0 and 63 bytes, inclusive (short packets)
127	Between 64 and 127 bytes, inclusive
255	Between 128 and 255 bytes, inclusive
511	Between 256 and 511 bytes, inclusive
1023	Between 512 and 1023 bytes, inclusive
1518	Between 1024 and 1518 bytes, inclusive
Inf	Packets greater than 1518 bytes (long packets)

You can use this packet size distribution information for network optimization purposes. If a network is consistently using smaller packets when the protocol supports larger packets, you may wish to investigate the reason for using the smaller packet size (such as a NetWare router that does not support larger packet sizes). By increasing packet sizes, you can reduce the amount of overhead required for communications and, ultimately, increase network efficiency. Databases can be tuned so that record sizes support more efficient data transfer to the client.

The total number of packets and kilobytes is also listed across the top of the screen. The number under the packet heading indicates the total number of packets that have occurred on the network since the test began. As activity increases, the total number of packets also increases. Comparing this number for a one-hour test period against an earlier one-hour test period provides a quick determination of recent network traffic patterns.

The total number of kilobytes column indicates the number of kilobytes that have traversed the network since the application began. This indicates the network throughput—how much information is being transmitted on the wire during the time period. Once again, you can compare this information against earlier statistics information to determine if the network throughput has increased.

The average utilization over sampling periods is recorded on the graph at the top center of the screen, as shown in Figure 18.3.

The sampling periods are listed on the left side of the bar graph: 1 second, 5 seconds, 10 seconds, and 20 seconds. The utilization is averaged over each

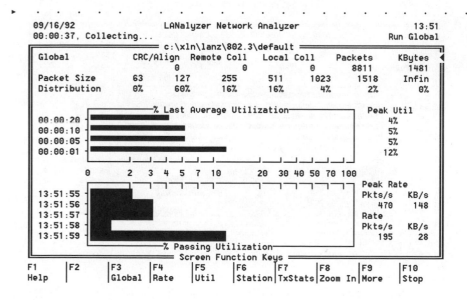

FIGURE 18.3

The average utilization (upper bar graph) indicates the utilization average of various sampling periods.

of the time periods and plotted on the bar graph. These sampling periods can be changed to reflect 1, 5, 10, and 20 times a selected sampling period. For example, you can configure the application to gather statistics each minute instead of each second. In that case, this column would include sampling averages for the last 1 minute, 5 minutes, 10 minutes, and 20 minutes.

On the right side of the screen, the average kilobytes per second (for the time the application has been running) are recorded. Below this indicator are the peak kilobytes per second during the application time period. You can use these indicators to determine if the current throughput is typical.

The utilization for the current sampling period is listed below the average utilization bar graph. This graph indicates the bandwidth utilization for the last 5 seconds, 1 second at a time. You can compare this information to the average listed above it to determine if utilization is increasing or decreasing. On small percentages that do not show up on the graph, the LANalyzer provides the ability to "zoom in" on the graph, as shown in Figure 18.4.

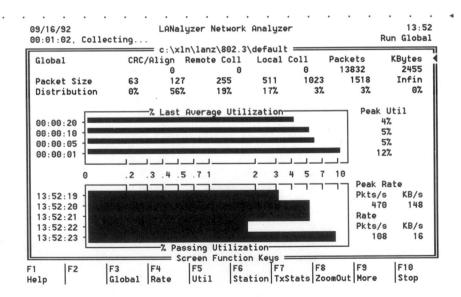

FIGURE 18.4

Zooming in allows viewing of smaller percentages.

Statistics that you can gather over time on a network include the following:

- ▶ Utilization
- ▶ Kilobytes/second
- ▶ Packets/second
- ▶ Errors/second

The total packets and total kilobytes may also be useful in situations where you are benchmarking or testing the network, such as bridge or router throughput. It is important to know current utilization when troubleshooting, but it is also important to note how bandwidth utilization has increased or decreased over time. Figure 18.5 shows the LANalyzer for NetWare Detail Utilization screen. You can notice a dramatic increase in utilization.

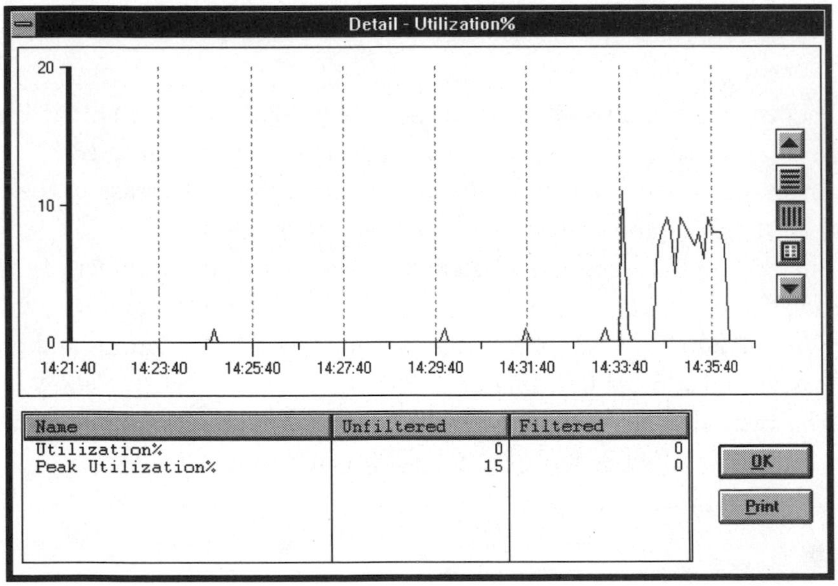

F I G U R E 18.5
Utilization statistics indicate increases or decreases in bandwidth use over time.

Kilobytes-per-second statistics indicate the increase or decrease in throughput on the network, as shown in Figure 18.6.

FIGURE 18.6

Kilobytes-per-second
statistics indicate
throughput over time.

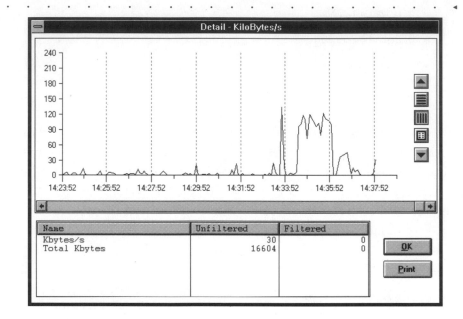

Packets-per-second statistics indicate the number of packets that have been transmitted on the network over time, as shown in Figure 18.7.

Errors-per-second statistics illustrate the increase or decrease in the errors occurring on the network, as shown in Figure 18.8.

The errors table provides a detailed breakdown of the number of fragments, short packets, long packets, CRC/alignment errors, and so on. As shown in Figure 18.8, statistics tables accompany the line graphs and provide peak and average information.

Analyzers also provide information for troubleshooting and optimizing the network with short-term and long-term, or trend, statistics.

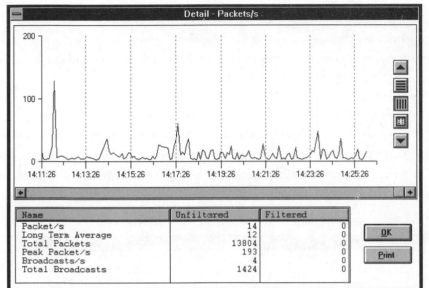

*Packets-per-second
statistics indicate the
number of packets on the
network for each sampling
period.*

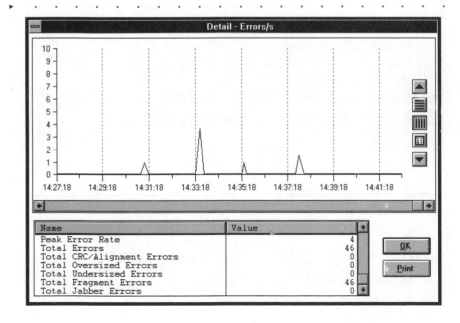

*Errors-per-second statistics
indicate increasing or
decreasing errors on the
LAN.*

Short-Term Statistics

Short-term statistics provide a "snapshot" of network performance in real time. These statistics are generally plotted each second and can be compared against the long-term statistics to determine if current network activity is typical.

In Figure 18.9, you are viewing a LANalyzer for NetWare screen that depicts short-term utilization statistics. This indicates that the network bandwidth utilization has increased dramatically over the last 15 minutes.

In order to provide a comparative graph, it is important to create a baseline report.

FIGURE 18.9

Short-term utilization statistics indicate a steady increase in bandwidth utilization over the last 15 minutes.

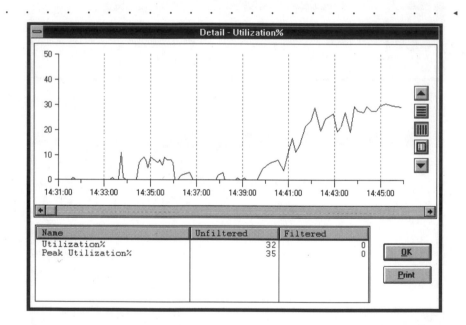

Long-Term (Trend) Statistics

Baseline reports include trend information on utilization, kilobytes per second, errors per second, and packets per second. The long-term (or trend) statistics indicate typical network performance over time. These statistics can span several days, weeks, or months. In Figure 18.10, you are viewing long-term statistics for network errors. As you can see, this network typically experiences an insignificant number of errors.

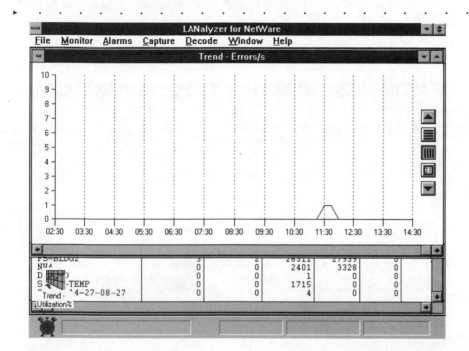

You can use this information for comparison with short-term statistics. If the short-term statistics show a dramatic rise in errors, you can see—based on the trend information—that this is not typical. Some error has occurred on the network recently. The next step for troubleshooting is to identify the type of error and the source.

You can use trend information for utilization to determine if the current utilization is typical. For example, if utilization has risen over the last 30 minutes, you can compare this current information against your long-term statistics. You may find that this is typical because network backup is being performed at this time or large files are being printed for the end-of-month reports.

You can also use trend information to determine the most appropriate time to back up the network. For example, in Figure 18.11, you are viewing trend statistics indicating that the best time for backup would be between 9:00 P.M. (21:00 hours) and 8:00 A.M.

You can export trend and short-term statistics into spreadsheet format. You can then import statistics information into spreadsheets and plot it for further analysis.

FIGURE 18.11

Trend statistics provide an indication of the best time to back up the network.

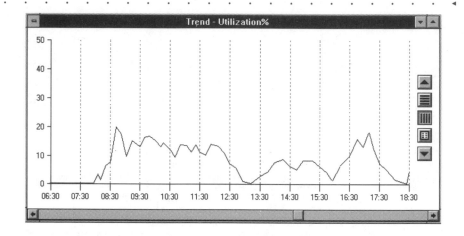

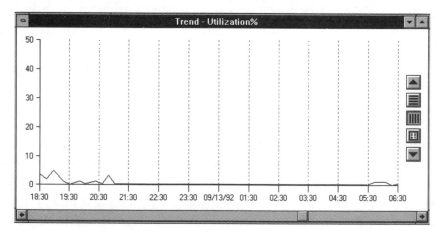

In this chapter you learned that you can use trend statistics, in conjunction with short-term real-time statistics, for troubleshooting. In addition, you learned that trend statistics are also an important part of a baseline report and that short-term statistics provide a "snapshot" of current network health.

In addition to these network statistics and trends, it is useful to have information on specific network stations. The next chapter discusses station monitoring on the network.

CHAPTER 19

Station Monitoring

The last chapter reviewed some of the statistical information available for networks. If a problem on a network becomes evident when you are viewing this statistical information, it is necessary to isolate the station or stations causing the problem. It may be necessary to determine which stations are responsible for utilization overload, errors, or excessive requests to the NetWare server. Once a station has been identified as causing a network problem, you can examine the error and take corrective action.

This chapter uses station monitoring to locate the following stations:

▶ Most active clients and/or servers

▶ Stations using the most bandwidth

▶ Stations generating errors on the network

The chapter also looks at name-gathering (collecting workstation and/or server names) features that are available. First, let's take a look at the network characterization and troubleshooting uses of station monitoring.

Determining the Most Active Clients/Servers on the Network

By filtering on traffic between a server and any station on the network, you can determine which client is communicating with the server most often. This requires the following steps:

1 · Record all traffic to the NetWare server.

2 · Sort the station names based on the total number of packets transmitted.

In Figure 19.1, you are viewing a network that supports 16 users and a single NetWare server. This is the server whose address you will filter on to determine the most active users.

FIGURE 19.1

*NetWare LAN consisting of
one server and 16 clients*

STEP 1: RECORD ALL TRAFFIC TO THE NETWARE SERVER

If your NetWare server is a router—that is, it has more than one network interface board installed with attached segments—traffic from a station on one network segment to the server will not be routed to the other network segment. When you are baselining or troubleshooting, the analyzer should be placed at a strategic location to avoid having packets filtered out before being seen by the analyzer.

NOTE
Filtering is covered in detail in Chapter 21.

In order to determine which workstations are sending the most requests to the server, you will run the LANalyzer for NetWare and filter on any traffic to the server. You can do this by filtering on the Ethernet source address. The source address field should contain the physical address of the server's network interface card. You could also filter on the server's internal IPX address (in the destination network address field of the IPX headers).

Figure 19.2 depicts the LANalyzer for NetWare Capture Filter dialog box, which you can use to capture all traffic to the server. You use the top portion of the dialog box to create a filter between stations.

At the bottom of this dialog box is the option Apply Filter to Station Monitor. If this box is checked, only stations that are communicating with the server will show up on the LANalyzer for Netware Station Monitor screen, shown in Figure 19.3. Check this box to ensure that you are viewing only clients that are communicating with the server you specified. While the application runs, the Station Monitor screen is displayed.

Across the top of the Station Monitor screen is a count of the number of stations the LANalyzer for NetWare has "seen" on the network. Stations are

FIGURE 19.2

Filtering on all traffic to the
NetWare server

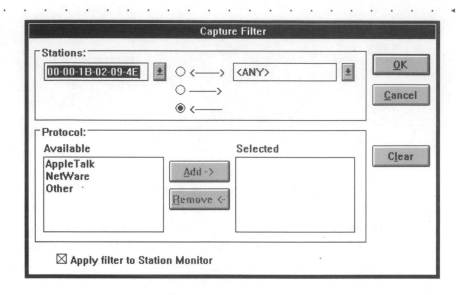

FIGURE 19.3

The LANalyzer for
NetWare Station Monitor
screen

Capture Filter

Stations:

00-00-1B-02-09-4E ○ ←——→ <ANY>
                   ○ ——→
                   ◉ ←——

OK
Cancel

Protocol:

Available
AppleTalk
NetWare
Other

Add ->
Remove <-

Selected

Clear

☒ Apply filter to Station Monitor

LANalyzer for NetWare

File   Monitor   Alarms   Capture   Decode   Window   Help

Station Monitor(Filtered) - 15 Stations

Name	Pkts/s Out	Pkts/s In	Pkts Out	Pkts In	Errors	KBytes
VIVIAN	0	0	802	0	0	
BPRATT	0	0	412	0	0	
08-00-20-0C-0D-33	0	0	9	0	0	
08-00-20-0C-07-01	0	0	135	0	0	
08-00-20-0B-F8-2A	0	0	627	0	0	
08-00-20-0B-E6-A9	0	0	65	0	0	
JOSINE	0	0	16	0	0	
08-00-20-0B-DA-A7	0	0	410	0	0	
NW4	0	0	3921	0	0	
This_Workstation	0	0	218	0	0	
00-00-1B-1E-E9-00	0	0	3	0	0	
LAPICHEL	0	0	23	U	0	
VVAL	0	0	284	0	0	
FS-BLDG2	0	0	0	27005	0	
00-00-1B-02-84-80	0	0	650	0	0	

added to the Station Monitor screen each time their node address is contained in either the source or destination address field of a properly formed frame that fits your filter criteria. If a new station enters the network and transmits an improperly formed frame on the network, it will not be added to the Station Monitor screen. This ensures that malformed or corrupt packets on the wire do not cause erroneous station numbers to be added to the Station Monitor table.

All stations listed in the Station Monitor screen are communicating with the server, based on the filter you defined earlier. In the next step, you will determine which station is communicating with the server most often, based on the number of packets sent to the server.

STEP 2: SORT THE STATION NAMES BASED ON THE TOTAL NUMBER OF PACKETS TRANSMITTED

You can sort any column of the LANalyzer for NetWare Station Monitor screen. Since you know that all stations listed are communicating with the server, the next step is to determine who is sending the most requests to the server. By sorting on the Packets Out column, you can determine the most active client, as shown in Figure 19.4.

Figure 19.5 shows the graphed results of the test. Users are plotted based on the total number of packets sent to the server during a 20-minute sampling. The graph has plotted only the top ten workstations communicating with FS-BLDG2.

Based on the results of sorting the station monitor screen, you can see that Vivian is communicating with the server most often. If the server indicates it is overloaded by transmitting a Request Being Processed packet, you can use this method to determine which workstation is making the most requests of the server. If the server indicates an overload condition, you may decide to move Vivian's applications to a less-burdened server on the network.

FIGURE 19.4

*Sorting the Packets Out
column leaves the most
active client at the top of
the list.*

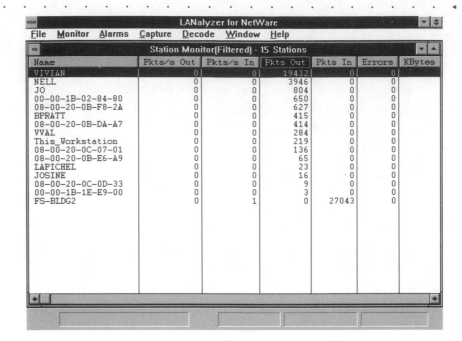

Using the Station Monitor screen, you have identified the client making the most requests of a particular server. Next, you will determine which client is using most of the bandwidth.

Determining the Stations Using the Most Bandwidth

On a heavily loaded network cabling system, you can determine which user is using up the most bandwidth on the network and, if possible, transfer that user to another network that is relatively idle and able to support such use. The following steps are required to determine the client using

▶ . . . . ◀

F I G U R E 19.5

Top-ten list for stations
communicating with the
server

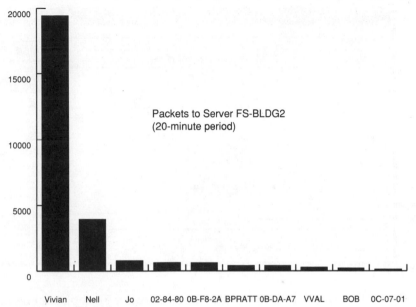

most of the bandwidth:

1 · Remove any station filters.

2 · Sort the station monitor screen by kilobytes out.

STEP 1: REMOVE ANY STATION FILTERS

Since you want to determine which user on the entire network is using up most of the bandwidth, you do not want any station filters, such as FS1 to FRED, defined. To set up the LANalyzer for NetWare to perform the utilization test, the station option <ANY> has been selected for the source and destination fields, as shown in Figure 19.6.

STEP 2: SORT THE STATION MONITOR BY KILOBYTES OUT

Since bandwidth in use is based on the number of kilobytes transmitted from each station, sorting on the Kilobytes Out column provides you with

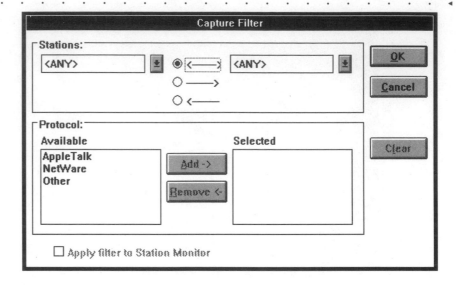

a list of clients and their bandwidth utilization. For example, in Figure 19.7, you can see that NW386-1 is responsible for using most of the bandwidth.

It is expected that servers and routers will use most of the bandwidth on the network since they answer requests from a number of stations. Be certain to scroll past any servers and routers to find the first network user name. In this example, Mary is the first user name. Mary is the user who is using the most bandwidth on the network.

If the cabling system became overloaded—if utilization and local collisions are high—you may wish to move Mary to another network that can support the bandwidth requirements.

Locating Stations Generating Errors on the Network

The Station Monitor screen of the LANalyzer for NetWare also provides an Errors column. This column "credits" errors to the station that transmitted them.

Name	KBytes Out	KBytes In	Pkts/s Out	Pkts/s In	Pkts In	Err
NW386-1	1626	23	1	0	328	
FS-BLDG2	535	32	2	1	401	
MARY	286	0	0	0	0	
NW4	277	16	0	0	268	
CAROLYN	214	0	0	0	0	
SALES-TEMP	208	0	0	0	0	
This_Workstation	133	11	0	0	133	
RTR-1264-264	110	0	0	0	0	
DOLAND	36	0	0	0	0	
CATHYD	34	0	0	0	0	
CHRISTIE	32	0	0	0	0	
TOMP	32	2	0	0	32	
VIVIAN	28	3	0	0	28	
BPRATT	28	3	0	0	28	
08-00-20-0B-DA-A7	27	3	0	0	27	
MONAL	18	0	0	0	0	
ALEXJ	16	0	0	0	0	
08-00-20-0C-07-01	12	1	0	0	12	
NANCYP	10	0	0	0	0	
PETEY	9	0	0	0	0	
08-00-20-0B-E6-A9	6	0	0	0	5	
LAPICHEL	2	0	0	0	2	
DEBBIES	2	0	0	0	2	
08-00-2B-24-CE-47	1	0	0	0	0	
00-00-1B-1E-3F-48	1	0	0	0	1	
08-00-20-0B-F8-2A	1	0	0	0	1	

LANalyzer for NetWare — Station Monitor - 40 Stations

FIGURE 19.7

Sorting the Station Monitor screen by kilobytes out

Sorting the station monitor information by the errors count will determine which station is responsible for transmitting most of the errors on the network. By capturing some of the packets from this station, you can determine the type of errors the station is generating, as shown in Figure 19.8.

Since CRC errors from a single workstation indicate a problem with the workstation's network interface card, you should replace the card and monitor the network for errors again. If CRC errors were seen from several stations, it most likely indicates a problem with the cable or segment the stations are on.

You have now determined the most active network stations based on packets addressed to a server, their bandwidth utilization, and stations generating errors. Next, you will examine the name-gathering features you can use for simplified interpretation of network communications.

NOTE
Refer to Chapter 5 for a listing of errors and possible causes.

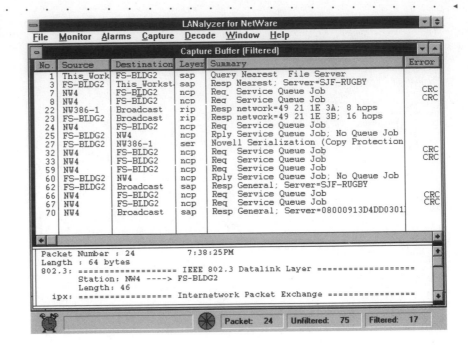

Name Gathering

Throughout this book you have been presented with screen shots of the LANalyzer and LANalyzer for NetWare products. In many of the screens, a name has been substituted in place of the 6-byte node address of a station. Server names have also appeared in many of the screens.

These names are kept in a name file, and when activated, the name file allows for substitute identifications (such as login names or server names) to replace physical node addresses displayed. Since an entire screen of node addresses can be somewhat difficult to interpret, the name-gathering feature simplifies the communication interpretation process.

Figure 19.9 shows a LANalyzer for NetWare Station Monitor screen that has names substituted for some of the node addresses on the network.

```
─                          LANalyzer for NetWare                    ▼ ↕
  File   Monitor   Alarms   Capture   Decode   Window   Help
─                      Station Monitor - 39 Stations                ▼ ▲
 Name              Pkts/s Out  Pkts/s In  Pkts Out  Pkts In  Errors  KByte ▲
 Broadcast              0           0          0       481       0
 CAROLYN                0           0        148         0       0
 CATHYD                 0           0         23         0       0
 CHRISTIE               0           0         23         0       0
 DEBBIES                0           0          1         1       0
 DEC_Console            0           0          0         7       0
 DEC_End_nodes          0           0          0        22       0
 DEC_LAT                0           0          0        43       0
 DEC_lcl_Bridges        0           1          0       360       0
 DEC_lv1_Router         0           1          0       124       0
 DEC_lv2_Router         0           0          0        22       0
 DOLAND                 0           0         24         0       0
 FS-BLDG2               1           1        366       267       0
 LAPICHEL               0           0          1         1       0
 MARY                   0           0        195         0       0
 MKTGTMP                0           0          0        12       0
 MONAL                  0           0         13         0       0
 NANCYP                 0           0          7         0       0
 NW386-1                2           2       1068       201       0
 NW4                    0           0        191       185       0
 PETEY                  0           0          6         0       0
 RTR-1264-264           0           0         74         0       0
 SALES-TEMP             0           0        146         0       0
 This_Workstation       0           0         66        67       0
 TOMP                   0           0         23        23       0
 VIVIAN                 0           0         18        18       0
```

FIGURE 19.9

Names replace node addresses if they are contained in the name table.

In the NetWare environment, you can perform name gathering by sending a SAP to servers on the network. NetWare v3.x servers reply with the name that is in their AUTOEXEC.NCF file. NetWare 2.x servers respond with the name assigned to them during the NETGEN process. Each server that replies is then listed in a name table that provides a translation to the server name. However, if you use this SAP method, NetWare client names cannot be gathered for the name file, since NetWare clients do not advertise as servers.

When Novell released the LANalyzer for NetWare, they took the name-gathering feature a step further. Using LANalyzer for NetWare's Active Name Gathering feature, you actually attach to a server by a specified user name, such as GUEST. Figure 19.10 shows the LANalyzer's name-gathering dialog box.

FIGURE 19.10

The application will log in to servers as the default user, GUEST, or another user, if desired.

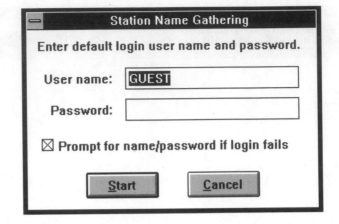

Once you are attached to a server, the application obtains the list of users and their node addresses. This is the same information received when you type **USERLIST /A** at the command line. Each known server is queried and all user names are automatically entered into the name table. This feature has added significantly to the name table capabilities, since you may now have user names listed instead of just station physical (node) addresses.

This chapter has covered the benefits of station monitoring and name gathering. You should be familiar with the steps required to determine the most active client communicating with a server, the client using the most bandwidth, and stations that are generating errors.

The next chapter views alarms and alarm thresholds.

Alarms and Alarm Thresholds

Chapters 18 and 19 covered network statistics and station monitoring techniques. These functions may occur without your continuously watching an analyzer; you want to be alerted when unusual conditions, such as increasing error counts, occur on the network. Alarms notify you of these unusual conditions.

This chapter discusses the two types of alarm threshold definitions: predefined and user-defined. When you work with user-defined alarm thresholds, you will set thresholds in accordance with the baseline information gathered for a network. You will also select actions to be taken when alarm thresholds are reached.

Calculating Network Statistics

Alarm thresholds are most commonly set based on statistics gathered, such as utilization, packets per second, or errors. As statistics are calculated, they are constantly checked to see if they have met the alarm threshold value. In Figure 20.1, you are viewing the general functions of a protocol analyzer.

As shown in Figure 20.1, the first step an analyzer performs upon receipt of a packet is processing the global statistics. *Global statistics* include information about all the packets seen on the network, regardless of any filtering you may have set up.

NOTE
Filtering is covered later in this chapter.

The second step is applying a pre-filter that defines the type of packet you want to copy into your trace buffer and calculate statistics for. The third step is to copy the packets into the buffer. If the buffer is full, you can configure the analyzer to remove the oldest packets to make room for the newest packets (first in, first out). The final step is to apply a post-filter, if one has been defined. The results of these four steps provide two sets of statistics (global and specifically defined) and a buffer filled with packets defined by a pre-filter.

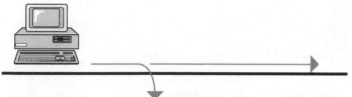

FIGURE 20.1

General functions of a
protocol analyzer

Protocol Analyzer Basic Functions

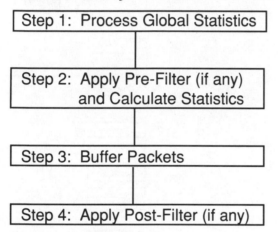

Step 1: Process Global Statistics

Step 2: Apply Pre-Filter (if any)
and Calculate Statistics

Step 3: Buffer Packets

Step 4: Apply Post-Filter (if any)

Global statistics that are calculated include

- Utilization percentage

- Kilobytes per second

- Errors per second

- Packets per second

- Packet size distribution

As shown in Figure 20.2, a 64-byte NetWare broadcast packet has been copied into the analyzer's buffer. Before being copied, however, it was

FIGURE 20.2

Counters are incremented based on the packet received.

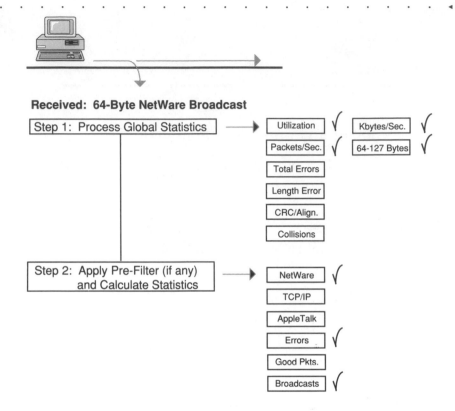

Received: 64-Byte NetWare Broadcast

calculated into the global statistics and met the pre-filter criteria. Global statistics that were affected include utilization, kilobytes per second, packets per second, and the appropriate packet size distribution counter (64- to 127-byte packets).

When an error packet is received, the Ethernet chipset reports the error. The LANalyzer, in turn, increments the errors-per-second counter as well as other affected global statistics counters. Global statistics can be tracked for the following errors:

- ► Local collisions
- ► Remote collisions

- ▸ Length errors

- ▸ CRC/alignment errors

In Figure 20.3, a NetWare packet longer than 1518 bytes has been seen by the analyzer on the local network. The long packet has incremented the associated statistics counters, including errors, NetWare packets, and length errors.

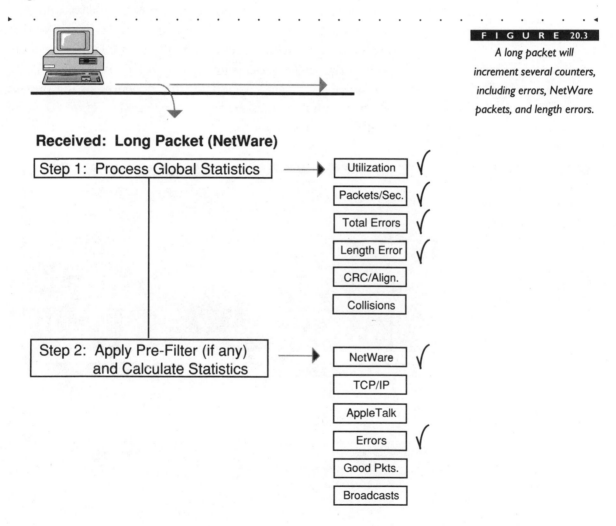

A long packet will increment several counters, including errors, NetWare packets, and length errors.

Alarm thresholds can be set on these counter values. If the value of 1 is set as an alarm threshold and a single long packet is received, an alarm is triggered. Alarm thresholds can be either predefined or user defined.

Predefined Alarm Thresholds

Predefined alarm thresholds are transparently set on an analysis product and generally cannot be changed by the user. For example, the LANalyzer for NetWare includes a predefined server alarm threshold. The server alarm threshold is defined to trigger an alarm when a server sends a Request Being Processed packet or no longer responds on the network. At the present time, this alarm threshold cannot be set by the user. In Figure 20.4, the server alarm has been triggered.

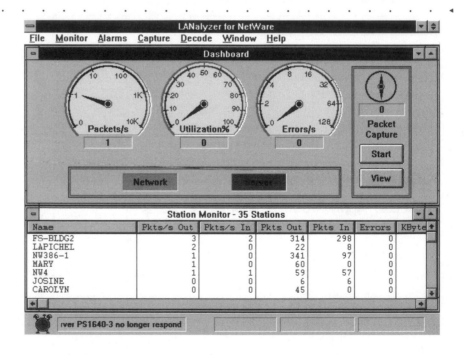

The alarm has caused an alarm clock icon and ticker-tape message to appear in the lower left-hand corner of the screen, an audible beep to sound, and an entry to be placed in the alarm log. The ticker-tape message states that server PS1640-3 no longer responds on the network. The server or an intermediary router may be down.

Figure 20.5 shows the alarm log that maintains a listing of alarms that have been triggered since the LANalyzer for NetWare was started. The alarm log indicates that the server has not been responding since 8:58 P.M. You can print the alarm log if desired.

For users who are new to protocol analysis, predefined alarm thresholds ensure that the user is notified of potential problems without having to learn to set the alarm thresholds. For experienced users, however, user-definable alarm thresholds allow more flexibility and customization for alarm triggering.

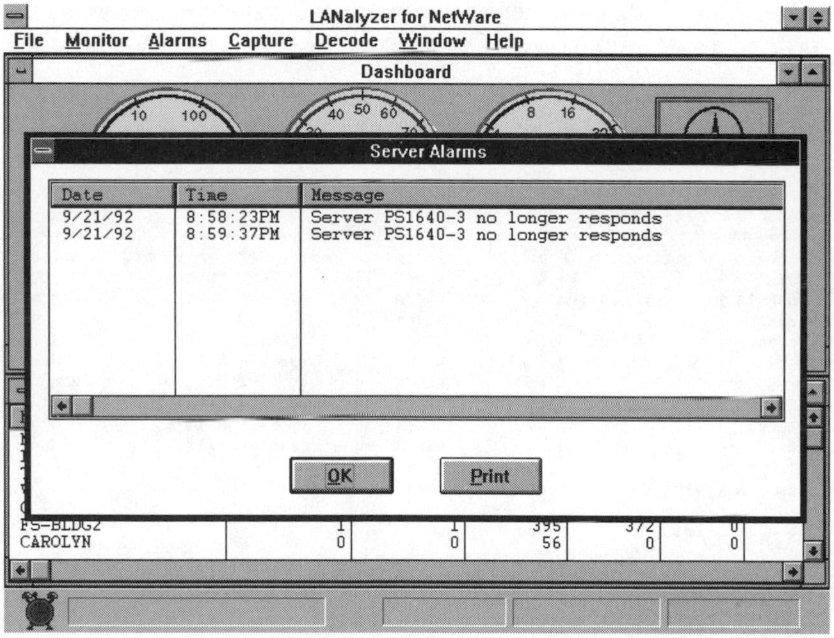

FIGURE 20.5

The alarm log lists the date and time that alarms were triggered.

User-Definable Alarm Thresholds

User-definable alarm thresholds can be set to trigger alarms when an unusual condition occurs on the network. You can determine these thresholds based on normal network operation. For example, if your network utilization peaks at around 23%, you may wish to set an alarm threshold at 27% utilization. If the utilization reaches 27%, an alarm will be triggered, indicating that an unusual condition is occurring on your network. By examining baseline information for your network, you can determine what thresholds are appropriate.

Alarm thresholds are set in various ways, depending upon the analysis tool. Figures 20.6 and 20.7 show two separate ways for defining alarm thresholds. Once again, you must examine your baseline information to determine what is normal activity on your network before you set alarms.

There are also various ways of indicating that an alarm threshold has been set. These indicators depend upon the analysis tool you are using. In Figures 20.8 and 20.9, you see the LANalyzer and LANalyzer for NetWare screens indicating that alarm thresholds have been set.

FIGURE 20.6

You can set alarm thresholds on each receive channel of the LANalyzer based on utilization or packets per second.

```
09/21/92                    LANalyzer Network Analyzer                    20 49
Press + or - to toggle                                            Edit Alarms
============================ c:\xln\lanz\802.5\default ============================
Channel      Utilization Threshold    Action    Packet Rate Threshold    Action
Global              30 %               Alarm          1000 Pkts/s         Alarm
GoodPkts       Disabled %              Alarm      Disabled Pkts/s         Alarm
Broadcas             1 %               Alarm            50 Pkts/s         Alarm
Promiscu       Disabled %              Alarm      Disabled Pkts/s         Alarm
MACpkts        Disabled %              Alarm      Disabled Pkts/s         Alarm
ErrMon               1 %               Alarm             2 Pkts/s         Alarm
NetBeui        Disabled %              Alarm      Disabled Pkts/s         Alarm
NetWare        Disabled %              Alarm      Disabled Pkts/s         Alarm
SNA            Disabled %              Alarm      Disabled Pkts/s         Alarm

When a new station is detected       take no action

Log alarms into file

Execute the following file when an alarm occurs and the action is Execute:


Ring bell when alarm is generated    Yes

F1      |F2      |F3     |F4      |F5    |F6     |F7      |F8    |F9      |F10
Help    |Revert  |Save   |Options |Mode  |       |Receive |Xmit  |Alarms  |Back
```

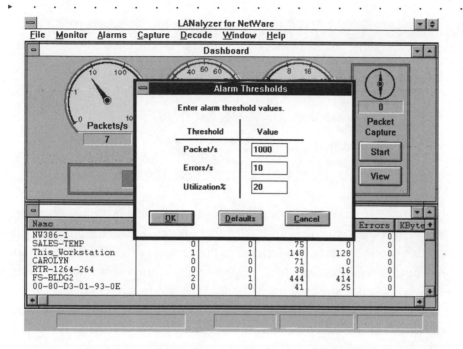

You can set three user-definable alarm thresholds on the LANalyzer for NetWare.

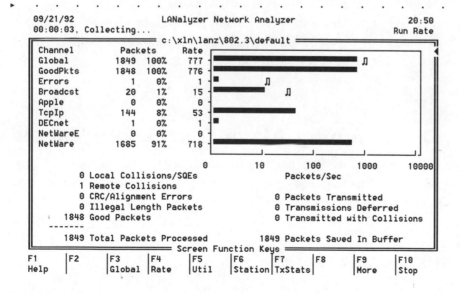

The LANalyzer displays a musical note at the value of the alarm threshold.

FIGURE 20.9

The LANalyzer for
NetWare displays alarm
threshold limits in red
(shown here with arrows)
on the dashboard gauges.

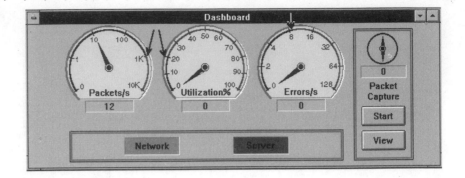

The LANalyzer also allows thresholds to be set on testing applications that are included with the product or that you have created. For example, perhaps you have recently given users the option of using the Burst Mode shell at their workstations. You created an application that filters on Burst Mode reads and writes (NCP type 7777). The results of the application will allow you to determine the average bandwidth used by Burst Mode reads and writes. If the current bandwidth used by Burst Mode transactions is 10%, you may wish to set an alarm threshold at 15%. This will alert you to increased bandwidth used by Burst Mode transactions.

The flexibility inherent in the LANalyzer product allows alarm thresholds to be set on any defined receive channel, including the Global channel.

Now, let's look at how to define typical alarm threshold values.

Determining Alarm Threshold Values

As mentioned earlier, alarm thresholds are set in accordance with baseline information. For example, perhaps the following peaks were observed when you documented your baseline information:

Peak utilization   22%

Peak packets per second   500

Peak errors per second   2

Based on these peak values, you may wish to set the following alarm thresholds:

Utilization alarm threshold   25%

Packets-per-second alarm threshold   600

Errors-per-second alarm threshold   3

When any of these thresholds is reached, an alarm is triggered. Since users may run tests unattended, there is a variety of alarm actions that can be defined, including those generating alarm logs or audible beeps.

Alarm Actions

You can customize the alert mechanism so that one or more of the following actions occur when an alarm is triggered:

- ▶ The alarm is logged to a file.

- ▶ A visual alarm notification appears.

- ▶ An audible alarm signal occurs.

- ▶ An executable file is launched.

The following sections examine each of these methods in order to help determine which is most appropriate for various situations.

ALARM LOG FILE

An *alarm log file* maintains a listing of alarms that have been triggered, as well as the date and time they were triggered. In Figure 20.10, you are viewing the alarm log file created by the LANalyzer.

FIGURE 20.10

*The alarm log file lists the
alarm triggered as well as
the date and time the entry
was made.*

```
Alarm: 09/21/92 07:58:59 Broadcst packet rate of 24 pkts/s exceeded threshold of 10
Alarm: 09/21/92 08:52:03 Broadcst packet rate of 13 pkts/s exceeded threshold of 10
Alarm: 09/21/92 08:52:57 Global packet rate of 725 pkts/s exceeded threshold of 500
Alarm: 09/21/92 08:52:59 Broadcst packet rate of 23 pkts/s exceeded threshold of 10
Alarm: 09/21/92 09:13:02 Global packet rate of 566 pkts/s exceeded threshold of 500
Alarm: 09/21/92 03:53:07 Broadcst packet rate of 15 pkts/s exceeded threshold of 10
Alarm: 09/21/92 03:53:16 Errors packet rate of 45 pkts/s exceeded threshold of 1
Alarm: 09/21/92 05:00:17 Global utilization of 47% exceeded threshold of 20%
Alarm: 09/21/92 05:03:19 Broadcst packet rate of 11 pkts/s exceeded threshold of 10
Alarm: 09/21/92 05:53:26 Errors packet rate of 3 pkts/s exceeded threshold of 1
Alarm: 09/21/92 05:53:30 Errors packet rate of 2 pkts/s exceeded threshold of 1
Alarm: 09/22/92 07:53:33 Broadcst packet rate of 42 pkts/s exceeded threshold of 10
Alarm: 09/22/92 07:53:36 Broadcst packet rate of 25 pkts/s exceeded threshold of 10
Alarm: 09/22/92 07:53:38 Errors packet rate of 2 pkts/s exceeded threshold of 1
Alarm: 09/22/92 07:53:40 Errors packet rate of 2 pkts/s exceeded threshold of 1
Alarm: 09/22/92 07:53:45 Errors packet rate of 3 pkts/s exceeded threshold of 1
```

As you can see from the alarm log, the network has exceeded several alarm thresholds: global utilization, broadcast packet rate, and errors packet rate. The alarm log provides the value of the alarm threshold, as well as the value that triggered the alarm. Based on the information contained in the log, you can see that the errors packet alarm threshold is set extremely low: 1 error packet per second. If this condition is not causing communications difficulties or sluggishness, you may wish to raise the alarm threshold to a more reasonable number, such as 5.

This alarm file is an ASCII text file that can be imported into a word processing program for formatting and printing. Some analyzers, such as the LANalzyer for NetWare, allow you to view an alarm log file from within the application, as shown in Figure 20.11.

As shown in the figure, alarms have been logged for the packet rate and utilization counters. Each has exceeded the alarm threshold. You can select the Print option in order to maintain a hard-copy version of the log file.

VISUAL ALARM NOTIFICATION

If you leave the analyzer running unattended, you can set up alarm notification to be visual so that when you return to the system, you can see that an alarm has been triggered.

For example, the LANalyzer displays a banner across the top of the screen that defines the alarm triggered. As shown earlier in Figure 20.4, the LANalyzer for NetWare also displays an alarm clock and a ticker-tape message that defines the alarm.

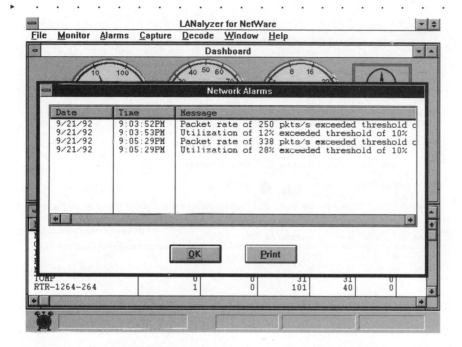

The LANalyzer for NetWare allows you to view the alarm log file from within the application.

AUDIBLE ALARM SIGNAL

Analyzers often provide an option for audible alarms (beeps) to alert the user when an alarm has been triggered. In a Windows-based product, such as the LANalyzer for NetWare, that is running in the background, an alarm will cause an audible beep, even if the LANalyzer for NetWare is not the active screen. In Figure 20.12, alarms have been configured to generate an audible alarm.

EXECUTABLE FILES

Many analyzers allow you to specify an executable file to be launched when an alarm is triggered. This capability adds to the effectiveness of the alarm notification system. For example, if the errors-per-second threshold is reached, perhaps you want the analyzer to launch an application that sends a message to the supervisor stating "Utilization high!"

FIGURE 20.12

You can specify audible alarms in the Edit Alarms screen of the LANalyzer.

```
09/21/92                    LANalyzer Network Analyzer                    20:54
Press + or - to toggle                                              Edit Alarms
═══════════════════════════ c:\xln\lanz\802.3\default ═══════════════════════════
Channel     Utilization Threshold    Action    Packet Rate Threshold    Action ◄
Global               20 %             Alarm            500 Pkts/s        Alarm
GoodPkts       Disabled %             Alarm       Disabled Pkts/s        Alarm
Errors                1 %             Alarm              1 Pkts/s        Alarm
Broadcst       Disabled %             Alarm             10 Pkts/s        Alarm
Apple          Disabled %             Alarm       Disabled Pkts/s        Alarm
TcpIp          Disabled %             Alarm       Disabled Pkts/s        Alarm
DECnet         Disabled %             Alarm       Disabled Pkts/s        Alarm
NetWareE       Disabled %             Alarm       Disabled Pkts/s        Alarm
NetWare        Disabled %             Alarm       Disabled Pkts/s        Alarm

When a new station is detected        take no action

Log alarms into file                  b:\alarm

Execute the following file when an alarm occurs and the action is Execute:


Ring bell when alarm is generated     Yes

F1      F2      F3      F4      F5      F6      F7       F8      F9       F10
Help    Revert  Save    Options Mode            Receive  Xmit    Alarms   Back
```

Using the LANalyzer, you must specify the alarm that will trigger the executable and the file name. In Figure 20.13, the batch file SEND.BAT will be launched when errors reach 5%. The LANalyzer can execute .COM, .EXE, and .BAT files.

The LANalyzer also has two additional features that give great flexibility to the Execute on Alarm option. One feature allows parameters to be passed to the batch file indicating which alarm was triggered. The other feature is the ability to restart the LANalyzer with a selected application. An example of their usefulness would be a general application such as the LANalyzer default application, which, when an alarm is set on a channel, such as the TCP/IP channel, would execute a batch file. This batch file could have the parameter indicate that the TCP/IP channel upon which the alarm was triggered restarts the LANalyzer running a TCP/IP-specific application.

```
 09/21/92              LANalyzer Network Analyzer              20:54
 Press + or - to toggle                                  Edit Alarms
╔════════════════════ c:\xln\lanz\802.3\default ═════════════════════╗
│Channel    Utilization Threshold   Action   Packet Rate Threshold   Action◀
│Global            Disabled %        Alarm       Disabled Pkts/s      Alarm
│GoodPkts          Disabled %        Alarm       Disabled Pkts/s      Alarm
│Errors               5 %           Execute      Disabled Pkts/s      Alarm
│Broadcst          Disabled %        Alarm       Disabled Pkts/s      Alarm
│Apple             Disabled %        Alarm       Disabled Pkts/s      Alarm
│TcpIp             Disabled %        Alarm       Disabled Pkts/s      Alarm
│DECnet            Disabled %        Alarm       Disabled Pkts/s      Alarm
│NetWareE          Disabled %        Alarm       Disabled Pkts/s      Alarm
│NetWare           Disabled %        Alarm       Disabled Pkts/s      Alarm
│
│When a new station is detected      take no action
│
│Log alarms into file                b:\alarm
│
│Execute the following file when an alarm occurs and the action is Execute:
│                                    c:\xln\send.bat
│
│Ring bell when alarm is generated   Yes
╚═════════════════════════════════════════════════════════════════════╝
 F1    │F2     │F3    │F4      │F5    │F6    │F7      │F8   │F9     │F10
 Help  │Revert │Save  │Options │Mode  │      │Receive │Xmit │Alarms │Back
```

F I G U R E 20.13

*The file SEND.BAT will
execute when the errors
reach 5% on the network.*

This chapter has examined the types of alarm definitions available: predefined and user-defined. You have also looked at some of the options for alarm notification, such as alarm logs, audible alarms, visual alarms, and executable files.

The next chapter examines the packet capture and filtering features available with many analyzers.

CHAPTER 21

Packet Capture

The previous chapters discussed the fact that you can create short- and long-term statistics to document network events such as errors, packet size distibution, and protocol types on the network. Some statistics, such as global utilization and errors, are calculated based on all packets seen. You can calculate other statistics, such as NetWare SAP traffic, RIP broadcasts, or Ethernet_802.2 frames, by applying a filter to the receive channels.

This chapter focuses on packet-capturing capabilities of analyzers and defines the filtering options available: pre-filtering (capture filtering) and post-filtering (decode filtering). The chapter also discusses the advantages and simplicity of point-and-click filtering. Finally, the chapter presents the purpose and advantages of enhanced filtering (filtering with Boolean operands).

Let's begin with an overview of packet-capturing abilities. Figure 21.1 depicts the general functions of a protocol analyzer.

FIGURE 21.1

General functions of a protocol analyzer that allows both pre- and post-filtering

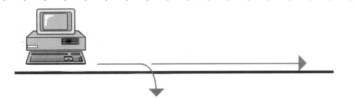

Protocol Analyzer Basic Functions

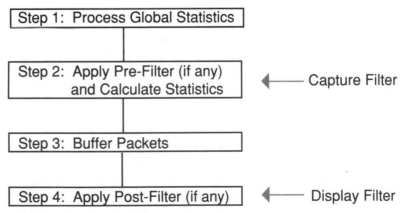

| Step 1: Process Global Statistics |
| Step 2: Apply Pre-Filter (if any) and Calculate Statistics | ◀── Capture Filter |
| Step 3: Buffer Packets |
| Step 4: Apply Post-Filter (if any) | ◀── Display Filter |

When a packet is seen on the network, the appropriate global statistics are calculated. In order to narrow down the scope of packets that are being captured and saved in the buffer, however, a filter can be applied: the *pre-filter*. Packets that meet the criteria defined in the pre-filter will be buffered either on the card or in system memory (product dependent). You can also capture the packets to disk if desired.

If no pre-filter is defined and an application is configured to capture all packets, the resulting trace buffer may be quite large and contain packets that do not relate to the information being sought. In this case, it may be difficult to view the important or problem packets because they are obscured by the large amount of extraneous traffic. In this situation, if an application has been run without the isolating pre-filters applied, you can filter the packets that are displayed from the trace buffer using a *post-filter*.

As shown in Figure 21.2, packets must meet the pre-filter criteria before being buffered. Packets must then meet the post-filtering criteria in order to be displayed.

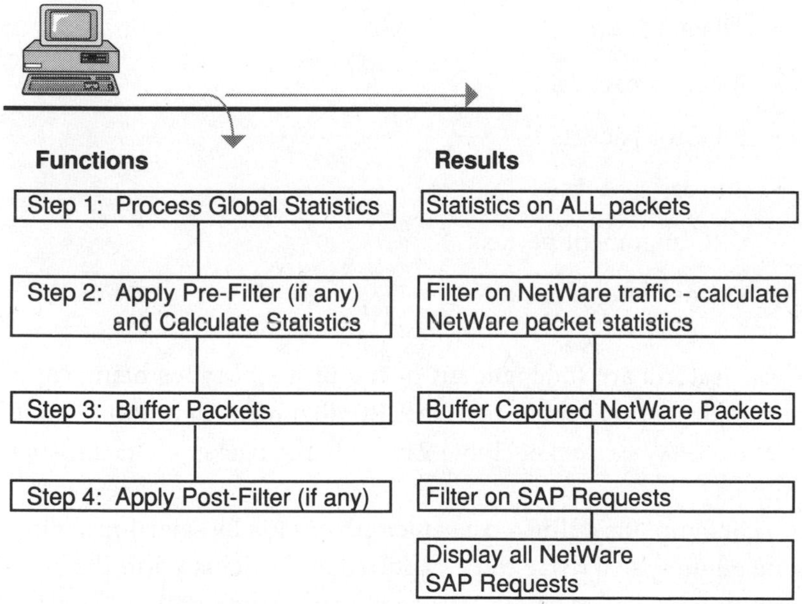

FIGURE 21.2

Packets must meet both pre- and post-filtering definitions before being displayed.

Functions

| Step 1: Process Global Statistics |

| Step 2: Apply Pre-Filter (if any) and Calculate Statistics |

| Step 3: Buffer Packets |

| Step 4: Apply Post-Filter (if any) |

Results

| Statistics on ALL packets |

| Filter on NetWare traffic - calculate NetWare packet statistics |

| Buffer Captured NetWare Packets |

| Filter on SAP Requests |

| Display all NetWare SAP Requests |

Figure 21.2 shows an application that has been configured with a pre-filter for NetWare packets. Although all packets will be calculated into the global statistics, only NetWare packets will be saved in the trace buffer. A post-filter has then been applied to the packets in the trace buffer. The post-filter allows only NetWare SAP packets to be displayed.

Pre-Filtering Criteria

There are two types of pre-filtering criteria that can be defined: packet characteristics and field values.

PACKET CHARACTERISTICS

Many analyzers, such as the LANalyzer, allow you to define the packet characteristics for pre-filtering. These characteristics are based on the overall packet formation and validity. Packet characteristics include

- All packets
- All good packets
- All error packets
- Size error packets
- CRC/alignment packets
- Defined length packets

These criteria are independent of the protocol types being captured. For example, a packet that fits the CRC/alignment definition could be a TCP/IP or NetWare packet. Table 21.1 lists the packet characteristics and definitions.

You configure the defined packet length criteria by selecting a minimum and maximum packet size to be captured and calculated in the statistics. You can use the packet length criteria in conjunction with other criteria.

PACKET CHARACTERISTIC	DEFINITION
All packets	All good and error packets
All good packets	All packets without error
Size error packets	Packets with a valid CRC that are less than 64 bytes or greater than 1518 bytes
CRC/alignment packets	Packets with invalid CRC values or packets that do not end on an 8-bit boundary (valid length)
Defined length packets	Packets that meet the defined length criteria

For example, you may wish to capture all short packets (packets less than 64 bytes with a valid CRC value). Since there is no packet characteristic called "short packets," you can use the defined length packet criteria in conjunction with the size error packets. In Figure 21.3, a channel, SHORT, has been defined that filters only on size error packets that are less than 64 bytes in length.

```
 09/22/92              LANalyzer Network Analyzer              01 23
 Press + or - to toggle, or Enter decimal number(s)      Edit Receive
=================== c:\xln\lanz\802.3\temp\temp ===================
┌RECEIVE                                          Simple Filter Mode ◄
│Channel         Size Range               Collect Start  Stop
│Name     Active From   To    Packets Allowed  Stats.  Count  Count
│SHORT    Yes    0      Min   Size-Errors     Yes     Off    Off
│Rx2      No     Min    Max   Good Packets    Yes     Off    Off
│Rx3      No     Min    Max   Good Packets    Yes     Off    Off
│Rx4      No     Min    Max   Good Packets    Yes     Off    Off
│Rx5      No     Min    Max   Good Packets    Yes     Off    Off
│Rx6      No     Min    Max   Good Packets    Yes     Off    Off
│Rx7      No     Min    Max   Good Packets    Yes     Off    Off
│Rx8      No     Min    Max   Good Packets    Yes     Off    Off

│TRIGGERS
│Start collecting at once
│Fire stop trigger never
│Once stop trigger has fired, collect an additional      0  packets.
│When the trace buffer is full, overwrite old packets.

│DATA COLLECTION

 F1      |F2     |F3    |F4      |F5    |F6    |F7     |F8   |F9     |F10
 Help    |Revert |Save  |Options |Mode  |Filter|Receive|Xmit |Alarms |Back
```

The value Min is used to indicate 64 bytes. The value Max is used to indicate 1518 bytes. The size range specified in the application shown is 0 to 64, inclusive, yet 64 is a valid length. You want to capture only packets shorter than 64 bytes. To define this, the packets allowed field has been toggled to Size-Errors. This ensures that 64-byte packets will not be captured in the buffer since they are legal-sized frames. Only short packets will be saved in the trace buffer.

NOTE
On the LANalyzer
Capture Filter screen,
the value **XX** is a
wildcard and denotes
that any value will be
accepted in this byte
position.

FIELD VALUES

In order to capture packets based on their Ethernet header type, network-layer protocol, transport-layer protocol, or upper-layer protocol information, you can indicate specific field values as pre-filtering criteria. Field values are defined based on a solid knowledge of the protocols in use. For example, to capture all RIP broadcasts on a NetWare LAN, you would define the values 0x0453 in the source socket field (IPX header) and FF-FF-FF-FF-FF-FF in the destination address field (Ethernet header), as shown in Figure 21.4.

FIGURE 21.4

The LANalyzer pre-filtering criteria are defined to capture all RIP broadcasts.

```
09/22/92              LANalyzer Network Analyzer            01 25
Enter a name, or Enter hexadecimal number(s)        Edit Simple Filter
======================= c:\xln\lanz\802.3\temp\temp =======================
↓Rx2                                    Link Protocol Ethernet

Station FF-FF-FF-FF-FF-FF <---- XX XX XX XX XX XX
Type    NetWare

Data:
Offset   Label               Value
0000     Checksum            XXXX
0002     Length              XXXXX
0004     Transport Ctl       XXX
0005     Packet Type         XXX
0006     Dest Network        XX XX XX XX
000A     Dest Node           XX XX XX XX XX XX
0010     Dest Socket         XXXX
0012     Src  Network        XX XX XX XX
0016     Src  Node           XX XX XX XX XX XX
001C     Src  Socket         0453
001E     Req Type            XXXX
0024     Function Code       XXX

F1     |F2    |F3     |F4   |F5     |F6   |F7     |F8   |F9   |F10
Help   |Copy  |Paste  |     |EBCDIC |     |Clear  |     |     |Back
```

The following list describes several field values that may be useful for pre-filtering on a NetWare LAN:

▸ **NetWare packets using Ethernet_802.3 frame types:** Filter on the value FFFF in the checksum field of the IPX header. You can also use a binary filter. (Binary filtering is discussed later in this chapter.)

▸ **NetWare packets using Ethernet_802.2 frame types:** Filter on the value 0xE0 in both the DSAP and SSAP fields.

▸ **NetWare packets using Ethernet_SNAP frame types:** Within the SNAP header, filter on the value 0xAA in the DSAP and SSAP fields and the value 0x8137 in the Ethernet type field.

▸ **NetWare packets using Ethernet_II frame types:** Filter on the value 0x8137 in the type field of the Ethernet header.

▸ **NetWare SAP broadcasts:** Filter on the value 0x0452 in the source socket (IPX header) and FF-FF-FF-FF-FF-FF in the destination address field (Ethernet header).

▸ **NetWare Get Nearest Server SAP requests:** Filter on the value 0x0452 in the source socket (IPX header), 0x0003 in the SAP type field, and 0x0004 in the server type field.

▸ **Burst Mode reads/writes:** Filter on the value 0x7777 in the NCP request type field.

You can define field values to capture a variety of NCP requests and replies on the network as well. To filter on a specific NCP request or reply, refer to Table 7.1 in Chapter 7 for a listing of NCP function and subfunction codes.

Figure 21.5 shows a filter set up on NCP Erase File requests (function code 68) from the client 0x00-00-1B-09-32-8E that is using the Ethernet_802.2 frame format. The LANalyzer has substituted the word "novell" in place of 0x00-00-1B to indicate that this is the vendor ID assigned to Novell's network interface cards (NE1000, NE2000, etc.).

NOTE

Novell has transferred ownership of network interface card manufacturing to a third-party company; however, the new manufacturer is still using the vendor ID number originally assigned to Novell by Xerox.

FIGURE 21.5

Filtering based on frame type, destination socket, source node address, and NCP function

```
| 09/22/92                      LANalyzer Network Analyzer
       01:32
   Press + or - to toggle, or Enter hexadecimal number(s)      Edit
Simple Filter
╔════════════════════ c:\xln\lanz\802.3\temp\temp═══════════════════════╗
║↑Station XX XX XX XX XX XX <---- novell09328E                           ◄
║Length  XXXXX
║DSAP NetWare                    SSAP NetWare              Control XX
║
║Data:
║Offset    Label              Value
║0000      Checksum           XXXX
║0002      Length             XXXXX
║0004      Transport Ctl      XXX
║0005      Packet Type        XXX
║0006      Dest Network       XX XX XX XX
║000A      Dest Node          XX XX XX XX XX XX
║0010      Dest Socket        0451
║0012      Src  Network       XX XX XX XX
║0016      Src  Node          XX XX XX XX XX XX
║001C      Src  Socket        XXXX
║001E      Req Type           XXXX
║0024      Function Code      68
║0025      Function Len       XXXXX
╚════════════════════════════════════════════════════════════════════════╝

F1     |F2     |F3     |F4    |F5     |F6    |F7     |F8    |F9    |F10
Help   |Copy   |Paste  |      |EBCDIC |      |Clear  |      |      |Back
```

Some analyzers also allow binary filtering criteria to be defined. *Binary filtering* permits filtering based on bit values rather than byte values. For example, if you wish to capture all packets that have crossed between four and seven routers to reach the local network, you need to place a binary filter value in the hops field of the IPX header. This bit value filter would be 00000000 000001XX. This filter requires 13 0's to precede a 1 in the hop count field. The last two bits can contain either 0 or 1. This allows the following values to be accepted by the filter:

00000000 00000100   Four hops

00000000 00000101   Five hops

00000000 00000110   Six hops

00000000 00000111   Seven hops

NOTE
Appendix D contains a binary-decimal-hexadecimal conversion chart that you may find helpful when assigning binary filters.

Some analyzers, such as the LANalyzer for NetWare, allow field prefiltering based on preset values, as shown in Figure 21.6. In this figure, a

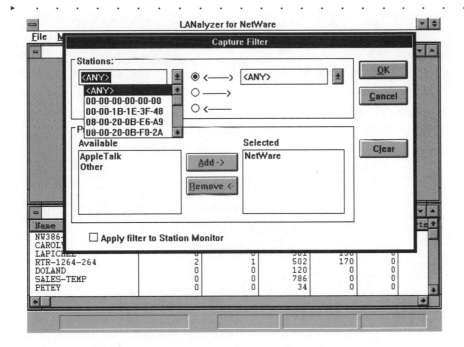

pre-filter on NetWare packets has been set. Packets that do not meet the criteria, such as AppleTalk or TCP/IP, will not be saved in the buffer. These pre-filter options are available and preconfigured, requiring a user to simply click on the desired pre-filtering criteria. This simplified method of pre-filtering may be more desirable for users who are new to protocol analysis.

Now that you've learned about pre-filtering options for protocol analysis, let's examine the post-filtering options you can use to isolate packets in the buffer.

Post-Filtering

You can use post-filtering (also referred to as display filtering) to apply additional filtering criteria to packets in the buffer. This ensures that packets in the buffer meet a more specific filter criterion before being displayed.

For example, perhaps you have captured all NetWare packets that use the Ethernet_802.2 frame type in your buffer. The result is over 200 packets in the buffer. In order to isolate and view only NetWare SAP packets in the buffer, you can apply a NetWare SAP post-filter to the captured packets.

The packets that met the pre-filtering criteria remain in the buffer; post-filters can be changed to show different packets saved in the trace buffer.

Figure 21.7 shows the steps taken to isolate SAP broadcast packets or Burst Mode connection requests from a single buffer of packets that met pre-filtering criteria.

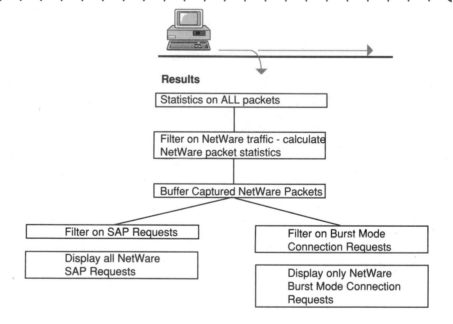

F I G U R E 21.7

A variety of post-filters can be applied to the trace buffer.

Analyzer products provide several methods for post-filtering. The LANalyzer for NetWare contains preconfigured post-filters, as shown in Figure 21.8.

In this figure, the post-filter option NetWare has been selected; this provides you with a list of various post-filter options you can select, such as NCP, SAP, RIP, SER (Serialization packets), WDOG (Watchdog packets), and so on.

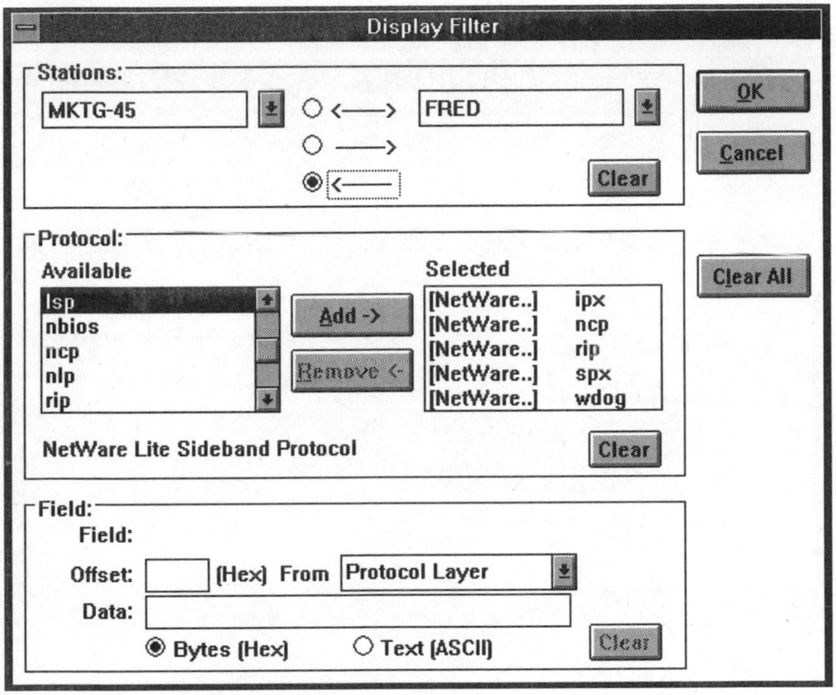

FIGURE 21.8

The LANalyzer contains
predefined post-filtering
criteria.

The LANalyzer for NetWare also introduced a new post-filtering technique known as point-and-click filtering. *Point-and-click filtering* allows users less familiar with frame structures to use advanced post-filtering techniques.

For example, perhaps a user is viewing a Burst Mode connection request in the buffer, as shown in Figure 21.9, and would like to filter on similar types of packets.

Using point-and-click filtering, the user need only double-click on "Function Code: 101" to automatically input the appropriate value in the postfilter. Figure 21.10 shows the values that are placed in the post-filter.

You can also use point-and-click filtering to isolate conversations between two stations. If you double-click on a line in the Summary screen that contains a packet being transmitted between the two stations, the station node addresses (or names, if a name table is used) are placed in the

FIGURE 21.9

*Point-and-click filtering
allows you to select a filter
value directly from the
trace buffer.*

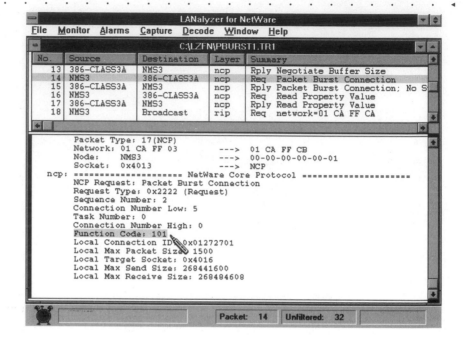

post-filter. As shown in the upper portion of Figure 21.11, you can use either names (contained in the name table), such as Josine and FS-BLDG2, or node addresses. You can also change the direction arrow to indicate the direction of the conversation you are interested in.

Enhanced Filtering

As shown in this chapter, you can use pre-filtering and post-filtering to isolate packets captured and displayed in the trace buffer. In addition to the basic techniques already covered, advanced users require additional filtering functionality. The following is an overview of enhanced filtering capabilities.

```
┌─────────────────────────────────────────────────────────────┐
│ ─            Display Filter                                   │
│ ┌─Stations:─────────────────────────────────┐  ┌────────┐   │
│ │ <ANY>          ▼   ⦿ <———>  <ANY>      ▼ │  │   OK   │   │
│ │                    ○  ———>                │  └────────┘   │
│ │                    ○ <———      [ Clear ]  │  ┌────────┐   │
│ └───────────────────────────────────────────┘  │ Cancel │   │
│ ┌─Protocol:──────────────────────────────────┐  └────────┘   │
│ │ Available              Selected             │  ┌──────────┐ │
│ │ [AppleTalk..]          [NetWare..]   ncp    │  │ Clear All│ │
│ │ [LinkLevel..]   [ Add -> ]                  │  └──────────┘ │
│ │ [NetWare..]     [ Remove <- ]               │              │
│ │                                             │              │
│ │                              [ Clear ]      │              │
│ └─────────────────────────────────────────────┘              │
│ ┌─Field:─────────────────────────────────────┐              │
│ │   Field:  Function Code: 101                │              │
│ │   Offset: [0006] (Hex)  From [Protocol Layer ▼] │          │
│ │   Data:   [65                              ] │              │
│ │        ⦿ Bytes (Hex)  ○ Text (ASCII)  [ Clear ] │          │
│ └─────────────────────────────────────────────┘              │
└─────────────────────────────────────────────────────────────┘
```

F I G U R E   21.10

The value 0x65 is placed at offset 0x0006 from the protocol header to indicate that the user is looking for Burst Mode connection request and reply packets only.

Enhanced filtering allows the use of Boolean operands, such as AND, OR, AND NOT, and NOT, when defining filters. These operands allow more flexibility and further definition of packets to be captured or displayed. For example, perhaps you would like to capture all SAP packets on a network that supports 20 servers. You do not, however, want to capture SAP traffic from FS1 or FS2. If you did not have the option of using enhanced filtering, you would have to define a filter based on SAP traffic and then simply ignore the trace buffer entries from FS1 and FS2.

Enhanced filtering on the LANalyzer permits the use of up to 16 filter patterns. Each pattern is a separate filter itself. By using the Boolean operands when mixing and matching patterns, you can define a single channel that includes various filtering criteria.

FIGURE 21.11

If you double-click on a packet's station information, the station node addresses are placed in the post-filter.

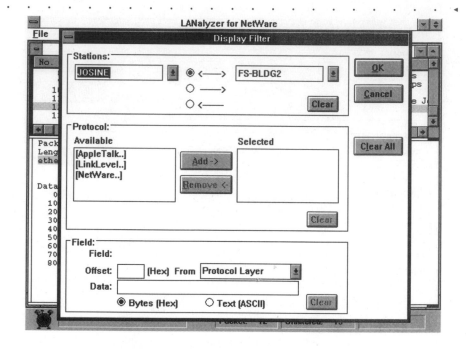

For example, perhaps you have defined the following patterns:

Pattern 1	All broadcast packets	Ethernet header: destination address FF-FF-FF-FF-FF-FF
Pattern 2	SAP-Source Socket	IPX header: source socket number 0x0452
Pattern 3	SAP-Destination Socket	IPX header: destination socket number 0x0452
Pattern 4	RIP-Source Socket	IPX header: source socket number 0x0453
Pattern 5	RIP-Destination Socket	IPX header: destination socket number 0x0453

| Pattern 6 | From FS2 | IPX header: source network address C9-00-00-01, node address 00-00-00-00-00-01 |
| Pattern 7 | To FS2 | IPX header: destination network address C9-00-00-01, node address 00-00-00-00-00-01 |

By using Boolean operands, you can define the following channel filters:

▶ (All broadcasts) AND NOT (SAP broadcasts)

▶ (All broadcasts) AND NOT (RIP broadcasts)

▶ (All broadcasts) AND NOT (RIP broadcasts) or (SAP broadcasts)

▶ (All broadcasts) AND NOT (from FS2)

Figure 21.12 shows a LANalyzer application, FILEVIEW, that uses enhanced filtering. The patterns DIRECTOR, PURGE, ERASE, SRC ADDR, and DEST ADDR are associated using Boolean operands.

The FILEVIEW application uses enhanced filtering to provide a variety of filter options by combining the patterns defined at the bottom of Figure 21.12. Each pattern is a separate filter that contains filter information in the type, function, subfunction, destination address, or source address field.

Enhanced filtering is only as limited as your imagination and knowledge of the protocols. As you become more familiar with the protocols and communications, you will find that enhanced filtering permits greater flexibility in isolating specific packets on the network.

This chapter has presented two methods for isolating specific packets in a buffer: pre-filtering and post-filtering. By using pre-filtering, you can set the initial definition for packet capturing based on packet characteristics or field values. Post-filtering allows you to further define the packets to be

FIGURE 21.12

The LANalyzer application FILEVIEW is defined using enhanced filtering.

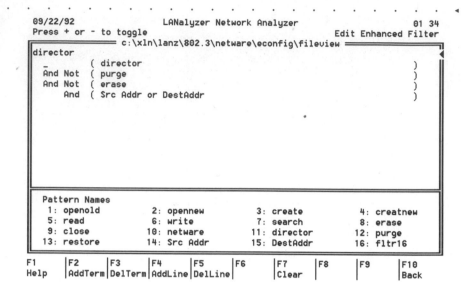

```
09/22/92              LANalyzer Network Analyzer              01 34
Press + or - to toggle                        Edit Enhanced Filter
                 c:\xln\lanz\802.3\netware\econfig\fileview
director
  _       ( director                                            )
  And Not ( purge                                               )
  And Not ( erase                                               )
      And ( Src Addr or DestAddr                                )




  Pattern Names
   1: openold       2: opennew      3: create      4: creatnew
   5: read          6: write        7: search      8: erase
   9: close        10: netware     11: director   12: purge
  13: restore      14: Src Addr    15: DestAddr    16: fltr16

F1    |F2      |F3      |F4      |F5      |F6  |F7      |F8  |F9  |F10
Help  |AddTerm |DelTerm |AddLine |DelLine |    |Clear   |    |    |Back
```

viewed from the buffer by using techniques such as field value definition and point-and-click filtering. Enhanced filtering allows users to capture very specific information.

The next chapter focuses on packet transmission techniques.

CHAPTER 22

Packet Transmit

Although most analysis techniques are based on packet receipt as defined in the previous chapter, many packet tests include packet transmission to test a network cabling system or component and gather or verify network information.

This chapter examines the three primary reasons for using packet transmit tests and provides examples of manual and automatic packet transmit tests. The chapter also discusses transmit options such as building packets from scratch or copying a captured packet onto a transmit channel.

The chapter begins with an overview of the three primary uses of packet transmit tests:

- ► Load testing

- ► Component testing

- ► Event re-creation

Load Testing

Two types of load tests have been defined in this book: intelligent load tests and dumb load tests. On a NetWare Ethernet LAN, you can use a transmit test to determine how high bandwidth utilization can become before users complain of performance degradation. For example, in Figure 22.1, the LANalyzer GENLOAD application has been configured to generate a 9% load on the network to a fictitious node address (0x00-00-00-00-00-00).

It has been specified that the packets being transmitted by GENLOAD will be filled with 0x00 in the data portion. Since the GENLOAD application is included with the LANalyzer, creating a "dumb load" test is quite simple.

NOTE
For more examples of load testing, refer to Chapter 3.

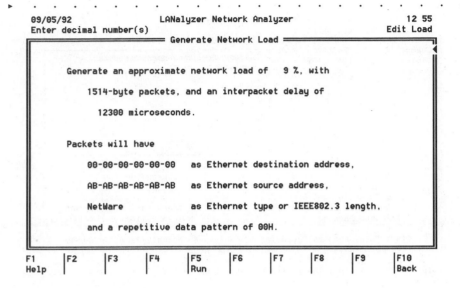

You can use the GENLOAD application to transmit a dumb load.

Component Testing

You can use intelligent loads to test a single component on the network, such as a server, bridge, or router. By addressing packets to a network device and, optionally, requesting a reply (using a diagnostic protocol such as the Diagnostic Responder), you can determine whether the component is able to keep up with requests under varying load conditions.

The LANalyzer's SERVERVU application, shown in Figure 22.2, allows you to transmit an intelligent load to a NetWare server. The application is designed to transmit SAP requests, thereby causing the server to reply with SAP replies. If the server cannot reply because of an overload condition, the SERVERVU application can also be configured to report the number of Request Being Processed packets from the server.

FIGURE 22.2

You can use the SERVERVU application to stress-test a NetWare file server.

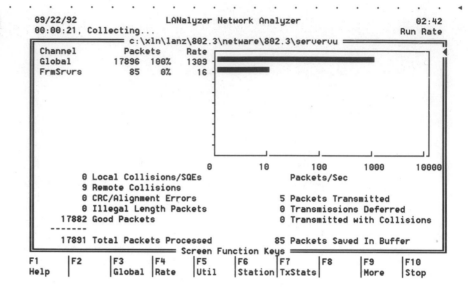

In Figure 22.2, the SERVERVU application has been configured to transmit SAP broadcasts on the network. Five packets have been transmitted and 85 replies have been received. In order to stress-test a server, place the server's network and node address in the IPX header and gradually increase the number of packets transmitted. The server will begin replying to clients with Request Being Processed packets when it cannot keep up.

Event Re-Creation

You can also use analyzers to capture and retransmit a single packet or a sequence of packets. This is useful when an event has occurred on the network that you must re-create in order to analyze it.

For example, perhaps you have noticed a small amount of short packets on the network but have been too busy to replace the LAN drivers causing the problem. You are now installing a new bridge on the network that continues to crash intermittently throughout the day. To determine whether the bridge crashes are linked to the short packets, you can use the LANalyzer

This type of analysis technique was used when an application developer complained that his SPX-based program was causing the NetWare server to ABEND. Because he sent in his trace to Novell, it was possible to re-create the situation and verify that the application was the cause of server ABEND. The developer had used an unsupported value in the SPX connection setup routine; this was evident upon examination of the SPX header used for his connection establishment. Novell, in turn, created a patch that would allow the server to accept these types of SPX packets without abending.

to capture a short packet, copy it into a transmit channel, change the destination address, and transmit it directly to the bridge. This enables you to test the bridge and determine whether the short packets are causing the crashes.

The LANalyzer also provides a method for replaying an entire trace buffer out onto the network. For example, if an SPX-based application is suspected of causing the server to ABEND, you can capture the connection setup packets that are transmitted to the server and analyze the server's response.

When using packet transmits to test a network component or re-create an event, there are three methods you can use for creating the test:

- ▶ Create transmit packets from scratch.

- ▶ Copy a packet from a receive channel and paste it into the transmit channel.

- ▶ Capture a sequence of packets into the buffer and replay the entire sequence.

Create Transmit Packets from Scratch

Experienced users may wish to create a transmit packet from scratch. This requires a thorough knowledge of the data link, network, transport, and upper-layer protocol structures. For example, if you wish to create a Diagnostic Request packet to send to the server on the network, you must know the length of the Diagnostic Request packet and each field value within the packet.

Figure 22.3 shows a diagnostic packet that has been created from scratch. The packet is shown in hexadecimal format.

F I G U R E 22.3

A Diagnostic Request packet was built from scratch.

```
09/22/92                    LANalyzer Network Analyzer                02:44
Press + or - to toggle, or Enter decimal number(s)              Edit Packet
═══════════════════ c:\xln\lanz\802.3\netware\802.3\nodeview ══════════════
 XmtNodes                          Protocol Type  DATA
 Packet Length (Generated: 60     Transmitted: as generated)

 Ethernet
         Destination Address                 Broadcast
         Source Address                      exos651575
         Type                                0022

 Data Length   46                         Data Offset 0       ASCII display
 0000   FF FF 00 22 00 11 00 00    00 00 FF FF FF FF FF FF    ..."..........
 0010   04 56 00 00 00 00 08 00    14 65 15 75 40 06 00 03    .V.......e.u@...
 0020   00 04 00 00 00 00 00 00    00 00 00 00 00 00          ..............
```

```
F1      |F2      |F3      |F4      |F5      |F6      |F7      |F8    |F9    |F10
Help    |Copy    |Paste   |Type    |EBCDIC  |Zoom In |Fill    |      |      |Back
```

In order to view the fields of the packet in their proper locations, you can apply a *template* to the packet. You can place templates over data to define field labels, field lengths, and field offsets. In Figure 22.4, a template called DIAG has been created and applied to the packet created earlier. As you can see from the example, this diagnostic packet contains no exclusion addresses. (Remember from Chapter 11 that the exclusion addresses specify which nodes are not required to respond.)

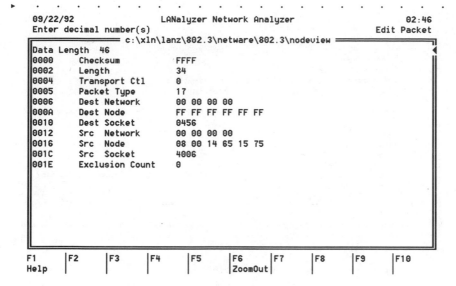

A template makes packet creation easier.

Copy-and-Paste Method

The copy-and-paste method provides a quick way to create a packet. After capturing a packet that is similar to the type of packet you wish to send, you can copy the packet into a buffer and paste it into a transmit channel. The fields within the packet, however, may need to be changed for your test.

For example, to create a test that transmits Get Nearest Server packets, you can run any LANalyzer application and copy a packet from the trace buffer, as shown in Figure 22.5.

The LANalyzer screen displays a notification message in the upper left-hand corner indicating that the packet has been copied. You can then paste the packet into a transmit channel and edit the packet fields. In Figure 22.6, the packet has been pasted into a transmit channel.

If desired, you can change the destination address to contain the node address of the device you want to send the packet to.

The COPY option allows you to copy the packet into the LANalyzer clipboard.

```
09/22/92                    LANalyzer Network Analyzer               02 50
Packet 36 copied to clipboard
=========================== Trace Buffer ===========================
Frame: Number: 36          Length:     64 bytes
       Errors: None
       Receive Channels: SAP
802.3: ================= IEEE 802.3 Datalink Layer =================
       Station: novell1EF22C      ----> Broadcast
       Length:   34
  ipx: ============= NetWare Internetwork Packet Exchange Protocol ========
       Checksum: 0xFFFF           Length: 34
       Hop Count:  0              Packet Type: 17 (NCP)
       Network: 00 00 00 00       ---> 00 00 00 00
       Node:    novell1EF22C      --->  Broadcast
       Socket:  0x4006            --->  SAP
  sap: ============= NetWare Service Advertising Protocol ============
       Type: 3 (Nearest Service Query)
       Server Type: 4 (File Server)



F1     |F2     |F3     |F4      |F5     |F6      |F7    |F8    |F9    |F10
Help   |Copy   |Print  |Options |EBCDIC |AltDisp |Prev  |Next  |Go To |Back
```

After pasting the packet, you can edit the fields for your application.

```
09/22/92                    LANalyzer Network Analyzer               02:51
Packet pasted
==================== c:\xln\lanz\802.3\temp\temp ====================
SAP REQ                     Protocol Type  DATA
Packet Length (Generated: 60    Transmitted: as generated)

Ethernet
    Destination Address                  Broadcast
    Source Address                       novell1EF22C
    Type                                 0022

Data Length  46                    Data Offset 0      ASCII display
0000   FF FF 00 22 00 11 00 00   00 00 FF FF FF FF FF FF   ...".............
0010   04 52 00 00 00 00 00 00   1B 1E F2 2C 40 06 00 03   .R.........,@...
0020   00 04 A5 A5 A5 A5 A5 A5   A5 A5 A5 A5 A5 A5         .............




F1     |F2     |F3     |F4      |F5     |F6       |F7    |F8    |F9    |F10
Help   |Copy   |Paste  |Type    |EBCDIC |Zoom In  |Fill  |      |      |Back
```

Replay Network Events

The LANalyzer provides a utility called REPLAY, shown as the fourth utility in Figure 22.7, that allows you to retransmit the entire contents of a trace buffer or trace file onto the network. The REPLAY utility enables technicians to test various network configurations under identical conditions. The REPLAY utility is one of the many utilities that are included with the LANalyzer product.

The REPLAY utility does not, however, allow you to change the packets that are being transmitted onto the network. In order to transmit a variety of different packets, you must create or edit an application and define transmit channels.

The LANalyzer has six transmit channels, allowing up to six packet types to be transmitted from a single application, as shown in Figure 22.8.

```
 LANalyzer   Release 3.11A                                    2:52 am

┌─────────────────────────────────────────────────────────────────┐
│                 Utilities - c:\xln\lanz\utility                   │
│ ┌───────────────────────────────────────────────────────────────┐│
│ │ GENNAME   - Generate a Name File                              ││
│ │ IP2NADDR  - Map Internet Addresses to Network Addresses       ││
│ │ NAME      - Edit Name Files                                   ││
│ │ REPLAY    - Transmit Trace File Back Onto The Network         ││
│ │ STATS     - Display Statistics                                ││
│ │ TEMPLATE  - Edit Template                                     ││
│ │ TRACEIPA  - Interpacket Arrival Time Analysis - IPA           ││
│ └───────────────────────────────────────────────────────────────┘│
└─────────────────────────────────────────────────────────────────┘

F1        |        |        |F5      |        |        |F8      |F10
Help      |        |        |Run     |        |        |DOS     |Back
```

FIGURE 22.7

The REPLAY utility is one of the many utilities that are included with the LANalyzer product.

The LANalyzer Transmit

screen supports six transmit

channels.

```
09/22/92                    LANalyzer Network Analyzer                    02:53
Press + or - to toggle                                             Edit Transmit
┌══════════════════════════ c:\xln\lanz\802.3\temp\temp ═══════════════════════╗
║TRANSMIT                                                                       ◄
║Channel              Delay                   Preamble    Coll.
║Name    Active  Count (100us)  CRC  Collide  Bytes       Backoff
║Tx1     Yes     1     0         Good No       8 (normal)  Normal
║Tx2     Yes     1     0         Good No       8 (normal)  Normal
║Tx3     Yes     1     0         Good No       8 (normal)  Normal
║Tx4     Yes     1     0         Good No       8 (normal)  Normal
║Tx5     Yes     1     0         Good No       8 (normal)  Normal
║Tx6     Yes     1     0         Good No       8 (normal)  Normal
║─────────────────────────────────────────────────────────────────────────────
║MULTIPACKET TRANSMISSION
║Txall   No      6     0         Good No       8 (normal)  Normal
║
║Transmit serially with the following relative frequencies:
║          Tx1       1       Tx2       1       Tx3       1
║          Tx4       1       Tx5       1       Tx6       1
║
║Transmit after _    99:00:00 hours or  _
└───────────────────────────────────────────────────────────────────────────────

F1    |F2     |F3    |F4      |F5   |F6     |F7      |F8    |F9     |F10
Help  |Revert |Save  |Options |Mode |Packet |Receive |Xmit  |Alarms |Back
```

The LANalyzer also provides a variety of options for packet transmission. These options include

▶ **CRC Validity:** The packet transmitted from that channel can have either a good or a bad CRC value. Packets with bad CRCs can be transmitted to a single network device to evaluate its handling of error packets.

▶ **Intentionally Collide:** The packet can be forced to collide when transmitting. (Wait for the line to become busy, and then transmit). You can force collisions onto the network to determine how devices are filtering (or not filtering) the collisions and their reactions to excessive network collisions.

▶ **Perform Backoff Algorithm:** Once you detect a collision, you can immediately retransmit the packet, without performing the backoff algorithm and waiting. This simulates an aggressive node that does not wait the allotted time before attempting retransmission after a collision.

The LANalyzer also allows you to determine the number of packets that will be transmitted from each channel. If desired, you can set the transmit number to INF (infinity). This indicates that the application will transmit packets continuously, until manually stopped.

Multipacket transmission is another feature of the LANalyzer. This enables several or all of the packets to be transmitted in serial or random order. As shown in Figure 22.9, you can configure an application to serially transmit 64-byte packets, 633-byte packets, and 1082-byte packets, to create a varying load on the network.

```
09/22/92               LANalyzer Network Analyzer              02:54
Enter a name                                           Edit Transmit
================ c:\xln\lanz\802.3\general\varload ===============┐
TRANSMIT                                                          ◄
Channel               Delay                  Preamble    Coll.
Name       Active  Count  (100us)  CRC  Collide   Bytes    Backoff
64byte     No        1       0     Good   No    8 (normal)  Normal
633byte    No        1       0     Good   No    8 (normal)  Normal
1082byte   No        1       0     Good   No    8 (normal)  Normal
           No        1       0     Good   No    8 (normal)  Normal
           No        1       0     Good   No    8 (normal)  Normal
           No        1       0     Good   No    8 (normal)  Normal
                                                                 
MULTIPACKET TRANSMISSION
Txall      Yes      Inf     200    Good   No    8 (normal)  Normal

Transmit serially with the following relative frequencies:
         64byte     30       633byte    20      1082byte   50
                     0                   0                  0

Transmit after _      00:00:00 hours or  _
                                                                 
F1     |F2     |F3    |F4       |F5   |F6     |F7      |F8   |F9    |F10
Help   |Revert |Save  |Options  |Mode |Packet |Receive |Xmit |Alarms|Back
```

FIGURE 22.9

An application can serially transmit packets defined in the transmit channels.

The final option that is available on the packet transmission screen determines when packets will be transmitted. The options include

▸ Transmit at a certain time of day (transmit at HH:MM:SS).

▸ Transmit after a certain amount of time has passed (transmit after HH:MM:SS).

▸ Transmit when a packet has been received on one of the receive channels.

Transmit-time options allow an application to be started automatically, without operator intervention. For example, to test a router during the evening, you can elect to transmit after two hours have passed. If you start the application at 5:30 P.M., when you leave the office, the LANalyzer will begin transmitting packets at 7:30 P.M.

You can also configure a LANalyzer test to start transmitting at a specific time of day—at 8:00 A.M., for example. This time is based upon the workstation clock time.

Finally, you can choose to begin transmission after receipt on one of the application's receipt channels. For example, upon receipt of a SAP request, you can transmit a SAP reply to simulate a server answering a client that is looking for a service on the network.

These options enhance the LANalyzer's capability for testing NetWare LANs and applications.

This chapter has presented the primary reasons for using packet transmit tests: load testing, component testing, and event re-creation. You examined three options for creating transmits, including packet replay. You also learned about transmit options for multipacket and automatic transmission.

The final chapter of this book examines protocol decodes that are available for analysis tools.

CHAPTER 23

Protocol Decodes

Throughout this book, you have seen screens that provide decodes of NetWare packets. Analyzers that can decode NetWare protocols provide an interpretation of the information within the packet. For example, function code 68 is interpreted as an Erase File NCP call.

This chapter examines decodes that are available with analysis products such as the LANalyzer and LANalyzer for NetWare. The chapter also provides an overview of decoding options available and a description of templates that can be applied when no decode is available.

First, a word of warning regarding decodes. Analyzers differ in their decoding capabilities. If a product claims to decode NetWare, it may be able to decode most NetWare 2.x and NetWare 3.x communications but not NetWare Lite and/or Burst Mode Protocol. If your network uses these protocols, you will have to manually decode them from a hexadecimal display of the packet contents—a time-consuming task. Since all analyzers differ in their decoding capabilities, check with the manufacturer to ensure that the desired decodes are available.

Some analysis products also charge for decodes. When you purchase the product, you pay one flat fee for the analysis product itself; additional fees are charged for each decode you wish to add to the system. For users who decode a variety of network protocols, such as AppleTalk, TCP/IP, NetWare 2.x, 3.x, NetWare Lite, and DECnet, these types of analysis systems may not be cost efficient.

Let's begin this chapter with a comparison of a packet that has been decoded and one that has not. Figure 23.1 shows a NetWare NCP packet that has been decoded.

The decoded packet fields are interpreted and presented in English with each field labeled, such as "hops" and "function code." Decodes may also change the numerical representation style from hexadecimal to decimal, ASCII, or EBCDIC when appropriate. For example, in a packet that contains data, you can see hexadecimal values translated into ASCII values, as shown in Figure 23.2.

If an analyzer doesn't support decoding (or has decoding turned off, as shown in the undecoded upper layers in Figure 23.3), the packets are displayed in hexadecimal format, with no labels applied and no translations

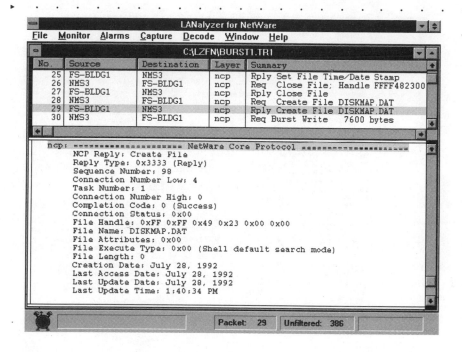

F I G U R E 23.1

Decoded NetWare NCP

reply

performed. In this case, you would need to manually decode the packet. Since this is a time-consuming and laborious task, it is desirable to have an analyzer that includes decodes for the protocols you will be using.

Some analyzers, such as the LANalyzer, include a large selection of decodes with the product; decodes do not need to be purchased separately. The LANalyzer product includes decodes for most of today's most popular protocols, such as

> NetWare (v2.x, v3.x, Lite)
>
> TCP/IP
>
> AppleTalk (Phase I and II)
>
> DECnet
>
> DEC LAT
>
> OSI

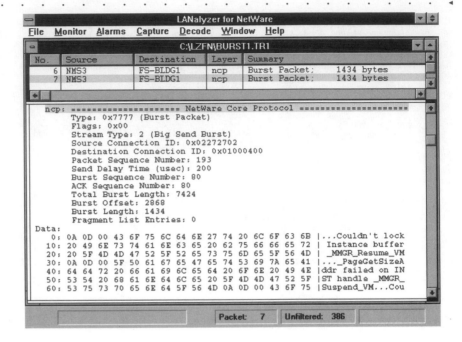

NFS

Banyan Vines

SNA

NetBEUI

XNS

SMB (LAN Manager/LAN Server)

The LANalyzer provides three decoding options: No Decode, Brief Decode, and Expanded Decode. Let's look at each of these decoding options.

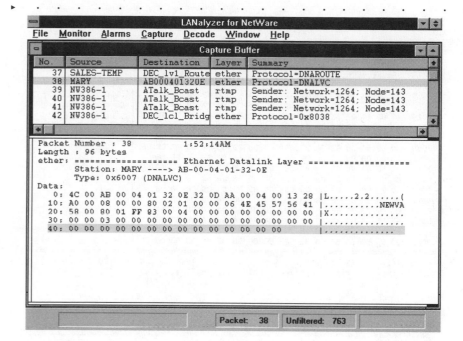

No Decode Option

If you configure a trace buffer to use No Decode, you basically get a hexadecimal "dump" of the packet contents, as shown in Figure 23.4. This can be valuable if you want to apply a template that would display only the few fields of interest to you.

Some products, such as the LANalyzer for NetWare, allow related fields of the decoded and undecoded data to be highlighted for easier correlation. As shown in Figure 23.5, the file handle field has been highlighted in the decoded portion. The same field has automatically been highlighted in the hexadecimal representation of the packet.

F I G U R E 23.4

If you elect to turn off decoding, as shown in this example, or if your analyzer cannot decode the protocol, you are presented with a hexadecimal "dump."

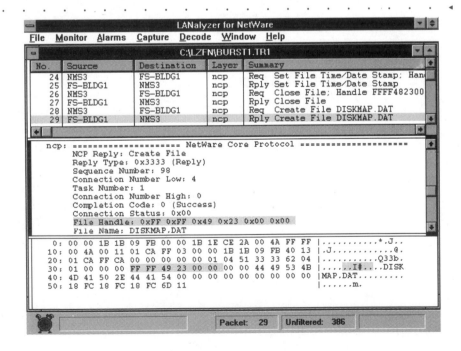

```
09/22/92                    LANalyzer Network Analyzer              03 30
                                                                Trace Decode
╔════════════════════════════ Trace Buffer ════════════════════════════╗
│↓Frame: Number: 2491        Length:    594 bytes                        │
│        Errors: None                                                    │
│        Receive Channels: GoodPkts NetWare                              │
│Data:                                                     ASCII display │
│0000  00 00 1B 1E 62 06 00 00  1B 03 E1 12 02 40 FF FF  ....b.......@.. │
│0010  02 40 01 05 C9 99 00 06  00 00 1B 1E 62 06 40 0C  .@..........b.@.│
│0020  10 00 86 03 00 00 00 00  00 01 2F 90 40 00 12 5A  ........../.@..Z│
│0030  97 59 43 5D C7 CB C7 CB  42 53 4C 42 03 00 0A 00  .YC]....BSLB....│
│0040  C9 C7 03 00 01 00 06 02  00 00 00 00 00 00 00 00  ................│
│0050  00 00 00 00 00 00 00 00  00 00 00 00 00 00 00 00  ................│
│0060  00 00 00 00 00 00 00 00  00 00 00 00 00 00 00 00  ................│
│0070  00 00 00 00 00 00 00 00  00 00 00 00 00 00 00 00  ................│
│0080  00 00 00 00 00 00 00 00  00 00 00 00 00 00 00 00  ................│
│0090  00 00 00 00 00 00 00 00  00 00 03 05 04 80 20 00  .............. .│
│00A0  00 85 E7 BE 2A 00 00 00  00 00 00 00 00 00 00 00  ....*...........│
│00B0  00 00 00 7E 00 00 00 00  00 01 00 00 00 DD 00 41  ...~...........A│
│00C0  49 42 80 99 48 00 DD 00  04 00 00 00 00 00 01 5E  IB..H..........^│
│00D0  00 11 00 00 00 00 00 24  06 01 01 03 01 03 10 00  .......$........│
│00E0  00 00 00 00 00 00 00 00  00 00 00 00 00 00 00 00  ................│
╚═══════════════════════════════════════════════════════════════════════╝
F1     │F2    │F3    │F4      │F5    │F6      │F7   │F8    │F9    │F10
Help   │Copy  │Print │Options │EBCDIC│AltDisp │Prev │Next  │Go To │Back
```

F I G U R E 23.5

The file handle field is highlighted in both the decoded and hexadecimal portions of the screen.

```
─                            LANalyzer for NetWare                      ▼ ▲
File   Monitor  Alarms  Capture  Decode  Window  Help
─                            C:\LZFN\BURST1.TR1                         ▼ ▲
┌────┬──────────┬─────────────┬───────┬──────────────────────────────────┐
│ No │ Source   │ Destination │ Layer │ Summary                          │
│ 24 │ NMS3     │ FS-BLDG1    │ ncp   │ Req  Set File Time/Date Stamp; Han│
│ 25 │ FS-BLDG1 │ NMS3        │ ncp   │ Rply Set File Time/Date Stamp     │
│ 26 │ NMS3     │ FS-BLDG1    │ ncp   │ Req  Close File; Handle FFFF482300│
│ 27 │ FS-BLDG1 │ NMS3        │ ncp   │ Rply Close File                   │
│ 28 │ NMS3     │ FS-BLDG1    │ ncp   │ Req  Create File DISKMAP.DAT      │
│ 29 │ FS-BLDG1 │ NMS3        │ ncp   │ Rply Create File DISKMAP.DAT      │
└────┴──────────┴─────────────┴───────┴──────────────────────────────────┘

ncp:  ===================== NetWare Core Protocol =====================
      NCP Reply: Create File
      Reply Type: 0x3333 (Reply)
      Sequence Number: 98
      Connection Number Low: 4
      Task Number: 1
      Connection Number High: 0
      Completion Code: 0 (Success)
      Connection Status: 0x00
      File Handle: 0xFF 0xFF 0x49 0x23 0x00 0x00
      File Name: DISKMAP.DAT

 0: 00 00 1B 1B 09 FB 00 00  1B 1E CE 2A 00 4A FF FF  |...........*.J..
10: 00 4A 00 11 01 CA FF 03  00 00 1B 1B 09 FB 40 13  |.J............@.
20: 01 CA FF CA 00 00 00 00  00 01 04 51 33 33 62 04  |...........Q33b.
30: 01 00 00 00 FF FF 49 23  00 00 00 00 44 49 53 4B  |......I#....DISK
40: 4D 41 50 2E 44 41 54 00  00 00 00 00 00 00 00 00  |MAP.DAT.........
50: 18 FC 18 FC 18 FC 6D 11                           |......m.

                            Packet:  29   Unfiltered: 386
```

Brief Decode Option

The LANalyzer provides a Brief Decode option that presents only the most significant fields within a packet to be shown on the Trace Decode screen, as shown in Figure 23.6.

NetWare packets look the same whether you use brief or expanded decode since there are so few fields in the IPX, SPX, and NCP portions. Other protocols, such as TCP/IP, will look quite different in each decode type.

```
 09/22/92              LANalyzer Network Analyzer              03:31
                                                           Trace Decode
┌────────────────────────── Trace Buffer ──────────────────────────┐
│Frame: Number: 2491        Length:    594 bytes                    ◄
│       Errors: None                                                 │
│       Receive Channels: GoodPkts NetWare                           │
│802.3: Station: FS4              ----> novell1E6206                 │
│       Length:  576                                                 │
│  ipx: Checksum: 0xFFFF          Length: 576                        │
│       Hop Count:  1             Packet Type: 5 (SPX)               │
│       Network: 10 00 86 03      ---> C9 99 00 06                   │
│       Node:    00-00-00-00-00-01 ---> novell1E6206                 │
│       Socket: 0x2F90            ---> 0x400C                        │
│  spx: Connection Control: 0x40 (Send Acknowledgement; )           │
│       Datastream Type: 0                                           │
│       Source Connection ID: 4698     Destination Connection ID: 38745 │
│       Sequence Number: 17245                                       │
│       Acknowledge Number: 51147                                    │
│       Allocation Number 51147                                      │
│Data:                                      ASCII display            │
│0000  42 53 4C 42 03 00 0A 00  C9 C7 03 00 01 00 06 02 │BSLB........... │
│0010  00 00 00 00 00 00 00 00  00 00 00 00 00 00 00 00 │............     │
└────────────────────────────────────────────────────────────────────┘
 F1     │F2    │F3    │F4      │F5    │F6     │F7   │F8   │F9    │F10
 Help   │Copy  │Print │Options │EBCDIC│AltDisp│Prev │Next │Go To │Back
```

Expanded Decoded Option

The final decode option is the Expanded Decode option. When you use expanded decode, the packet is completely decoded throughout—from the Ethernet header to the data field. This is the default decode option for the LANalyzer and LANalyzer for NetWare products.

Figure 23.7 shows a LANalyzer Expanded Decode screen.

FIGURE 23.7

*The LANalyzer defaults to
the Expanded Decode
option.*

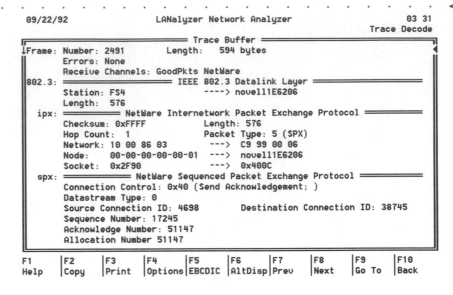

```
09/22/92                    LANalyzer Network Analyzer                    03 31
                                                                    Trace Decode
┌──────────────────────── Trace Buffer ────────────────────────┐
│↓Frame: Number: 2491        Length:     594 bytes               ◄
│        Errors: None
│        Receive Channels: GoodPkts NetWare
│802.3: ═══════════════════ IEEE 802.3 Datalink Layer ═══════════
│        Station: FS4              ----> novell1E6206
│        Length:  576
│   ipx: ═══════════ NetWare Internetwork Packet Exchange Protocol ═══════
│        Checksum: 0xFFFF          Length: 576
│        Hop Count:  1             Packet Type: 5 (SPX)
│        Network: 10 00 86 03      ---> C9 99 00 06
│        Node:    00-00-00-00-00-01 ---> novell1E6206
│        Socket:  0x2F90           ---> 0x400C
│   spx: ═══════════ NetWare Sequenced Packet Exchange Protocol ═══════
│        Connection Control: 0x40 (Send Acknowledgement; )
│        Datastream Type: 0
│        Source Connection ID: 4698        Destination Connection ID: 38745
│        Sequence Number: 17245
│        Acknowledge Number: 51147
│        Allocation Number 51147
└───────────────────────────────────────────────────────────────┘
F1    |F2    |F3    |F4      |F5    |F6     |F7    |F8    |F9    |F10
Help  |Copy  |Print |Options |EBCDIC|AltDisp|Prev  |Next  |Go To |Back
```

Expanded decodes provide a comprehensive interpretation of the protocols used on the network. If new protocols are developed and used in the
industry, however, decodes may not be available. In this case, some
analyzers, such as the LANalyzer, enable you to create templates that can
be placed on the packets to interpret the information.

Using Templates

A template is not an intelligent utility, whereas a decode is. Decodes interpret packet contents based on the values within a packet. For example,
a packet that contains the value 0x8137 in the type field is known to be a
NetWare packet using an Ethernet_II frame. In the destination socket, the
value 0x0456 indicates that the packet is a diagnostic packet.

Templates, on the other hand, must be manually "placed" on a packet to
provide interpretation. A template is simply an aid for viewing packets on
the network. You create a template by defining a field, the field length,
and the hexadecimal offset, as shown in Figure 23.8.

```
09/22/92                  LANalyzer Network Analyzer              03:34
Enter decimal number(s)                                    Template Edit
══════════════════════ c:\xln\lanz\Template\nettrans ═══════════════════
Offset from Data: 0
Byte Ordering for 'word' and 'long' Type: high, low

Offset   Label             Type       Format        Length  Bit-offset,Length
0000     Checksum          word       hexadecimal   2
0002     Length            word       decimal       2
0004     Packet Type       byte(s)    decimal       1
0005     Time To Live      byte(s)    decimal       1
0006     Source Network    byte(s)    hexadecimal   4
000A     Source Node       byte(s)    hexadecimal   6
0010     Source Socket     word       hexadecimal   2
0012     Dest Network      byte(s)    hexadecimal   4
0016     Dest Node         byte(s)    hexadecimal   6
001C     Dest Socket       word       hexadecimal   2
001E     Sequence Number   byte(s)    decimal       1
001F     Fragment Number   byte(s)    hexadecimal   2




F1     F2     F3     F4      F5      F6      F7     F8     F9     F10
Help   Load   Save   Insert  Delete  Append                       Back
```

F I G U R E 23.8

A template defines fields, field lengths, and hexadecimal offsets.

In Figure 23.8, a template has been created for a fictitious protocol named Network Transport Protocol. If the LANalyzer product group did not release a decode for this protocol, you can still apply the template to the packets for interpretation, as shown in Figure 23.9.

The LANalyzer provides a group of template files you can use for transmit channels, receive channels, or decode screens. These template files include

   NetWare

   NetWare Lite

   DECnet

   AppleTalk

   TCP/IP

   ARP

   RARP

   OSI

SMB

ICMP

FIGURE 23.9

A template applied to the packet provides interpretation.

```
10/20/92                      LANalyzer Network Analyzer                      11:44
                                                                        Trace Decode
┌══════════════════════════ Trace Buffer ══════════════════════════┐
│Frame: Number: 1          Length:    64 bytes                      ◄
│       Errors: None
│       Receive Channels: director
│0000     Checksum           0000
│0002     Length             6915
│0004     Time to Live       100
│0005     Packet Type        72
│0006     Dest Network       00 00 1B 1E
│000A     Dest Node          87 B3 00 2A FF FF
│0010     Dest Socket        0029
│0012     Src  Network       00 11 C9 40
│0016     Src  Node          83 46 00 00 00 00
│001C     Src  Socket        0001
│001E     Sequence Number    0451
│0024     Fragment Number    0
│Data:                                              ASCII display
│0000   00 1B 1E 87 B3 40 03 22  22 E1 1E 08 00 16 00 02   |.....@."".......|
│0010   15 0C 01 01 03 AA 00                                |.......         |
│
└────────────────────────────────────────────────────────────────┘
F1      |F2      |F3      |F4       |F5      |F6       |F7     |F8    |F9     |F10
Help    |Copy    |Print   |Options  |EBCDIC  |AltDisp  |Prev   |Next  |Go To  |Back
```

Many of these templates are shown in Figures 23.10 through 17.

As mentioned in Chapter 22, templates are also useful when you are creating packets to transmit on the network.

This chapter has defined the advantage of purchasing an analysis system that supports the protocols found on your network. You also examined the three decode options: No Decode, Brief Decode, and Expanded Decode. Finally, the chapter provided a listing and display of templates that are included with the LANalyzer product.

This book has explained technology, protocols, implementations, analysis techniques, and analysis features for NetWare Ethernet LANs. You should now have a strong foundation regarding Ethernet network systems, NetWare protocols, and testing strategies.

```
09/22/92                    LANalyzer Network Analyzer                    03 44
Enter decimal number(s)                                          Template Edit
┌──────────────────── c:\xln\lanz\Template\nwlite ════════════════════════◄
│Offset from Data: 0
│Byte Ordering for 'word' and 'long' Type: high, low
│
│Offset  Label           Type       Format       Length  Bit-offset,Length
│0000    Checksum        word       hexadecimal  2
│0002    Length          word       decimal      2
│0004    Transport Ctl   byte(s)    decimal      1
│0005    Packet Type     byte(s)    decimal      1
│0006    Dest Network    byte(s)    hexadecimal  4
│000A    Dest Node       byte(s)    hexadecimal  6
│0010    Dest Socket     word       hexadecimal  2
│0012    Src  Network    byte(s)    hexadecimal  4
│0016    Src  Node       byte(s)    hexadecimal  6
│001C    Src  Socket     word       hexadecimal  2
│001E    Sequence Number byte(s)    decimal      1
│001F    Connection Numb word       decimal      2
│0021    Task Number     word       decimal      2
│0023    NLP Function    word       hexadecimal  2
│0025    Completion Code word       hexadecimal  2
└─────────────────────────────────────────────────────────────────────────

F1     F2     F3     F4     F5     F6     F7     F8     F9     F10
Help   Load   Save   Insert Delete Append                       Back
```

FIGURE 23.10

NetWare Lite template

```
09/22/92                    LANalyzer Network Analyzer                    03 37
Enter decimal number(s)                                          Template Edit
┌──────────────────── c:\xln\lanz\Template\Netware ═══════════════════════◄
│Offset from Data: 0
│Byte Ordering for 'word' and 'long' Type: high, low
│
│Offset  Label           Type       Format       Length  Bit-offset,Length
│0000    Checksum        word       hexadecimal  2
│0002    Length          word       decimal      2
│0004    Transport Ctl   byte(s)    decimal      1
│0005    Packet Type     byte(s)    decimal      1
│0006    Dest Network    byte(s)    hexadecimal  4
│000A    Dest Node       byte(s)    hexadecimal  6
│0010    Dest Socket     word       hexadecimal  2
│0012    Src  Network    byte(s)    hexadecimal  4
│0016    Src  Node       byte(s)    hexadecimal  6
│001C    Src  Socket     word       hexadecimal  2
│001E    Req Type        word       hexadecimal  2
│0024    Function Code   byte(s)    decimal      1
│0025    Function Len    word       decimal      2
│0027    SubFunction Code byte(s)   decimal      1
└─────────────────────────────────────────────────────────────────────────

F1     F2     F3     F4     F5     F6     F7     F8     F9     F10
Help   Load   Save   Insert Delete Append                       Back
```

FIGURE 23.11

NetWare template

```
09/22/92                    LANalyzer Network Analyzer              03 37
Press + or - to toggle                                         Template Edit
╔═══════════════════════ c:\xln\lanz\Template\tcpip ═══════════════════════╗
↑Byte Ordering for 'word' and 'long' Type: high, low                      ◄

 Offset  Label            Type       Format       Length  Bit-offset,Length
 0000    Version/IHL      byte(s)    hexadecimal  1
 0001    Type of Service  byte(s)    hexadecimal  1
 0002    Total Length     word       decimal      2
 0004    Identification   word       decimal      2
 0006    Flags/Frg Offset byte(s)    hexadecimal  2
 0008    Time to Live     byte(s)    decimal      1
 0009    Protocol ID      byte(s)    hexadecimal  1
 000A    Header Checksum  word       hexadecimal  2
 000C    IPSource Address byte(s)    decimal      4
 0010    IPDest Address   byte(s)    decimal      4
 0014    Source Port      word       decimal      2
 0016    Dest Port        word       decimal      2
 0018    Sequence Number  long       decimal      4
 001C    Ack Number       long       decimal      4
 0020    Data Offset/Flag byte(s)    hexadecimal  2
 0022    Window           byte(s)    hexadecimal  2
╚═══════════════════════════════════════════════════════════════════════════╝
F1     F2     F3     F4      F5      F6      F7     F8     F9     F10
Help   Load   Save   Insert  Delete  Append                       Back
```

```
09/22/92                    LANalyzer Network Analyzer              03 42
Enter decimal number(s)                                        Template Edit
╔═══════════════════════ c:\xln\lanz\Template\decnet ══════════════════════╗
 Offset from Data: 0                                                       ◄
 Byte Ordering for 'word' and 'long' Type: low, high

 Offset  Label            Type       Format       Length  Bit-offset,Length
 0000    Data Count       word       decimal      2
 0002    Flags            byte(s)    hexadecimal  1
 0003    Dst. Area        byte(s)    hexadecimal  1
 0004    Dst. Sub-Area    byte(s)    hexadecimal  1
 0005    Dst. ID          byte(s)    hexadecimal  6
 000B    Src. Area        byte(s)    hexadecimal  1
 000C    Src. Sub-Area    byte(s)    hexadecimal  1
 000D    Src. ID          byte(s)    hexadecimal  6
 0014    Next Lvl 2 Routr byte(s)    hexadecimal  1
 0015    Visit Count      byte(s)    hexadecimal  1
 0016    Service Class    byte(s)    hexadecimal  1
 0017    Protocol Type    byte(s)    hexadecimal  1



╚═══════════════════════════════════════════════════════════════════════════╝
F1     F2     F3     F4      F5      F6      F7     F8     F9     F10
Help   Load   Save   Insert  Delete  Append                       Back
```

```
09/22/92                    LANalyzer Network Analyzer                    03 42
Enter decimal number(s)                                           Template Edit
┌══════════════════ c:\xln\lanz\Template\vinesip ══════════════════════════┐
│Offset from Data: 0                                                       ◄│
│Byte Ordering for 'word' and 'long' Type: high, low                        │
│                                                                           │
│Offset  Label            Type        Format       Length  Bit-offset,Length│
│0000    Checksum         word        hexadecimal  2                        │
│0002    Length           word        decimal      2                        │
│0004    Unused           mask byte   binary       1        0,1             │
│0004    Error            mask byte   binary       1        1,1             │
│0004    Metric           mask byte   binary       1        2,1             │
│0004    Redirect         mask byte   binary       1        3,1             │
│0004    Transport Cntrl  mask byte   binary       1        4,4             │
│0005    Protocol Cntrl   byte(s)     hexadecimal  1                        │
│0006    Destnetnum       byte(s)     decimal      4                        │
│000A    Destsubnetnum    byte(s)     decimal      2                        │
│000C    Srcnetnum        byte(s)     decimal      4                        │
│0010    Srcsubnetnum     byte(s)     decimal      2                        │
│                                                                           │
│                                                                           │
└───────────────────────────────────────────────────────────────────────────┘
F1    |F2    |F3    |F4     |F5     |F6     |F7   |F8   |F9   |F10
Help  |Load  |Save  |Insert |Delete |Append |     |     |     |Back
```

FIGURE 23.14

VINES IP template

```
09/22/92                    LANalyzer Network Analyzer                    03 43
Enter decimal number(s)                                           Template Edit
┌══════════════════ c:\xln\lanz\Template\vinessmb ═════════════════════════┐
│Offset from Data: 0                                                       ◄│
│Byte Ordering for 'word' and 'long' Type: low, high                        │
│                                                                           │
│Offset  Label             Type       Format       Length  Bit-offset,Length│
│0002    Length            word       decimal      2                        │
│0004    Transport Cntrl   byte(s)    hexadecimal  1                        │
│0005    Protocol Cntrl    byte(s)    hexadecimal  1                        │
│0006    Destnetnum        long       decimal      4                        │
│000A    Destsubnetnum     word       decimal      2                        │
│000C    Srcnetnum         long       decimal      4                        │
│0010    Srcsubnetnum      word       decimal      2                        │
│0012    Source Port       word       decimal      2                        │
│0014    Destination Port  word       decimal      2                        │
│0016    Packet Type       byte(s)    decimal      1                        │
│0017    Control Byte      byte(s)    decimal      1                        │
│0020    Window            word       decimal      2                        │
│0022    SMB Indicator     byte(s)    hexadecimal  4                        │
│0026    Function          byte(s)    hexadecimal  1                        │
│002C    Return Code       byte(s)    decimal      2                        │
└───────────────────────────────────────────────────────────────────────────┘
F1    |F2    |F3    |F4     |F5     |F6     |F7   |F8   |F9   |F10
Help  |Load  |Save  |Insert |Delete |Append |     |     |     |Back
```

FIGURE 23.15

VINES SMB template

```
09/22/92                    LANalyzer Network Analyzer              03 43
Enter decimal number(s)                                       Template Edit
╔══════════════════════ c:\xln\lanz\Template\ipicmp ═════════════════════╗
 Offset from Data: 0                                                      ◄
 Byte Ordering for 'word' and 'long' Type: high, low

 Offset  Label            Type       Format        Length  Bit-offset,Length
 0000    Version/IHL      byte(s)    hexadecimal   1
 0001    Type of Service  byte(s)    hexadecimal   1
 0002    Total Length     word       decimal       2
 0004    Identification   word       decimal       2
 0006    Flags/Frg Offset byte(s)    hexadecimal   2
 0008    Time to Live     byte(s)    decimal       1
 0009    Protocol ID      byte(s)    hexadecimal   1
 000A    Header Checksum  word       hexadecimal   2
 000C    IPSource Address byte(s)    decimal       4
 0010    IPDest Address   byte(s)    decimal       4
 0014    Type             byte(s)    hexadecimal   1
 0015    Code             byte(s)    hexadecimal   1
 0016    Checksum         word       hexadecimal   2
 0018    Identifier       word       hexadecimal   2
 001A    Sequence Number  word       hexadecimal   2
╚═════════════════════════════════════════════════════════════════════════╝
 F1      F2     F3      F4      F5      F6      F7     F8     F9     F10
 Help    Load   Save    Insert  Delete  Append                        Back
```

```
09/22/92                    LANalyzer Network Analyzer              03:44
Press + or - to toggle                                        Template Edit
╔════════════════════════ c:\xln\lanz\Template\osi ══════════════════════╗
 ↑Byte Ordering for 'word' and 'long' Type: high, low                    ◄

 Offset  Label            Type       Format        Length  Bit-offset,Length
 0000    netwk protcol id byte(s)    hexadecimal   1
 0001    length indicator byte(s)    decimal       1
 0002    version/prot ext byte(s)    hexadecimal   1
 0003    lifetime         byte(s)    decimal       1
 0004    SP/MS/ER         mask byte  binary        1       5,3
 0004    CLNP type        mask byte  binary        1       0,5
 0009    dest addr length byte(s)    decimal       1
 000A    afi              byte(s)    hexadecimal   1
 000B    net entity title byte(s)    hexadecimal   8
 0013    nsap selector    byte(s)    hexadecimal   2
 0015    srce addr length byte(s)    decimal       1
 0016    afi              byte(s)    hexadecimal   1
 0017    net entity title byte(s)    hexadecimal   8
 001F    nsap selector    byte(s)    hexadecimal   2
 0021    data unit id     word       hexadecimal   2
 0025    total length     word       hexadecimal   2
╚═════════════════════════════════════════════════════════════════════════╝
 F1      F2     F3      F4      F5      F6      F7     F8     F9     F10
 Help    Load   Save    Insert  Delete  Append                        Back
```

Glossary

Alarm log file   A file, generally in ASCII (American Standard Code for Information Interchange) format, that contains a listing of alarms that have occurred, as well as the date and time each alarm occurred.

Backoff algorithm   A computation that each Ethernet card is required to perform in order to determine available transmission times after a collision. The backoff algorithm process is formally called the "truncated binary exponential backoff."

Baseline   The process of determining and documenting network performance characteristics under normal conditions. Network characteristics might include utilization, errors per second, kilobytes per second, packets per second, and most active users/servers.

Binary filtering   Filtering on bit values (0 or 1) instead of a full byte value.

Bindery   A special-purpose database maintained by NetWare servers. The bindery contains information about clients and resources on the network, such as passwords, client accounts, and client restrictions.

Bridge   An internetworking device that connects two network segments on the same logical LAN. A bridge filters traffic between segments based on hardware (MAC) addresses and is unaware of upper-layer protocols being used.

Burst Mode window   The Burst Mode window is the amount of data that can be transferred in a Burst Mode session before an acknowledgment is required. The window size is dynamically adjusted based upon error conditions or lack thereof.

Collision fragment   The result of two or more stations transmitting simultaneously on the cabling system. Fragments are defined as packets that are fewer than 64 bytes in length and contain an invalid CRC value. The presence or absence of a collision detection signal differentiates local collisions from remote collisions.

Crosstalk Interference caused by electromagnetic sources, such as motors. Crosstalk is detected as bandwidth utilization that is not a result of packets on the wire.

Cyclical Redundancy Check (CRC) A calculation performed by the transmitting and receiving stations to validate the integrity of frames. Transmitting stations place the CRC value in the frame check sequence (FCS) field; receiving stations perform the same calculation and compare the result to the value in the FCS field. The CRC is performed on all fields of the packet except the preamble, start frame delimiter, and frame check sequence field itself.

Deaf node An Ethernet node that does not adhere to the CSMA/CD requirement of "listen first, then transmit." A deaf node either will not listen to the cabling system for activity or will ignore the activity on the wire before transmitting.

Default server The server that is specified by the client's default drive mapping.

Deferral time The amount of time that a node must wait before transmitting once it has noticed the cable is "busy." Nodes must wait 9.6 microseconds after the cable has become idle before beginning transmission.

Deterministic protocols Protocols that provide assurance of an opportunity to transmit on the medium. Token Ring is considered a deterministic protocol since the token (right to transmit) passes logically from one station to the next.

Dumb loads Packets that are transmitted onto the network and contain no information regarding destination or purpose. Dumb loads are used to test the network cabling system performance abilities under varying levels of utilization.

Enhanced filtering   A filtering technique available with the LANalyzer that permits up to 16 filter patterns to be combined using Boolean operands.

Exclusion address   A node address of a station that will not be required to respond to a diagnostic configuration packet (Diagnostic Responder). A maximum of 80 nodes can be excluded in each diagnostic configuration packet.

Frames   Encapsulation bits that provide synchronization services, addressing, upper-layer protocol definition, and integrity checking of information transmitted across a network.

Global statistics   Statistics regarding all the traffic on the network, including errors, utilization, kilobytes, packets per second, and so on.

Hardware address   Address assigned to a network interface card by either a manufacturer or, in some cases, the network administrator. The hardware address identifies the local device address to which a packet is destined. Hardware addresses can also be referred to as the physical, MAC, or Ethernet addresses.

Intelligent loads   Packets that are transmitted to a specific device or upper-layer protocol on the network. Intelligent loads are used for component testing.

Internetwork address (NetWare environment)   A software address that consists of a 4-byte network address and 6-byte node address. A station's internetwork address denotes the network it is located on, as well as the physical address of the device.

Jabber   A "packet" that is greater than the maximum size allowed (1518 bytes) that contains a bad CRC value. A common cause of jabber on the network is a faulty transceiver.

Jabbering transceiver   A transceiver generating transmissions that exceed the maximum transmission time duration allowed by the 802.3 specification. The maximum transmission time cannot exceed 150 milliseconds, as defined by the IEEE 802.3. Properly functioning transceivers are required to inhibit transmission (jabber suppression) once the allowable time duration has been reached.

Jam   A 32-bit transmission that follows detection of a collision by a transmitting station. Jam is used to ensure that the collision can be detected by all transmitting stations on the segment. The content of jam is unspecified but cannot be equal to the CRC value of the partial frame transmitted prior to jam.

Key (login encryption)   An encryption sequence provided by a NetWare server to clients that wish to gain access to services. A maximum of two keys is provided to clients during each Net-Ware login attempt.

Late collision   A collision that occurs later than 64 bytes into a packet. Late collisions indicate either a deaf node or a cabling problem, such as cable length exceeding the maximum allowable by the 802.3 specifications.

Load test   A test that is developed to determine the capabilities of either a single component on the network or the network cabling system. There are two types of load tests: dumb and intelligent.

Local collisions   Collisions that occur on the same network segment as the observer. Local collisions are detected by monitoring the node's collision-detect circuitry for a signal that equals or exceeds the possible signal produced by two or more MAUs (Medium Access Units).

Long frames   Frames that are greater than 1518 bytes in length and contain a valid CRC value. Long frames can be transmitted by stations that are using a faulty LAN driver.

Ping   To transmit a packet to a defined node on the network in order to test connectivity. In the NetWare environment, a diagnostic configuration packet can be transmitted to test station connectivity and gather configuration information. The term "ping" is common in the TCP/IP environment.

Point-and-click filtering   A post-filtering (display filtering) technique provided by the LANalyzer for NetWare. Point-and-click filtering allows a user to configure post-filtering values by clicking on a field shown in the decode.

Post-filter   A filter that is applied to packets that are saved in the trace buffer or on disk. Post-filters are used to focus on packets that meet a defined post-filter criterion.

Pre-filter   A filter that is applied to the packet before saving it in the trace buffer or on disk. Pre-filters are used to reduce the number and types of packets saved to the buffer.

Predefined alarm threshold   An alarm threshold that is determined and set by the analysis software manufacturer. These predefined alarms alert new users to potential problems before they learn how to set alarm thresholds.

Preferred server   A NetWare server that is explicitly defined either in a NET.CFG file or at the command line during the login process.

Primary server   The server to which the workstation shell attached upon execution. If a preferred server has been requested, the primary server will provide routing information to the shell in order to enable the shell to request attachment to the preferred server.

Relative format (time-stamping)   A time-stamping format that bases all packet time stamps on the first packet within the buffer. The first packet is assumed to have been received at time

00:00:00. Each subsequent packet in the buffer will have a receipt time relative to the first.

Remote collisions Collisions that occur on the other side of a repeater. Remote collisions are identified as packets that are fewer than 64 bytes and contain an invalid CRC value. Remote collisions cannot be detected by a node's collision-detection circuitry.

Routers Devices used to connect two or more similar or dissimilar networks and provide routing services based on logical end-to-end connections. Routers utilize addressing information contained in the network header of a packet to determine the source and destination address on an internetwork.

Short frames Frames that are fewer than 64 bytes in length and contain a valid CRC value. The detection of short frames indicates that a node is using a faulty LAN driver.

Signal Quality Error (SQE) A signal on the collision-detection circuitry of a transceiver. An SQE signal indicates that an improper signal exists on the medium or that a collision has occurred. An SQE test is performed to test the collision-detection circuitry of the transceiver after each frame is transmitted.

Software addressing Addressing that defines the logical address of a device on an internetwork and is independent of the physical address of a device. Software addresses are used by routers to forward packets through a network.

SPX handshake A connection establishment sequence that must be performed before using connection-oriented services provided by SPX (Sequenced Packet Exchange).

Template A defined format for protocol decoding that includes byte offset, field labels, and field lengths. When used in conjunction with packet transmission, templates label fields for easier packet creation.

Token   A 24-bit sequence in Token Ring that allows the receiving station to transmit. Upon completion of transmission, a Token Ring station releases the token, allowing the next station to acquire the right to transmit. There can be only one token on a ring at a time.

APPENDIX B

Bibliography

Comer, Douglas. *Internetworking with TCP/IP: Principles, Protocols and Architectures*. Prentice-Hall, 1989.

IEEE Standard 8802-5 (ANSI): 1992. *Carrier Sense with Collision Detection (CSMA/CD) Access Method and Physical Layer Specifications*. Institute of Electrical and Electronic Engineers, 1992.

IEEE Standard 802.3i-1990 (ANSI). *Supplement to CSMA/CD: Systems Considerations for Multisegment 10 Mb/s Baseband Networks (Section 13), and Twisted-Pair Medium Attachment Unit with Baseband Medium, Type 10BASE-T (Section 14)*. Institute of Electrical and Electronic Engineers, 1992.

International Standard ISO/IEC 8802-5: 1989. *Token Ring Access Method and Physical Layer Specifications*. Institute of Electrical and Electronic Engineers, 1989.

NetWare System Interface Technical Overview. Novell, 1991.

Novell Education. *Advanced LANalyzer v3.11A (Ethernet-TCP/IP)*. Novell, Inc., 1992. [Pentin, Josine; Spicer, Roger]

Novell Education. *Advanced LANalyzer v3.11A (Token Ring-IPX/SPX)*. Novell, Inc., 1992. [Hakes, Dan]

Novell Education. *LANalyzer for NetWare Self-Paced Course*. Novell, Inc., 1992. [Pentin, Josine]

Novell Education. *Networking Techniques Course*. Novell, Inc., 1992.

Novell Research. *NetWare Application Notes*, "NetWare Communication Processes." Novell, Inc., September 1990.

Novell Research. *NetWare Application Notes*, "A Comparison of NetWare IPX, SPX and NetBIOS." Novell, Inc., August 1990.

Novell Research. *NetWare Application Notes*, "NODEVIEW: LANalyzer Filters for IPX Protocol Diagnostics on a Locally-Attached Network Segment" and "SERVERVU: LANalyzer Filters for Service Advertising Protocol (SAP) Diagnostics on a Locally-Attached Network Segment." Novell, Inc., December 1990.

Novell Research. *NetWare Application Notes,* "OVERVIEW: LANalyzer Applications for NetWare File Server Access Characterization on a Locally-Attached Network Segment" and "FILEVIEW: LANalyzer Applications for NetWare File Service Diagnostics on a Locally-Attached Network Segment." Novell, Inc., January 1991.

Novell Research. *NetWare Application Notes,* "Resolving Performance Problems on a NetWare Network." Novell, Inc., February 1991.

Novell Research. *NetWare Application Notes,* "Analyzing LAN/WAN Internets: Testing IPX Routes Using Novell's LANalyzer." Novell, Inc., June 1991.

Sherman, Ken. *Data Communications. A User's Guide,* 3rd edition. Prentice-Hall, 1990.

Stallings, William. *Local Networks,* 3rd edition. Macmillan, 1990.

Tanenbaum, Andrew S. *Computer Networks,* 2nd edition. Prentice-Hall, 1988.

LANalyzer
Product Information

The LANalyzer product provides a hardware/software analysis solution and includes the LANalyzer card (Ethernet and/or Token Ring) and LANalyzer software (Ethernet and Token Ring combined). The LANalyzer card has an on-board processor, as well as a 2-megabyte buffer for packet capturing.

The LANalyzer software includes the Automated Troubleshooting System (ATS). ATS is a set of over 170 predefined tests for baselining, troubleshooting, and monitoring Ethernet and Token Ring LANs. The LANalyzer also includes decodes for the most common LAN protocols in use today:

NetWare (v2.x, v3.x, Lite)

TCP/IP

DECnet

DEC LAT

Banyan

NFS

AppleTalk (Phase I and II)

OSI

SNA

NetBEUI

XNS

SMB

The LANalyzer for NetWare is a Windows-based application that provides a software-only analysis solution. The LANalyzer for NetWare can be run over any network interface card using drivers developed in accordance with the NetWare 4.0 specifications.

The LANalyzer for NetWare currently includes decoding for all NetWare protocols, including Burst Mode, NetWare Lite, NetWare v2.x, and NetWare v3.x. A set of defined pre-filters and post-filters allows easy creation of customized applications. You can use point-and-click filtering to quickly apply customized post-filters to packets saved in the trace buffer.

The main screen of the LANalyzer for NetWare displays a "dashboard" showing gauges indicating real-time statistics, such as utilization, packets per second, and errors per second.

The LANalyzer for NetWare and LANalyzer products are manufactured by Novell, Inc. The LANalyzer for NetWare product is available through Novell Authorized Resellers. The LANalyzer is available through specialized Novell LANalyzer Resellers.

Call 1-800-NETWARE (within the United States and Canada), 801-429-5533 (outside the U.S. and Canada), or your local Novell office for the number of your nearest Authorized Reseller.

Education courses are also available for the LANalyzer for NetWare and LANalyzer. For information regarding the nearest Novell Authorized Education Center or LANalyzer Authorized Training Center, call 1-800-233-EDUC or 801-429-5508.

NOTE
Trace files from the LANalyzer for NetWare and LANalyzer are interchangeable.

Hex to Decimal
Conversion Chart

NOVELL'S GUIDE
TO NETWARE
LAN ANALYSIS

Hex to decimal
conversion chart.

Dec.	Hex	Binary		Dec.	Hex	Binary		Dec.	Hex	Binary	
0	00	0000	0000	46	2E	0010	1110	92	5C	0101	1100
1	01	0000	0001	47	2F	0010	1111	93	5D	0101	1101
2	02	0000	0010	48	30	0011	0000	94	5E	0101	1110
3	03	0000	0011	49	31	0011	0001	95	5F	0101	1111
4	04	0000	0100	50	32	0011	0010	96	60	0110	0000
5	05	0000	0101	51	33	0011	0011	97	61	0110	0001
6	06	0000	0110	52	34	0011	0100	98	62	0110	0010
7	07	0000	0111	53	35	0011	0101	99	63	0110	0011
8	08	0000	1000	54	36	0011	0110	100	64	0110	0100
9	09	0000	1001	55	37	0011	0111	101	65	0110	0101
10	0A	0000	1010	56	38	0011	1000	102	66	0110	0110
11	0B	0000	1011	57	39	0011	1001	103	67	0110	0111
12	0C	0000	1100	58	3A	0011	1010	104	68	0110	1000
13	0D	0000	1101	59	3B	0011	1011	105	69	0110	1001
14	0E	0000	1110	60	3C	0011	1100	106	6A	0110	1010
15	0F	0000	1111	61	3D	0011	1101	107	6B	0110	1011
16	10	0001	0000	62	3E	0011	1110	108	6C	0110	1100
17	11	0001	0001	63	3F	0011	1111	109	6D	0110	1101
18	12	0001	0010	64	40	0100	0000	110	6E	0110	1110
19	13	0001	0011	65	41	0100	0001	111	6F	0110	1111
20	14	0001	0100	66	42	0100	0010	112	70	0111	0000
21	15	0001	0101	67	43	0100	0011	113	71	0111	0001
22	16	0001	0110	68	44	0100	0100	114	72	0111	0010
23	17	0001	0111	69	45	0100	0101	115	73	0111	0011
24	18	0001	1000	70	46	0100	0110	116	74	0111	0100
25	19	0001	1001	71	47	0100	0111	117	75	0111	0101
26	1A	0001	1010	72	48	0100	1000	118	76	0111	0110
27	1B	0001	1011	73	49	0100	1001	119	77	0111	0111
28	1C	0001	1100	74	4A	0100	1010	120	78	0111	1000
29	1D	0001	1101	75	4B	0100	1011	121	79	0111	1001
30	1E	0001	1110	76	4C	0100	1100	122	7A	0111	1010
31	1F	0001	1111	77	4D	0100	1101	123	7B	0111	1011
32	20	0010	0000	78	4E	0100	1110	124	7C	0111	1100
33	21	0010	0001	79	4F	0100	1111	125	7D	0111	1101
34	22	0010	0010	80	50	0101	0000	126	7E	0111	1110
35	23	0010	0011	81	51	0101	0001	127	7F	0111	1111
36	24	0010	0100	82	52	0101	0010	128	80	1000	0000
37	25	0010	0101	83	53	0101	0011	129	81	1000	0001
38	26	0010	0110	84	54	0101	0100	130	82	1000	0010
39	27	0010	0111	85	55	0101	0101	131	83	1000	0011
40	28	0010	1000	86	56	0101	0110	132	84	1000	0100
41	29	0010	1001	87	57	0101	0111	133	85	1000	0101
42	2A	0010	1010	88	58	0101	1000	134	86	1000	0110
43	2B	0010	1011	89	59	0101	1001	135	87	1000	0111
44	2C	0010	1100	90	5A	0101	1010	136	88	1000	1000
45	2D	0010	1101	91	5B	0101	1011	137	89	1000	1001

Dec.	Hex	Binary	Dec.	Hex	Binary	Dec.	Hex	Binary
138	8A	1000 1010	184	B8	1011 1000	230	E6	1110 0110
139	8B	1000 1011	185	B9	1011 1001	231	E7	1110 0111
140	8C	1000 1100	186	BA	1011 1010	232	E8	1110 1000
141	8D	1000 1101	187	BB	1011 1011	233	E9	1110 1001
142	8E	1000 1110	188	BC	1011 1100	234	EA	1110 1010
143	8F	1000 1111	189	BD	1011 1101	235	EB	1110 1011
144	90	1001 0000	190	BE	1011 1110	236	EC	1110 1100
145	91	1001 0001	191	BF	1011 1111	237	ED	1110 1101
146	92	1001 0010	192	C0	1100 0000	238	EE	1110 1110
147	93	1001 0011	193	C1	1100 0001	239	EF	1110 1111
148	94	1001 0100	194	C2	1100 0010	240	F0	1111 0000
149	95	1001 0101	195	C3	1100 0011	241	F1	1111 0001
150	96	1001 0110	196	C4	1100 0100	242	F2	1111 0010
151	97	1001 0111	197	C5	1100 0101	243	F3	1111 0011
152	98	1001 1000	198	C6	1100 0110	244	F4	1111 0100
153	99	1001 1001	199	C7	1100 0111	245	F5	1111 0101
154	9A	1001 1010	200	C8	1100 1000	246	F6	1111 0110
155	9B	1001 1011	201	C9	1100 1001	247	F7	1111 0111
156	9C	1001 1100	202	CA	1100 1010	248	F8	1111 1000
157	9D	1001 1101	203	CB	1100 1011	249	F9	1111 1001
158	9E	1001 1110	204	CC	1100 1100	250	FA	1111 1010
159	9F	1001 1111	205	CD	1100 1101	251	FB	1111 1011
160	A0	1010 0000	206	CE	1100 1110	252	FC	1111 1100
161	A1	1010 0001	207	CF	1100 1111	253	FD	1111 1101
162	A2	1010 0010	208	D0	1101 0000	254	FE	1111 1110
163	A3	1010 0011	209	D1	1101 0001	255	FF	1111 1111
164	A4	1010 0100	210	D2	1101 0010			
165	A5	1010 0101	211	D3	1101 0011			
166	A6	1010 0110	212	D4	1101 0100			
167	A7	1010 0111	213	D5	1101 0101			
168	A8	1010 1000	214	D6	1101 0110			
169	A9	1010 1001	215	D7	1101 0111			
170	AA	1010 1010	216	D8	1101 1000			
171	AB	1010 1011	217	D9	1101 1001			
172	AC	1010 1100	218	DA	1101 1010			
173	AD	1010 1101	219	DB	1101 1011			
174	AE	1010 1110	220	DC	1101 1100			
175	AF	1010 1111	221	DD	1101 1101			
176	B0	1011 0000	222	DE	1101 1110			
177	B1	1011 0001	223	DF	1101 1111			
178	B2	1011 0010	224	E0	1110 0000			
179	B3	1011 0011	225	E1	1110 0001			
180	B4	1011 0100	226	E2	1110 0010			
181	B5	1011 0101	227	E3	1110 0011			
182	B6	1011 0110	228	E4	1110 0100			
183	B7	1011 0111	229	E5	1110 0101			

FIGURE D.I

Hex to decimal conversion
chart (continued)

Index

O

software-only solutions for
protocol analyzer, 285–286
sorting, station names by total
number of packets transmitted,
305–306
source address for Ethernet_802.3,
59, 60
source connection ID
in Burst header, 156
in SPX header, 116
source network number in IPX
header, 105
source node field in IPX header,
105
Source Service Access Point field
in Ethernet_802.2 frame, 65
in Ethernet_SNAP frame, 69
spacing, cable taps, 92
spreadsheet programs
importing network statistics to,
227–228
plotting server performance data
on, 265–266
SPX Close Connection request, 117
SPX diagnostic socket number
field, Diagnostic Response
packet, 203
SPX handshake, 117, 118, 377
SPX header, 100, 114–118, 122
SPX protocol, 100, 114
advantages and disadvantages, 101
customizing connection
parameters, 121–122
establishing and terminating connection, 117
monitoring connection, 117
terminating session, 120

SPXCONFG utility, 121
SQE (Signal Quality Error) test, 11
SQL VAP, type code, 168
star configuration, 46
start frame delimiter, 58
Station Monitor screen, 303–305
Station Name Gathering dialog
box, 312
station node address, 5
stations. *See* workstations
statistics. *See* network statistics
stream type in Burst header, 156
stress tests, 36–41, 240–242
subfunction codes, 130
Sub-Network Access Protocol, 67.
See also Ethernet_SNAP
synchronization services, NCP
function codes for, 142–142
synchronizing receiving stations, 58
SYS flag in Burst header, 156
System Packet value (connection
control field), 115

T

task number (NCP request
header), 127
T-connectors, 5, 45
TCP/IP protocol, 78
Ethernet_SNAP support for, 67
template, 368
TDR (time domain reflectometer),
278
templates, 350, 364–370, 377